KASHMIR DURING BRITISH RULE

ENCYCLOPAEDIA OF KASHMIR SERIES - 3

Kashmir During British Rule

Edited by

Suresh K. Sharma & S.R. Bakshi

ANMOL PUBLICATIONS PVT LTD

New Delhi

ANMOL PUBLICATIONS PVT LTD
4374/4B, Ansari Road, Daryaganj
New Delhi-110 002

Kashmir During British Rule

First Edition 1995
Reprint 1996
ISBN 81-7488-056-9

PRINTED IN INDIA

Published by J.L. Kumar for Anmol Publications Pvt. Ltd., New Delhi and Printed at Mehra Offset Press.

Preface

The picturesque valley of Kashmir situated on the northern extremity of India, occupies a position of unique and strategic importance in the sub-continent of India. It excels in beauty, art, architecture, culture and tradition, rivers, mountains, flora and fauna than several regions of the world. So far so, some eminent writers have compared this Himalayan range with that of Switzerland. Whereas, Kashmir bore the pangs of various onslaughts from North-West, Switzerland enjoyed peaceful postures for centuries.

The present volume is the collection of selected documents which throw valuable light on the economic, political and social history of Kashmir during British regime.

We have collected the material from several libraries and some of them are—Nehru Memorial Museum and Library, Indian Council of World Affairs Library, Gandhi National Museum and Library, Indian Council of Historical Research Library, University of Delhi Library, etc.

We feel much beholden to the authorities of these institutions for their academic support during our researches.

Finally, we owe a deep sense of admiration for Usha Sharma, Jyotsna Tewari, Gagan, Shilpa and Naresh with regard to their constant help provided in many ways.

Editors
Suresh K. Sharma
S.R. Bakshi

Contents

	Preface	*v*
1.	The Revolt in Kashmir, 1846 *R. R. Sethi*	1-12
2.	Siyahat-I-Kashmir (Kashmir Nama or Tarikh-i-Kashmir) *Ganeshi Lal*	13-66
3.	The Government of India and the Maharaja of Kashmir *William Digby*	67-199
4.	Kashmiri Pandits in British India *Jia Lal Kilam*	200-225
5.	Dogras *G.L. Kaul*	226-323

CHAPTER 1

THE REVOLT IN KASHMIR, 1846

By

R.R. Sethi

By the terms of the Treaty, which in March, 1846, closed the First Sikh War, amongst other things, the Sikhs ceded to the British all the hill country between the rivers Beas and Indus,. "including the provinces of Kashmir and Hazara;" and "in consideration of the services rendered by Raja Gulab Singh, of Jammu, to the Lahore State towards procuring the restoration of the relations of amity between the Lahore and British Governments," the British agreed to recognise "the independent sovereignty of Raja Gulab Singh in such territories and districts in the hills as may be made over to the said Raja Gulab Singh, by separate agreement between himself and the British Government, with the dependencies thereof, which may have been in the Raja's possession since the time of the late Maharaja Kharak Singh"; further the British Government, "in consideration of the good conduct of Raja Gulab Singh," agreed "to recognise his independence in such territories, and to admit him to the privileges of a separate treaty with the British Government."

A week later, on March 16, 1846, was signed this separate Treaty with Gulab Singh, by which the British Government "transferred and made over, for ever, in independent possession, to Maharaja Gulab Singh and the heirs male of his body, all the hilly and mountainous country, with its dependencies, situated to the eastward of the river Indus and westward of the river Ravi, including Chamba and excluding Lahoul, being part of the territories ceded to the British Government by the Lahore State." In consideration of this transfer Gulab Singh was to pay the British Government seventy- five lacs of rupees (Nanakshahi), fifty lacs to be paid on ratification of the Treaty, and twenty-five lacs on or before October 1, 1846, and in token of the supremacy of the British Government, was "to present annually to the British Government one horse, twelve perfect shawl-goats of approved breed (six male and six female), and three pairs of Kashmir shawls." He further engaged "to join with the whole of his military force the British troops when employed within the hills, or in the territories adjoining his possessions"; and on their part the British Government engaged "to give its aid to Maharaja Gulab Singh in protecting his territories from external enemies."

Thus it was that Gulab Singh, the great grandfather of the present Maharaja, became the ruler of Kashmir. But he did not acquire actual possession of his new province without much difficulty.

The Revolt of Shaikh Imam-ud-din, Governor of Kashmir

One can easily imagine the jealously which would be felt by a power at giving over, "in sackcloth and ashes", a rich tract of its territory to one who, only lately, was a subject of its own—a powerful subject, all but independent, but still a subject acknowledging, perhaps, a more perfect allegiance than he paid. Then began intrigues, month after month passed away and still Gulab Singh was not in possession of Kashmir. We shall examine concisely the cause of this.

Kashmir was annexed to the Sikh dominions in 1819, and had thence-forward been administered by Governors from Lahore who were frequently changed. In 1846, the Sikh Governor, in charge of Kashmir affairs, was one Shaikh Imam-ud-din, who is thus described by a contemporary writer:

"The Shaikh is, perhaps, the best mannered and best dressed man in the Panjab. He is rather under than above the middle height; but his figure is exquisite, as far as it goes, and is usually set off with the most unrivalled fit which the unrivalled tailors of Kashmir could achieve for the Governor of the Province. His smile and bow are those of a perfect Courtier, whose taste is too good to be obsequious; his great natural intelligence and an unusually good education have endowed him with considerable conversational powers; and his Persian idiom would do no dishonour to a native of Shiraz. Beneath this smooth surface of accomplishment and courtesy lies an ill-assorted and incongruous disposition: ambition, pride, cruelty and intrigue, strangely mixed up with indolence, effeminacy, voluptuousness and timidity. From such pluses and minuses what result can be expected but a moral cypher?"

Deeply engaged in the intrigues and revolutions of Lahore, Shaikh Imam-ud-din was never to be found at any crisis and so completely were all his aspirations negatived by indecision, that he spent the six months of his Kashmir government in wavering between three different schemes for his own personal aggrandisement: doubtful whether to accept Gulab Singh's offer, and continue Governor on a salary of one lac per annum; to oppose the transfer of the Province to that Prince, which Raja Lal Singh told him should be a receipt in full for his Kashmir accounts; or to try to buy over the British, and make himself independent sovereign of the loveliest valley in the world. We shall see presently that he chose the most senseless of the three; and to save himself from the consequences, on the first appearance of danger, he turned "King's evidence," and sacrificed his accomplice.

In his choice he was urged, it is said, by the influence of a wife, the daughter of the Khan of Kohistan, "proud of her kin and blood," and bigoted in her Mohammedan faith. Imam-ud-din with the aid of feudatories took up arms to oppose the entry of Gulab Singh, and his troops obtained some advantages.

Gulab Singh could not himself drive the recalcitrant Shaikh out by force of arms and the British Government had to intervene and coercive measures were resorted to. Without an hour's hesitation, the Governor-General declared that the clause of the Treaty of Lahore by which Kashmir was to be transferred to Gulab Singh must be enforced and "that the British Government would give every possible support to the Maharaja Gulab Singh in compelling the servant of the Darbar, the Shaikh Imam-ud-din to evacuate Kashmir, holding the Darbar responsible for the acts of their officers, in this gross violation of the Treaty."

The Lahore Darbar was asked to place at Maharaja Gulab Singh's disposal from one-half to two-thirds of the force at any or all of the stations between the Ravi and the Attock and to desire their Officers Commanding within that tract instantly, on receipt of the Maharaja's requisition, to move on such points as he might desire and to act on his instructions. The Darbar was further instructed to proclaim to their border subjects that the property of persons taking up arms against Maharaja Gulab Singh would be confiscated. The Maharaja was advised to combine mercy with energy in coercing the rebels and to offer an amnesty for submission up to a certain date.

In the meantime a letter was addressed to the Sikh officers and soldiers in Kashmir, informing them that an English army had been ordered to support the Maharaja. "I warn you" wrote Henry Lawrence, "that if on receipt of this order you separate from the Shaikh and return to the Panjab, your lives will be spared and your arrears will be paid."

The Governor-General on September 15, 1846, ordered six Regiments of Native Infantry, two Regiments of Irregular Cavalry, and twelve Field Guns, under Brigadier Wheeler, commanding the Jullundur Doab, to be held in readiness to move fully equipped for field service from Jullundur towards Jammu, for the purpose of protecting the Maharaja's rear in his absence.

The Maharaja did not wish British troops to go to Kashmir but was anxious that they should hold Nowshera (above Bhimbar) for him for the double reason, that it was a troublesome country, and, that by so forward a movement, people might be led to suppose that they would advance into Kashmir.

Accordingly, the Governor-General on September 22, 1846, addressed the Commander-in-Chief, requesting him that the Brigadier might be ordered to advance. "The object of the movement," the Governor-General wrote," is to enable Maharaja Gulab Singh to move all his disposable forces on Kashmir, by protecting his rear from the confines of our frontier up to Jammu, a distance probably of between 60 and 70 miles, in the country between the Ravi and Chenab rivers at the foot of the hills which divide the Maharaja's territory from the plains.

The troops selected by the Lahore Darbar for the Kashmir expedition were:-

Under Sardar Sher Singh—his own troops, the Kohistani (Mountaineers), about 5,000 in number; four guns.

Under General Doab Singh—two regiments.
Under General Kahan Singh—two regiments.
Lahore troops, under General Imam Singh—
two regiments; two guns.

Moreover ten other guns and all necessary munitions were got ready at Lahore under the direction of Captain Brind. Various officers were despatched to collect carriage and supplies in Rawalpindi, Jhang, etc.

And then was seen the very remarkable spectacle of the British Agent marching at the head of the Sikh troops, supported by British forces, to wrest Sikh territory from Imam-ud-Din in order to hand it over to the last of those Rajput brothers, who had always inspired the Sikhs themselves with intense jealousy.

These vigorous measures had the desired effect of showing not only to Gulab Singh, but also to the Shaikh in Kashmir, and the Vazir in Lahore, that no difficulties which could be created by hostile combinations, or intrigues, would be allowed to stand in the way of carrying out the Treaty. The very first fruits were the revelation of Raja Lal Singh's treachery. No sooner did Puran Chand, the Shaikh's Vakil, find that the British were in earnest, than with admirable decision he chose his side, and determined to save his master by throwing Raja Lal Singh overboard.

The Surrender of Shaikh Imam-ud-Din

Lieut. H.B. Edwardes, the Assistant Political Agent, who had been deputed by the Governor-General to keep Government informed about the proceedings in Kohistan and Kashmir and to advise Maharaja Gulab Singh 'at the present juncture,' reporting the substance of conversations he had held with Puran Chand, the Shaikh's Vakil, in a letter dated the 17th September, 1846, observed that the Vakil, repeatedly asserted that his master, the Shaikh, had been secretly instigated in his resistance to Maharaja Gulab Singh in Kashmir, by communications sent to him by the Vazir, Raza Lal Singh, and that the Shaikh possessed letters to that effect written by his Vakil and signed by Raja Lal Singh at Lahore.

"If these suspicious circumstances shall subsequently be verified," wrote F. Currie to H.M. Lawrence, "Lieut. Edwardes may assure the Shaikh that if he (as his Vakil declares, he can) does prove the truth of the Vakil's declaration, the British Government will visit the offence of a Lahore servant, acting under the orders of his Government upon that Government, and not upon him, and will ensure his personal safety, it without further resistance he abandons his desperate enterprise and delivers himself up to the British Political Agent."

Negotiations were then opened between Lieut. Edwardes and Shaikh Imam-ud-Din, and the latter expressed his willingness to evacuate the valley and come over to Lahore but he was afraid that his Jullundur Jagirs would be confiscated and that he would be charged for the arrears of his troops. Hence he wavered and sought assurances before he finally gave up. He was assured that if he left kashmir immediately with the property he possessed, either with or without his troops, his life would be spared and his past conduct forgiven, and that if he could prove that he had resisted at the instigation of the Lahore authorities, he would retain his property and would be exempted from rendering any account to the Darbar. But he was told that his Jagirs in Jullundur could not be restored, for as a resident in the British territory and as a Jagirdar under the British Government he had disobeyed its orders. This caused the Shaikh to pause.

On October 6, the Adjutant-General of the Army ordered Col. Reed, commanding at Ferozepur, to march Her Majesty's 62nd Regiment, three regiments of Native Infantry, two regiments of cavalry and twelve guns on to Lahore. Major-General Sir John Littler was ordered to move Her Majesty's 80th Regiment, three regiments of Native Infantry and twelve guns on to Sailkot. Lieut. Lumsden was to join the Sikh troops, which had already left Lahore, at Rajourie, lest they should halt short of their destination. On October 11, Brigadier Wheeler was ordered to move the forces under his command so far as Bhimbar, but was instructed on no account to proceed beyond that. He, however, received instructions from General Littler, on October 19, ordering him to cross with his forces to the right bank of the Chenab, the forces under Littler being stationed on the left bank of the Chenab, the forces under Littler being stationed on the left bank ready in 24 hours to form a junction with

Brigadier Wheeler to advance on Bhimbar or Nowshera, whenever required to do so.

This mobilisation of troops further proved to the Shaikh, the hopelessness of his resisting any longer, and detached from him some of his most valuable adherents.

Reports now, from different quarters, confirmed the news that the Shaikh was yielding to the persuasions of the deputies and had made preparations for his departure to Lahore. Puran Chand and Fateh Khan arrived in Kashmir on October 1, and delivered the written pledge of Lieut. Edwardes to Imam-ud-Din. No sooner had the Shaikh read this encouraging letter, than trusting entirely to the leniency and generosity of the British Government he raised the siege of Hari Parbat; called in his men to their respective camps, exhorted the Kings of the Kohistan to put down the rebellious spirit they had raised and set himself to work in earnest to write similar orders to every part of the country, Maharaja Gulab Singh's servants imprisoned in Kashmir were released and Mirza Faqir Ullah was ordered to set free those in confinement at Rajourie.

Before leaving Kashmir, Imam-ud-Din wanted still to make sure of the action the British Government would take against him. So he sent Fateh Khah and Puran Chand and two of his confidential agents, Rattan Chand and Mirza Ahmed, with a letter to Lieut. Edwardes, whom they met at Seyouth, ten kos from Rajourie on October 15. Edwardes had already promised to meet the Shaikh on his way to Lahore. Imam-ud-Din requested him to come up to Bairamgulli, Edwardes offered to meet him at Thana, 8 or 9 miles from Rajourie, and wrote to him that the British Government would not interfere with his Kashmir property, nor allow the Lahore Darbar to call him to account, if he could prove the complicity of the Lahore Darbar in the rebellion. Arrangements would also be made to save any possibility of a collision between Imam-ud-Din's troops issuing from Kashmir and the Maharaja's and the Sikh forces marching into the valley.

In the meanwhile, on October 12, Mirza Faqir Ullah of Rajourie, the mainstay and ally of Shaikh Imam-ud-Din, had written a humble letter of submission to Edwards, wherein he declared his readiness to submit as soon as the latter reached the Rajourie border.

The Mirza wrote another letter to the Maharaja's Moulvi, offering to submit provided the Moulvi got him "the Maharaja's necklace as a pledge of good faith." Taking on himself the responsibility of his safety, Edwardes asked Faqir Ullah to come at once and the Maharaja too agreed to the request of the Mirza. On October 18, at 10 A.M., attended by about thirty followers, this master mechanician of the Shaikh's plans, the firebrand of the rebellion, the 'Lord and leader' of the insurgents and the deadly enemy of His Highness came and made his submission to Maharaja Gulab Singh.

The army still advanced, and had reached the fort at the Bairamgulli Pass into Kashmir.

Soon it was reported that the Shaikh was preparing to depart, having promised to start on the 9th Katik 1803 (October 23, 1846). He hoped and also believed that no crime would be "proved against him." "The British had ordered him to leave and leave he would," he gave out, "he would not stay another moment in that place, though he should be forced in consequence to halt a day or two on the road to collect coolies". On October 23, the Shaikh finally communicated, "I have this day departed from the city of Kashmir, though my preparations for the march were far from complete".

He proceeded about three miles from the city where it took him a day or two to complete his arrangements. He wrote to Maharaja Gulab Singh, "My Lord, I have ever been your servant and son. The reply which you sent to my humble epistle has inspired me with confidence. May God keep you on your throne to all eternity! You tell me to come and make my submission. I am honoured by receiving your commands and I hasten to obey them....You have taken me by the hand, now deal with me as you think I deserve... My good and bad qualities I have confided to you. It is for you to estimate the sum of them". Leaving the valley on October 25, and proceeding via Shopian the Shaikh, worn out with a forced mountain-march of forty miles, in the course of which he had been drenched in a snow-storm, reached Bairamgulli on October 31. Surrounded by his officers made his submission to Lieut. Edwardes, who on the following day, conducted him to the camp of Henry Lawrence at Thana, the latter having a few days earlier come up with the army. On the next day the forces under the command of Major-General Sir John Littler were ordered to withdraw and Brigadier Wheeler's soon followed. Thus ended this bloodless rebellion.

Maharaja Gulab Singh entered the city of Kashmir about 8 A.M. on November 9, 1846, (it had been declared the auspicious time by the astrologers) and found his sowars in entire possession of the place; Sardar Sujan Singh, with the garrison of Shergurhi, about 3,000 men, and the family of Shaikh Imam-ud-Din, having moved off two days previously. To avoid their line of march, the Maharaja made a detour on his road from Shopian, and fell in with Henry Lawrence at Pampur on the evening of the 8th. It was thought that His Highness would prefer entering his capital by himself, and therefore he was given the opportunity of doing so, but the meeting at Pampur led the British Agent to imagine that the Maharaja was willing to sink his dignity in the increased opinion of the British support that his formal accompaniment would afford His Highness.

Maharaja Gulab Singh having been established in power, Henry Lawrence, "with his usual energy" as Lord Hardinge describes it, returned at once to Lahore. The next thing to be done was to bring Raja Lal Singh to solemn trial and exposure before all the Sikh Chiefs, for secretly instigating Shaikh Imam-ud-Din in the treacherous opposition to Gulab Singh; the defeated Shaikh, having turned "King's evidence" against his late accomplice. He placed in Henry Lawrence's hand at Thana, three original documents, purporting to be instructions from Lal Singh to oppose Gulab Singh; and to the officers and soldiers in Kashmir, to be faithful and obedient to the orders of the Shaikh. These papers were put in as evidence at the subsequent trial of Raja Lal Singh for his complicity in this affair.

It would not be out of place here, before we close, to review the more striking features of this Kashmir expedition.

One cannot help noticing here that the Sikh troops, who had only very recently fought against the British under the same officers who now led them, unwilling as they were in their hearts to support Gulab Singh, whom the Khalsa hated thoroughly, acted admirably in these operations, and thus drew warm commendations from Lord Hardinge. Moreover, these operations afforded to the Sikh troops an opportunity of manifesting the improved state of their temper and discipline, by the alacrity with which they obeyed the order they received at Lahore, and the cheerfulness and patience with which they endured the privations of scanty supplies and long marches in a mountainous country. This service had been performed on the requisition of the British Government. "His Lordship," writes F. Currie to H.M. Lawrence, "will be much gratified by having the opportunity of acknowledging the services rendered in so admirable a manner by an army whose military qualities were last year experienced in the field on the banks of the Sutlej—and this year have been displayed in maintaining by the most zealous co-operation with the British forces and those of Maharaja Gulab Singh, an important article of the Treaty of Lahore, the violation of which was threatened by Shaikh Imam-ud-Din, employed by the Lahore Darbar in the Government of Kashmir".

Properly considered this feat of compelling the culpable Lahore Darbar, with its chief conspirator, Raja Lal Singh, at its head, to make over, in the most marked and humiliating manner, the richest province in the Panjab to the one man most detested by the Khalsa, was the real victory of the campaign; and its achievement must continue an enigma to every one who remembers that it was performed by 10,000 Sikh soldiers at the bidding and under the guidance of two or three British officers within eight months of the battle of Sobraon.

This conjuncture was described by Henry Lawrence in a letter to Kaye (published in his Lives of Indian Officers, Volume II, page 298) as—"that ticklish occasion when I took the Sikh army to Kashmir, and when I was obliged to tell Lal Singh's Vakil that if anything happened to me, John Lawrence was told to put the Raja (Lal Singh) in confinement. The fact was, I knew he was acting treacherously, but trusted to carrying the thing through by expedition, and by the conviction that the British army was in our rear to support and avenge us."

(Bengal Past and Present, 1933)

CHAPTER 2

SIYAHAT-I-KASHMIR
(Kashmir Nama or Tarikh-i-Kashmir)

By

Ganeshi Lal

To the traversers of the domains of intellect and the wanderers on the paths of wisdom it is manifest that the benefits of travel,like the company of the experienced and the observation of marvels of God, are innumerable and beyond description. An old adage has it, "so long as you remain confined to the precincts of your house you will not mature into manhood. Go roam about the world until you depart from it". Accordingly the exalted Sahibs, the leaders, the glorious ones, the statesmen and holders of high offices—Charles Hardinge and Captain Hardinge, sons of the Governor-General of India, planned to proceed to Kashmir, which has been accepted by the tourists of the world as the most beautiful and delightful place, on a pleasure trip. The writer of this account, Ganeshi Lal, was, at the instance of the Sahibs, called upon to accompany them on the said tour and thereby had an opportunity to see strange things on the journey. He was required to record events and information about the places on the way right from the start i.e., Ludhiana, up to the end—the City of Kashmir. It was enjoined on him that accounts should be prepared of whatever could be seen or investigated about things of interest and people inhabiting the region in the form of a daily Journal. Those who might read these pages would thus be informed about the nature and difficulties of the journey. May God enable me to achieve this purpose!

Twenty-eight March, 1846, Saturday. In company with the Honourable Charles Hardinge and Captain Hardinge, sons of the Governor-General of India, Lord Elphinstone, Dr. Walker, Captain Edward Lake, the Political Assistant at Ludhiana, marched this afternoon from Ludhiana, crossed the Sutlej and arrived at Phillaur. Through the negligence of the servants a box containing cash, goods and papers in English and Persian was carried away from the Bahngi at Talwandi.

Twenty-ninth March, Sunday. Spent the night in the Haveli of Jawahar Mal, Tehsildar. Passing by Bara pind, also called Koleta, and other villages, after a march of 10 coss, reached Phagwara, a town belonging to Sardar Nihal Singh, the Ahluwalia Chief. It is a pretty large town with long rows of shops but in common with all the towns of the Panjab, its streets are narrow and dirty. There is a fort outside. The camp was pitched to the west of the town.

Thirtieth March, Monday. After a march of 10 coss we arrived at Jullundur and pitched close to the camp of John Lawrence, the Commissioner of the Doab. In the course of journey we crossed a beautiful bridge lately built by Sheikhs of the Doab over the small stream—Bain. Jullundur is an ancient populous town, a number of large tombs and mosques and other building erected by the Moghal Kings, Mohammadan Zamindars and Afghan rulers are to be seen here. The streets are long, pucca and narrow. There is the strong fort adjoining the town. It is the centre of the commerce of the Doab and has a number of Nauhria merchants' shops. Silk is the staple article of trade. It is of various descriptions. The suburbs are beautiful. The numerous mango gardens, wells for irrigation—altogether form a delightful landscape. Since the time of Kings it has always been the seat of Government in the Doab.

Thirty-first March, Tuesday. Both the Camps, the Commissioner's and ours, moved together and after a March of 9 coss, reached Adampore, a large village belonging to the Sikh General, Ram Singh Jullehwalla. There are about 200 shops in this village, a small fort and an abundance of sugarcane cultivation. Sugar is made here plentifully.

First April, Wednesday. A march of about 9 coss brought us to Hoshiarpur, a pretty large town situated at the foot of the hills. It is populated by the Hindoos who are more numerous here than the Mohamedans and is a great entrepot of the hill commerce. The camp was pitched at Missur Rooplal's Baradaree. We separated from the Commissioner's camp at this place and Captain Bates, the Commander-in-Chief's Aide-de-Camp, joined us with a view to accompany us to Cashmere.

Second April, Thursday. Passing by Bussee Alfkhan, Bussee Moolwalee, Dolowal, Ajoowal, Ninyan Kasba, Huryana, King Bhoonga, Dhot, Pindouree Mochian and Goyundpore, we arrived at the village of Gudh Deewala, properly Gudh Dewalla, having been denominated from the circumstance of its having a temple of Devi "Dus Bhooj" (or Goddess with ten arms). The camp was pitched near Baba Dhuramdas's tomb. Scenery on the road is beautiful and the neighbourhood of the village bears a happy resemblance to that of Munee Muzra and Teera, being surrounded with a Jungle of mango trees and watered with a number of small artificial rivulets called Kools. The zamindars are Jats of Sehota denomination and are the proprietors of all the 4 Turrufs into which this old village is divided. The present Punch or Headman, named Mehan Singh, is a respectable old man of about 70 years of age and together with his son, Bishen Singh, has great influence with the people as well as with the rulers in the fort. This fort is situated to the east of the village, is built pukka, having a bastion on each corner and a strong one in the middle. A well, a temple and a few houses are situated inside. It was left rent- free to the ancestors of the present Zamindars; and Munsha Singh and Gursahai in Sambut

1857 (1800 A.D.) having built the middle bastion, were going to found others when the fort was suddenly attacked by Rajah Sansar Chand of Kangra. A battle took place in which about 2,000 men on either side are said to have been killed and the fort captured by the Rajah. In Sumbut 1872 (1815 A.D.) it fell a prey to the rising power of the "Lion of the Punjab", and is now in the hands of the British. There are about 2,000 shops and a Devi's temple in this village. It produces the best sugar and commands 132 villages.

Third April, Friday. We arrived at Dasooha, 5 coss, an old village built pukka and having more than 200 shops. The Zamindars are Mohammadan Rajpoots and Kanoongoes, Khutrees by caste. Together with 27 dependent villages it yields a revenue of 16,000 rupees a year and was given in Jagir by the late Maharaja Sher Singh to his brother Tara Singh. Some villages are now in the hands of Sher Singh Sindhanwalla. It has a pukka fort to the north on an elevated ground, a gun, some ammunition and store in it. About a 1/4 mile to the south of it is the village of Kaneit, belonging to the Sheikhs with 40 villages.

Fourth April, Saturday. Passing through Khanpore and Mukerian, a large old town, we arrived at Bhimgala, 11 coss, and encamped near Rambagh at the place of Baba Hurriedass, a Fakir of the "Oodassee" sect and devout pious man. At Mukerian there is a fort about 1/2 mile to the south of the town and has 84 villages under its jurisdiction. Bhungalas are two small and large villages about 1/2 mile from each other, the Zamindars are Mohammadan Rajpoots going under the title of Rai. The present Headman is Rai Futteh and the villages together with 27 hours are subject to Mukerian. These villages are inhabited by Bunjarahas, who keep about 500 bullocks and trade in rice, carrying that article from the Kangra hills by the Beas river to Ferozepore for the purpose of trade.

Fifth April, Sunday. After a short march of 3 coss we arrived by Gurdaspoora at Meelwan, a small thatched village of the Mohammadan Rajpoots on the Beas opposite to the Meerthul Ghat. Here we met the 44th Regiment native Infantry Sirdar Jhunda Singh, the Lahore agent, with 50 sowars, the Baboo and the Monshee on the part of Maharajah Golab Singh of Jammu with 100 sowars and as many infantry. They arrived from Meerthul and together with Dewan Ajoodhia Nath, Moonshee Shadeelal, and a Vuzeer of the Noorpore Rajah paid their respects to Mr. Lake, a strong wind blew the whole day. Mr. Lake granted me a very obliging testimonial.

Sixth April, Monday. Mr. Lake and the 44th remained at Meelwan, while our party, consisting of the sons of the Governor-General, Lord Elphinstone, Dr. Walker and Captain Bates, crossed the Beas at the Kathgurh ferry, and, passing by Nuzzle Bhore and Chhunee, arrived at Goomtal, 8 coss. This village belongs to the Noorpore Chiefshif and is held rent-free by Gopal Das, a Byragee mendicant, in whose garden we encamped. At the ghat we were saluted by the troops of Rajah Gulab Singh, who had formed an imposing line for the purpose. Goomtal is a large village, situated on the foot of the hill, having about 25 shops and very few houses of the Mohammadans, while the rest are occupied by the Hindoo, Rajpoot and Jat Zamindars. Its neighbourhood bears a great resemblance to that of Pinjore, being interested by small artificial rivulets, and has an abundance of the Rice, Wheat and Barley production but no gain and little or no trade. The Head mendicant, Baba Gopaldas, has a large house like a fort, and is erecting another which promises to rise into a noble building. The hand of the famous painter of Noorpore, Bishendas, has shown the utmost powers of his art at this place. The Baba is a handsome youngman dressed in the hill costume and gives rations to every beggar, who may call at his door, being supported in this charitable expense by the revenues of 3 other villages, and assisted by his numerous votaries in the neighbourhood. He received us very civilly. There are a Bolie and a

Goopha or recess. A tradition prevails that about 300 years ago the Goopha had a subterranean passage to Jaypore and another to Kooloo.

Seventh April, Tuesday. Starting from Gomtal in the morning we arrived at Puthankot, about 2½ coss. This seems to have been a pukka Sarai in former days; from its top a beautiful view is presented to the eye of the hills and the town, which consists of more than 200 pukka shops, besides, a number of the houses belonging to Mahajans, Rajpoots and Kashmiris. The Kashmiris run Shawl factories and form two parts of the populace while the third consists of other castes of the Hindus and Panjabi Muslims. The vicinity is beautiful, being surrounded with gardens and intersected with Kools. The cultivators are Rajputs. Passing further on, about 2½ coss, we reached Sujanpur Bhaganwalla and encamped at Maharaja Runjeet Singh's Baraduree situated about a 1/4 mile to the west of the town on the bank of the canal called "Hunslee". This is a nice delightful place abundantly watered and thickly shaded, having a pukka ghat and a flight of stairs built with bricks and mortar. The "Hunslee" is cut from the Ravee and is carried to Harmandir at Amritsar, the Shalamar gardens at Lahore and the Tarn Taran Tank. At Sujanpur, too, there are several Shawl factories of Kashmiris. The Kashmiri merchants and Sahukars carry manufactures of the place to Farukhabad, Banaras and Jagadhari. The cultivators in the area are Hindu Rajpoots. A tradition prevails that more than 200 years ago Rana Kullas, Chief of Noorpore, cut this famous canal at the village Goortha, alias Rani Ka Tala. The reason for undertaking these works is said to have been that Kullas, coming from Jumoo, was one day sitting at this place and happened to ask a parcel of the shepherd boys, whose place it was? They refused to give him this information, which incensed the Chief. The boys, however, not knowing who he was told him that he must not be angry, did he not know the name of Rana Kullas, their lord? This influence of his name seems to have pleased the Rana so much that he told the boys that he was the Chief they named and wished them to ask any favour they wanted. On this the boys said that their flocks were generally much distressed for want of water and the Rana was as good as his word in granting them their request and soon had the canal dug from the Ravee. But a more accurate history of the "Hunslee" appears to be that Nawab Allee Murdan Khan, in obedience to the orders of the Emperor Shahjehan, had this canal cut from the Ravee from the vicinity of the village of Madhopore, 5 coss below Shahpore, and making it pass by Soojanpore, Purmanand, Adeena Nuggar, Batala and Mujeetha (where it branches off into 3 canals), brought it to the Shalamar; a branch of it has been directed to Tarn Taran. And in the Hijra year 1238 (1822 A.D.), when Maharaja Runjeet was laying the foundation of the Rambagh at Amritsar another branch of the Hunslee was excavated to water it and fill the sacred tank at the place. There are beautiful gardens and buildings at Adeena Nuggar on its banks and a strong bridge over it near Batala; and the junction of it is annually dug and cleared by the orders of the Lahore Government.

The following is the genealogy of the Noorpore Rajas:-

Rana Kullas.
Raja Ingta.
Rajroop.
Daya Dhotta.
Mandhata.
Prithee Singh.
Beer Singh, died about 20 days ago.
Tikka Jaswant Singh, alive.

The annual revenue of this village is 1,200 rupees. After the death of Adeena Beigh, the Moghal satrap, the Sikhs of the Bugga denomination took possession of it and erected a fort. In Sumbut 1869 (1812 A.D.) Maharaja Runjeet Singh gave battle to Budh Singh Bugga; but after 15 days' skirmish he was obliged to return without effecting anything. The fort was, however, taken by him after 4 or 5 years, more by a stratagem than by force. In starting from Goomtal we had to cross a stream by the name of the Chuckee Mudee on the bank of which stands the shrine of some saint with a flag over it and a small hill over it, called Dhangee, is much frequented by the Fakeers and native botanists in their botanical researches. From Majitha Hansli canal is split into three branches, one going to Shalimar, the other to Amritsar and the third, when necessary, to Tarn Taran.

Eighth April, Wednesday. Leaving Sujanpur in the morning, crossing the small wooden bridge of the "Hunslee", and proceeding in the river at the distance of half a mile by boats, we arrived at Kathua, 5 coss, belonging to Jammu, and encamped in a garden. The road is much intersected with small rivulets and Kools which render it almost impassable and add to the cultivation. With reference to the Ravee and its Ghats, it is stated by Khyra, a boatman of Kathua, that water from various issues, being collected near the "Nun Muheis" hills, the residence of Fakeers and hermits, forms itself into a Nullah and, flowing via Chumba, Burmoore Hut, Bisohle and Shahpore; and receiving the Siyava and Sival rivers into it respectively at Hut and Simlee, swells into a river. It is crossed in the hills by a kind of suspension bridge at the lower ghats of Bisohlee Kuttooah by boats. The following is a list of its ghats, viz:-

	Coss
Theela, belonging to Jammu ..	7
Gidree, belonging to Jammu ..	1
Akhwara, belonging to Mujeetha ..	1/4
Jullala, belonging to Jummoo ..	1/4
Turmoon, belonging to Lahore ..	2
Sheikhoopore, belonging to Lahore ..	2
Duryaka Ghat, belonging to Jammu ..	3
Bheemka, belonging to Jammu ..	4
Durangla, belonging to Majeetha ..	5
Adde Ka Ghat, belonging to Majeetha ..	7

Deriaka, belonging to Lahore ..	10
Buddalla, belonging to Lahore ..	3
Boolakee Chuck, belonging to Lahore ..	4
Dera Baba Nanak, belonging to Lahore ..	5

At Kathua Dewan Jwalla Sahai, agent of Rajah Golab Singh, presented himself to the Chief of our party and gave 525 rupees at Zeeafut and sweetmeats. With reference to this village it was gathered that it formerly belonged to Rajah Ajaib Singh of Jasrota, the ancestor of the Jammu family, that it was subsequently taken possession of by Sirdar Amar Singh Bugga, that about 16 years ago Rajah Socheit Singh attacked the fort, situated half a mile to the east of the village, with about 10,000 troops and artillery, but the garrison, consisting of a handful of men (300), resisted and held out for a month after which it was taken by the besiegers. The village is inhabited like the hill villages, having few roofed and many thatched houses, a Nulla flows quite close to it and it contains 200 shops. Ishar Chowdree or the headman stated that Rice and Turmeric are produced here in abundance and are sent to Lahore and Amritsar as articles of trade. The Zamindars are Hindoo Rajpoots and the annual revenue 20,000 rupees.

Ninth April, Thursday. Passing by Khanpore, Mahee, Chuck and other villages on the road, crossing the ford of the Oojh river and leaving Jasrota, the Capital of the late Rajah Heera Singh, about 3 coss to our right, we arrived at Chungee, belonging to Jammu, after a long march of 10 coss. The road was almost entirely intersected with Kools from the Oojh and the whole neighbourhood so very fresh with an abundance of water and thick with cultivation and tree that it seemed considerably to outbeat the fresh scenery of Ambala, Ludhiana and those parts in the rainy season. Our camp was pitched in a thicket belonging to a devout hermit who died about 4 years ago. Dewan Jwalla Sahai sent a Zeeafut of 51 pitchers full of sweetmeats.

Tenth April, Friday. A long march of 14 coss brought us to Sambha, a large town having about 350 shops. The Hindoo Rajpoots are the Zamindars, the cultivators and people are generally dependent on the rain water, which is scarce. The Bussantar river, which flows towards the west, is dry except in the rains. The Sumyaloo Rajpoots held this town with its dependent villages under their rule subject to the Jammu principality; but the famine of Sumbat 1840 (1783 A.D.) caused a thorough ruination, and latterly the Futteh Singhia and Tara Singhia Sikhs took possession of it. About 25 years, since the present Jammu Rajas became masters of the place and assigned allowances to the original proprietors in lieu of service, which is still rendered by them at Jammu, Raja Sochet Singh, deceased, turned it into a military station, built a cantonment and a mud fort, formed good streets and gave encouragement to trade. But last year the Lahore Sikhs, after killing Raja Heera Singh, Sohan Singh, Labh Singh and Missar Jhalla, and others attacked this place and destroyed the fort and the lines. A great portion of the inhabitants fled and the place now presents a wretched appearance. But after the late war the British have put the Rajah of Jammu again in possession of it, and owing to the most abominable tyranny of the Sikhs, the change seems to have made the people happy. The Hindus are in majority and Mohammadans are artisans. The several hill productions are brought to this place and transported to the various parts of the Punjab. Sahukars of Amritsar had established their depots as Commission Agents; but presently all have moved away. Only the depot of Karam Chand Arora is there. Chintz is the staple produce and an article of exportation while the saber and leather trousers, used by a numerous population in the hills, are supplied from this place. After the death of Rajah Sochet Singh at the hands of Lahore Sikhs by the order of his own nephew, Heera Singh, 13 Ranees and slave girls of the deceased, and 3 widows of Vuzeer Kesari Singh, who fell with him sword in hand, became Sutteess at this spot and burnt themselves alive and their tombs have been erected here to commemorate this great, catastrophe. The Sumeergarh, alias Heera Nagar fort which was strongly built by Heera Singh was left by us to the right, 3 coss from the last ground, and there Mian Ranbir Singh, son of Raja Gulab Singh, had visited the Chief of our party and presented a Zeafut.

Eleventh April, Saturday. A difficult march of 14 coss brought us to a small river called Deoka or Oomaputtee. This place is supposed by the natives to be as sacred as Gyaji and is, therefore, called Gyaji or Autarbunee. The temple consecrated by Raja Gulab Singh to Devi is a nice building. It was visited by the gentlemen of our party, who also presented 25 rupees and received sweetmeats in return from the priests. There is also a peepal tree at this place on the bank of the river where an ablution is considered as holy as that at the Kashi. We did not, however, stop at this place and, crossing further on, arrived at Poormundal, 3 coss. This being the great religious day of the Hardwar fair, a large crowd of villagers had assembled at the holy place of Poormandal to bathe in the Oomaputtee and to worship the old Mahadev called Oomaputti over which a very splendid Sheewala (or Shivala) has been built by Raja Gulab Singh and the dome and the cornices are gold plated, which must have cost no less than a lakh of rupees. A number of other Lingas have been transported to this place from the Narbada amounting, it is said, to 360. Other splendid buildings stand here on either bank of the river, belonging to the several chiefs of the country and give the place an imposing appearance. The river is, however, dry except during the rainy season and at this time the people have been put to the necessity of digging temporary holes in its bed for the purpose of bathing. They offer suitable amounts in charity and pay homage to Mahadev. At the mela the sweetmeat sellers, general merchants and dealers in sundries open their shops in large numbers. The wood for ploughs is sold in abundance here. Its price is five or six annas. A duty of three annas per piece from the buyer and that of 2 annas from the seller is levied. None of the costlier articles are offered for sale. The mela was not largely attended this year. The people, however, seem very poor and needy and ready to do anything for a piece of bread or a pice. The women, generally fair, but with regard to their character and morals they are what a needy and uneducated people may be expected to be Poormandal is a sacred place mentioned in the Shastras. The nudee here is a tributary of the Ravi. Mian Ranbir Singh remained with the camp the whole day.

Twelfth April, Sunday. Travelling 8 coss, we encamped at Babuleana, a small village belonging to Jammu and only 3 coss distant from that town. A shower of rain came on in the afternoon. There is scarcity of water, there being only one well and a pukka tank, quite insufficient to meet the want of the people and the travellers in the hot weather, and two shops.

Thirteenth April, Monday. The gentlemen of the party went out shooting and in the afternoon, mounting the elelphants in company with Mian Ranbir Singh, we crossed the Tavi river by a ford about a coss this side of Jammu. Here we were received by Maharaja Gulab Singh, who presented 650 rupees as Sarwarna to all the officers and the camp was pitched in Raja Dhian Singh's stable and Baradurree and a newly constructed bungalow there. The Maharaja used every kind of civility, brought vegetables and presents and took leave. One thousand rupees were sent in the evening as Zeeafut together with 225 pitchers of sweetmeats with Dewan Jawala Sahai. The writer was lodged in the building along with Chanda Singh. The Tavi river takes its rise from these hills and flows constantly, swelling considerably in the rainy season. There being a great scarcity of water at Jammu the whole town is supplied with this element from the river. In the town there is only one tank and there is no other well, etc. Hence there is considerable scarcity of water. Across the river, to the east, stands the famous strongly built Bahoo fort on a hillock. It is said to have once been a well populated town before the existence of Jammu. On each side of the last named town there stands a thorny jungle which is protected by the Raja. No one is allowed to cut wood from it and it is supposed to be a strong defence, having only a narrow inlet into the town. It is also added that when the Sikh troops, about 50,000, had attacked Jammu after murdering Raja Hira Singh, they could not penetrate this natural defence, but were obliged to retreat before a small number of Jammu troops who took sure aims at them from their ambushes in this wood and succeeded in carrying off four guns of the invaders.

Fourteenth April, Tuesday, Jammu. All the gentlemen went to Raja Gulab Singh's house on elephants, were received with civility, accepted a Sarwarna of 775 rupees, a polite conversation lasted during the visit. Seventeen guns were fired. China furniture and dresses with figures of the Chinese gods on them, their curious caps and swords and other curiosities were shown. These things were brought as booty after the battle which took place between the Jammu and Lhasa troops on the Ladakh frontier in 1842, when Captain J.D. Cunningham had been deputed by the British Government to mediate between them. The Maharaja stated that there were still 3 Chinese Wazirs and sepoys as prisoners at Jammu, that his Wazir Zorawar Singh had been killed in that war and the tract of country then conquered by him was still in his hands. They further examined maps and charts and retired after inspecting the tents and camp accessories for journey to Kashmir. The Maharaja's palace and Dewan Khana looked no better than those of ordinary Sirdars or aristocrats of Delhi, which is the least indicative of his greatness and grandeur. In the bazar the writer met Kamudar Khan, son of Imam Bakhsh Khan, Vakil of Patiala, who had proceeded thither in search of service, and Moulvi Mazher Ali Khan.

Fifteenth April, Wednesday Jammu. The writer stayed at the Dera throughout the day but in the evening we went to see the town which seems to consist of about 500 shops, narrow streets, a famous shrine of Syed Mitha and a Shiwala, the residence of Sanyasi Faqirs, in company with Sardars Chanda Singh and Sham Singh. Lala Jugal Kishore, nephew of Lala

Harsarn Das, who had come for news-writing, came to see the writer. Through him several letters to friends at Ludhiana were sent. The buildings are poor and like those of any other hill towns and the more so for want of clay, water and other materials.

Sixteenth April, Thursday, Jammu. Sardar Chanda Singh, who was with us on deputation from Lahore got leave today on receipt of commendation letters. He holds for five generations a jagir yielding 20,000 rupees a year at Kulalwala, 25 coss from Jammu and 2 from Deok river. In the days of Moghal Kings, about 125 years ago, Sardar Dewan Singh was the principal heir to the territories of Kalalwala and held other Jagirs. He was succeeded by Charat Singh, son of Dhian Singh district and had long held out against the rising power of held these forts—Kulalwalla, Punwan and Pulpar, under him and his sister was married to the late Maharaja Kharak Singh. The other Sardar on deputation with him was Sham Singh, who also enjoys a jagir of three villages, 5 coss, from Amritsar and was in charge of Toshakhana under Kanwar Naunihal Singh. In the evening we were invited to an entertainment by the Maharaja from which we returned at about 10 p.m. much amused by seeing dances and fireworks.

Raja Ranjit Deo in times of his power brought 11 hill Chiefships on the east and as many on the west bank of the Ravi under his subjugation. The following is a list of them—

Between the Ravi and the Jhelum.	To the east of the Ravi.
Bhimber Raj under Muslim rulers.	Noorpur.
	Haripur.
Poonch.	Guler.
Rajaur.	Kangra and Kamlagarh.
Amthal, Chini Capital.	Shahpur.
Bunderhal, called Ramnagar.	Mandi and Sooket.

Bhuddo, the Somurta fort.	Bilaspur-Kuhloor.
Jasrota.	Hindoor-Nallagarh.
Mankot, Ramkote Capital.	Sirmore-Nahan.
Chamba and Bhadarwah.	Kulu.
Kishtwar.	

About 40 years ago this mighty Chiefship fell a prey to the blooming power of Lahore and Ranjit Singh, the Lion of the Panjab, made repeated inroads into it, took possession of its several parts, gave then over to his various Chiefs, Dewans and others and this state of things lasted about 12 years. The members of the present ruling family, i.e. Gulab Singh, Dhyan Singh and Sochet Singh were nothing more than private individuals, who had joined the service of the Maharaja as Sowars. Mian Dido, a descendant of the same Jammu family and a petty Jagirdar of Jagtee had not, however, allowed Ranjit a peaceful possesion of his new conquests and was always plundering the country with a large gang of followers, bidding open defiance to Ranjit's measures. He used to kill the Sikh officers and functionaries wherever he found them, always sneaked in the thick forests or hills difficult of access, never stopped in one place and in short had given Ranjit a great annoyance and trouble. The Maharaja was, however, advised by his friends to select Gulab Singh and his brothers to punish their relation, Didoo, and in pursuance of this plan Gulab Singh was, about 25 years ago, at Kanch kachuk, created Raja of Jammu. Dhyan Singh also got the title and was made Raja of Bhimber. Sambha or Ramnagar was assigned to Raja Sochet Singh and Jasrota to Raja Heera Singh, who was a favourite of the Maharaja since his infancy. Many of the Chiefships between the Ravi and Jhelum were incorporated with that of Jammu and others were subsequently taken possession of by force by the new Raja during their Wazarat or Ministry at Lahore. There is only a part of Rajaur and part of Chamba in the hands of their original rulers, the rest of the Chiefships have been absorbed by the Jammu principality. In the month of March, 1846, after the Panjab War, Raja Gulab Singh has been created Maharaja of Jammu and got Kashmir, Chuch and Hazara in addition to his former possessions by paying 75 lakhs of rupees, the remuneration promised by the Lahore Durbar for the expenses of the war. He is now entirely alienated from Lahore, is under the British protection and a line of demarcation has been drawn between his and the Lahore territories. In the evening Maharaja Gulab Singh paid us a visit and brought hill ponies for the officers to assist them in the long journey in the hills before them.

Eighteenth April, Saturday. We went to take our leave of the Maharaja today and were assisted in the ceremony by Captains Brown and Nicholson, who were already there to organise and train the troops of Raja Gulab Singh on his request.

Nineteenth April, Sunday. Having marched from Jammu in the evening we arrived and encamped at Nagrota in Jammu territory. Today nothing particular took place.

Twentieth April, Monday. A march of 7 coss over the summit of Murhal range by Dhukke and Bun brought us to Dumsal a village enjoyed, together with 18 others as a jagir, by Mian Bichatar Deo, grandson of Mian Mota, yielding altogether a revenue nominally of 12,000 rupees but really 7,000 rupees per annum. The whole is dry and waterless. The road rugged and difficult even to the foot passengers. The village contains 100 houses, 20 shops. The annual revenue is 300 rupees. The present headman is Chaudhari Sahoo Mian Bachittar remains in attendance at Jammu, to serve the Raja and furnishes 6 Sowars in lieu of the jagir. Dumsal is a parganah also called Dumsala.

Twenty-first, April, Tuesday. Crossing the confluence of the Jhajjar with the Tavi near Jammu, ascending the Krah range and then crossing Doadur, another tributary of the Tavi, we arrived at Guddhee. This place had a demolished fort; an open plain and an imposing scenery which invited us to take little rest and, after breakfast, recrossing the Deoka at Parmandal, we encamped at Udhampore, 3 coss from the last ground. This is the place where late Mian Udham Singh had ordered the creation of 20 ranges of shops about 100 in number as Bazars, crossing each other and inhabited by various artisans. The neighbourhood is beautiful. The country from the Kural range to the Kuramchee village is called Boolhatta, owing to the great abundance of water and of the spontaneous productions of nature. It is styled by the natives as little Kashmir. It is very fertile and productive and is a military station of Jammu troops. This village together with 20 others was given in jagir to the late Mian Udham, but has been resumed since his death. The day's journey was easy and clear.

Twenty-second April, Wednesday. The Deoka was crossed again and, passing by Sambhal, Jhakkar and the Ramsar villages we arrived at Kuramachee, 3½ coss, the boundary of the Boolhalta tract. Beyond this the country is called Bhootee, which yields about 9,000 rupees a year and formerly belonged to Raja Jai Singh Bhootial, but in Sambat 1890 (1833 A.D.) Raja Gulab Singh took possession of it and assigned a small maintenance to Jai Singh, now living at Jammu. There are about 50 shops and a dismantled mud fort here. We did not, however, stop here, but, passing on, reached the village Meer, 8 coss by the following villages on the road:

Mansur, Hamira, Trichee, Narneir, Khatgulara and across the Biscar range. the camp was pitched on a narrow spot, scarcely enough for our tents. Here the writer stayed in a beautiful house with Jagan Nath, Munshi of Elphinstone Sahib. The road abounds with beautiful valleys, delightfully watered with several rivulets and issues from the hills, enlivened by fresh verdure and diversified by a variety of odoriferous flowers. This scenery lasts to the Biscar range, where an increasing cold like that in the month of 'Poh' (December) in the plains becomes perceptible. Honey is produced here of the best kind.

Twenty-third April, Thursday. Passing by the Cholta village, crossing the Panthal, a tributary of the Chandar Bhaga or the Chenab, ascending the Panjaree range by the summit called Kumadhuk, we arrived at the Sundar fort and thence by Beemudah encamped at 'Kul', 7 coss, belonging to Bhotee. The villages here are universally scattered here and there, the road bad and tedious, intersected near Lander by the Bhonee Nullah, which pours itself into the Punthal. Lunder is the name of a newly built fort by Gulab Singh, but it is not strong. The annual revenue does not exceed 400 rupees. The people are very poor and extremely fearful of their rulers. Here we felt exceedingly cold weather—a cold wind scarcely to be met with in the plains and water intensely cold. The Zamindars are generally Hindu Rajputs and live chiefly on flesh.

Twenty-fourth April, Friday. Ascending the Singhpal range, Ladda- laddy, over the hills here and there covered with snow, we arrived by the Kurree and Solu villages at Bullot, 6 coss. The road was rugged and was with difficulty passed on foot. The village is smallish. The country is called Himta and the range is called Ludha, but is more generally known by the name of Singhpal. The Ladda-laddy, which means the bride and the bridegroom, is a shrine consecrated to a newly married couple who fell victims here to the severity of the snow under which they were buried by a sudden shower and the place is now generally respected by the mountaineers. The temple of god Singhpal, from which the name of the range is derived, is also situated here and is annually resorted to by about 2,000 people in the beginning of rains. It is much revered by the people who offer sacrifice of goats and presents in money to it. The cowherds of the neighbouring plains bring their flocks to the range in hot weather for the purposes of grazing and give two seers of butter per month to Jammu authority as their right for permission to graze. This right is called "Gheeana". The whole range is thickly covered with forest, consisting of the Sivahum or native Cypress, a very large trees exceeding 120 cubits—the "Cheel" the "Mohroo", the Deodar and other trees. The cold is intense and the road passable only when the snow has melted away.

Twenty-fifth April, Saturday. We passed the day at Meetra, a village 2 coss from the last place, on the east bank of the Chenab, and in the afternoon broke ground again and, crossing the river by a kind of Jhoolas or swings called Khrihra or Khuralee by the natives over an almost impassable ghat, reached Nasmun, 3 coss, belonging to Kunthee Parganah in the Kishtwar Chiefship. The river flows very deep, it is called Chandar Bhaga by the natives, deriving its name from two small rivers Chandar, crossing from Bhotan and Chamba via Kulu and Bhaga from an unknown source. These two rivers form a junction at Bhoordarkote in the Kishtwar district and thence flow on under the above name in the hills and the Chenab in the plains. The banks near Nasmun are covered with the spontaneous pomegrenates and lemon trees and flowers of various kinds. Owing to the immoderate rapidity of the stream intervened with huge rocks in the bed the river is unnavigable. Customs posts are established by the Jammu Raja at Meetra and Nasmun and their officers give a good deal of annoyance to passangers, the rate of payment depending upon their own will and pleasure.

Twenty-sixth April, Sunday. Walking the whole way on foot, owing to the difficulty of the road, we arrived by Smicha and Mogee, 4 coss, belonging to Bullote. Zorawar Singh Vazir, in attendance on the part of Jammu, got leave and Sehu, another officer, joined the camp in his place. The range on the west bank of Chenab is called Ooncote. It has an abundance of water throughout. The images cut in stone near Smicha are called by the people "Jwala Deotas". A fair takes place here on every Tuesday, after the new moon in the month of Sawan (August) when goats and sheep, milk and rice are offered as sacrifice to the deity and such petty fairs are said to be very common in these parts of hills.

Twenty-seventh April, Monday. The Loonkot, also called Manankot range, was crossed on foot and, descending down in the valley formed by the same range and, passing by the villages and streams noted in the margin, we arrived at Bathinder, a village in the Lorra valley in the Poogul Pargannah of Kishtwar and encamped on the bank of Bishuree river, coming from the Surrooloora range in the Bannihal country. The Purshlan Khud is the terminus of the Looncote range and beyond it commences the Poogul district. At Bathunder the 3 rivers i.e., the Purushlan from the east, the Neelkhud from the north and the Bishuree from the west, form a junction and flow together taking a southerly direction and all pour themselves into Chandar Bhaga near Gulee and Bhatta villages, about 5 coss from this place. From the junction to its confluence with Chandar Bhaga the river is called Bishuree alone and is a pretty rapid stream so as to be fordable with difficulty. The Poogul Paragannah yields only 2,000 rupees per annum and is very thinly inhabited by Mohammadans and Hindus, the latter being in no way better than the former and generally eating and drinking together. The Mohammadan Zamindars of Batlander are of Soolmut denomination and speak a mixture of the Kashmiri, Hill and Dogri languages. Their customs and manners bear strong resemblance to those of the Kashmiris. They groan under the oppression and extortions of the rulers. The productions are Chestnuts, Wheat, Makki, Koda Cheena and a small quantity or rice; but a peculiar grain is called "Kubroo, which resembles black pepper and is somewhat bitter in taste. The Zamindars state that formerly the Kishtwar country belonged to Raja Tegh Singh. A battle took place at Ussur which sealed the fate of Tegh Singh. He was taken prisoner, brought to Jammu and thence to Lahore. But he together with 2 wives died at the Capital. His 2 sons ruined by the misfortune sunk into thorough destitution, and one of them at last arriving at Ludhiana adopted the Christian religion under the protection of American missionaries who give him 5 or 6 rupees a month to support life.

Twenty-eighth April, Tuesday. Keeping along the bank of Bishuree by the small villages of Gangra, Neehungree and Norchlanath, boundary between Kishtwar and Kashmir, passing by Araor bank of Hyder Bunoo, thence crossing the Kidaree range called by the Kashmiris Lad Nazenturah, joining with the famous Peer Bannihal Chain, we arrived by Muchdulloo, Kharpoora and Adalkote at Deogool, 7 coss, belonging to Kashmir in the Bannihal Pargannah. The whole district is populated with Mohammadans, speaking the Kashmiri dialect. Its revenues under the past rulers stood thus:-

	Rs	
Dewan Kirpa Ram's time ..	4,000	of Kashmiri coins together with Zinot.
Genl. Mehan Singh's 2 years ..	5,000	Ditto
Genl. Mehan Singh's 3 years ..	6,000	Ditto
Sh. Ghulam Muhayyudin's one year ..	7,000	Ditto
From the last year ..	11,509	Ditto

Asadullah Meer, Zamindar of Churchil, a village of this district, is in charge of the revenues, the grazing rights, etc. etc., are settled on each village.

The table of Kashmiri weights was known to be thus:-

> Seventy-six Kashmiri or Hari Singhi rupees make one seer.
> One seer consists of 20 Peil.
> Half-seer makes one Munbatta.
> Four Munbattas make one Tunk and
> Sixteen Tunks make one Kharwar.

At Deogal a post is established for levying customs duties on goods and the rates of duty are as follows:-

On goods exported from Kashmir side;-

1 piece of Shawl cloth ..		6 pies Kashmir currency.
1 Seer of Saffron ..	4 As.	
1 Kharwar of Kooth ..	6 As.	

1 Kharwar of Ghee ..	1 Re.
1 Kharwar of Silk ..	6 Rs.
1 Kharwar of Black Zeera ..	12 As.
1 Kharwar of Bahee Dana ..	2 Rs.
1 Kharwar of Inkstand and white paper ..	2 Rs.
1 Tunk of Charas (extract of hemp) ..	8 As.
1 Kharwar of Banafsha ..	12 As.
1 Kharwar Kana Kucha ..	8 As.
Apples per headload ..	4 As.
Woollen cloth per piece ..	2 As.
Miscellaneous per headload ..	1 Re.

On goods imported into Kashmir from Panjab—

1 Kharwar of cloth of every kind, including silks and kinkhabs ..	4Rs.
1 Kharwar of cloth of every kind, including silks and kiriana ..	From Rs 3 to Re 1 and eight annas.
1 Kharwar of cloth of every kind including silks and sugar ..	Re 1 and eight annas.
1 Kharwar of cloth of every kind, including silks and Gur ..	Re 1.
Miscellaneous per headload ..	One rupee and eight annas.
1 Kharwar of salt brought via Yasman ..	2 As.

On salt 1/2 seer per Kharwar is taken as Zamindara and Chowkidara

Formerly 12 annas per 1,000 rupees was the amount levied on cash but the late General Mehan Singh gave it up.

Twenty-ninth April, Wednesday. Ascending the famous snowy range of Peer Bannihal by the Churbil village in the midst of cold, strong wind and clouds we reached Amoor in the Shahabad Pargannah, belonging to Kashmir and another Customs post where the duty is levied on articles.

The only item of Sayer receipt is carried to the government credit while the rest is appropriated by the Zamindars, Chowkidars and Harkaras, who remain in attendance. A 7th share of their wages is also taken from the poor bearers since the last two years and this imposition on their honest labours has excited great discontent and murmur among the labouring classes.

The famous Vernag or Byreenag fountain is situated about a coss and a half from Amoor. An abundance of water issuing forth from the earth flows out in the shape of a river. The fountain itself is very deep, said to be 10 yards and contains the clearest, bluish, cold and sweetest water that was ever tasted by man. It is inhabited by a swarm of fishes and surrounded with ruins of huge buildings apparently erected by Akbar the Great and his successor Jahangir. The following couplets in Persian are seen inscribed in black stone in one of the corners of the ruins. The date of the building appear to be 1036 Hijra (1626 A.D.) which is seen in the last line of the third couplet. The following prose and couplets in Persian were seen on another black stone in the fountain itself......

"The King of the 7 Kingdoms, the Justice spreading Emperor, Abu-ul-Muzzaffar Jahangir King, son of Akbar, the Ghazi, in the 15th year of his reign came to this beneficient fountain and this building was furnished by order of his Gracious Majesty".

The last line of the couplet gives the date of erection 1029 Hijra (1619 A.D.).

A tradition prevails among the Hindu part of the natives that the holiness of the fountain is testified in the sacred writings of the Puranas, that God Mahadev, happening to arrive at the place mounted on a bull in his usual form of a Fakir, found a "Rakshasa" or a giant sitting to obey, the God became angry and threw his trident on him so vehemently that it not only killed the giant but burst the ground and caused water to flow out of it. It is hence called "Byree Nag"—Byree meaning as enemy and Nag the fountain or issue of water.

Dewan Kishan Lal and Sheikh Shabad-ud-Din of Kashmir attended here and proceeding farther on by villages of Poolee, Cheemee, Gaund, Mooroo, we encamped at Daoroo, altogether 8 coss. The last named town was lately called Shahabad by the Mohammadans. It is inhabited by Kashmiris and has a good row of shops. On reaching this we had to cross the Sandrein river, descending from the snowy ranges of Bannihal.

Thirtieth April, Thursday. From Daoroo, alias Shahabad, we came by Bantheepore across Sandean, Larukpore, Poonth Diala, Boordiala and Isthajipura to Islamabad, 6 coss. This was called Anant Nag in the old days of Hindus, but has now been redesignated Islamabad.

About a mile and a half the famous Sheikh Imam-ud-Din, son of Sheikh Ghulam Mohiyuddin, Governor of Kashmir, came out in great pomp to receive us and brought presents in cash and sweetmeats. The former were, however, declined and the latter accepted.

At the place there are several issues of water which abound with fish of various sorts and are considered sacred by the Hindus. The Anantnag fountain, formed into two large reservoirs, is beset with images of Mahadeo and others. Another fountain, called Mulluknag, close to a Kashmiri's house, produces somewhat warmer water, such as may be found in wells of the plains in the cold weather and gives a sulphuric smell. It is much warmer in other seasons. A third called Sonanag has the most transparent cold water without any smell. The town is pretty large, or at least called so by the natives, consisting of shops and houses of the Kashmiris; but there is nothing in it worth attracting attention. Mattan Saheb is another holy fountain about 2½ miles from the town. The water in it issues forth from three openings formed into one deep reservoir and flows out into another large one which is almost like a long tank. It is surrounded by the houses of Kashmiri Pandits and for the purposes of ablutions, cutting hair of children and other religious rites it is considered as sacred as Gaya. Like all the holy places in India, such as the Ganges, Kurukshetra and others, Pandits and Brahmins swarm round the pilgrim, make him sign his name, which they write in their book or list of their votaries, and urge him to pay them something. Accordingly the writer got his name registered with Pandit Kaul, a resident of the place. About 2 or 3 coss from Islamabad there are some old buildings, or rather ruins, which are said to have belonged to Kurus and Pandavas of old.

First May, 1846, Friday. In company with Dewan Kishan Lal and Jagan Nath we went to Bijbabra, 2 coss, and thence embarking in a boat, 5 coss, arrived at Chursoo or Sursoo. The river by which we came is formed by the accumulation of the waters of several nullahs of "Bishuree". The "Khumbat" arising from the Vernag joins the Sanrein near Islamabad and their confluence is called by the Kashmiris "Vith" and "Bithushtha" by the Hindus. Near the Bighiara the Nullah Luddar falls into it and all these streams passing under the general name of "Vith" flow into the town of Kashmir which is inhabited on either bank of it. In its course it moreover receives the waters of the Chutbul and Doodh Ganga and other nullahs before it falls into Woolur Dal and thence, passing on via Soopore and Baramula, receiving in it the Nand Bhooroo from the Kamraj Pargannah, at Dulga, descends through the hills into the plains of the Punjab. This famous river, the fountain of which has been traced above, is called Bitushtha throughout the hills; but it changes its appellation into the Jhelum by which it is universally known in the plains.

Second May, Saturday. In our progress from Chursoo by the river we had to pass along Vinteepore now reduced to a village but said to have formerly been a large Capital of Raja Vinadatta and to have enjoyed great magnificance the marks of which are still observable in the ruins of large buildings and Ghat on the river. Thence along Buraree, Barus, Lutpore, Pampore, Shampore, Bulwara and the Butung garden, all situated on the bank, arrived in the town of Kashmir and encamped in the garden of Sheikh Ghulam Mohiyuddin. The road from Chursoo to Kashmir by land was only 13 coss but the winding of the river by which we came lengthened it to 20 and the villages are situated on its bank. At Shrompore in the Parnpur Pargannah were seen the famous saffron fields. This is the only place in the whole district which produces the precious specie. Its seed is something like the onion and its beds are small and narrow. It is planted and loose earth is thrown over it just as it is done with potatoes or ginger and it springs up into beautiful purple flowers which give the yellow fibres called the saffron. Its stem is like that of the Dubha kind of grass of the plains and it springs and is gathered in the month of Asooj and Katik (September and October). It is not necessary to sow the seed every year. Once scattered it lasts for 12 or 13 years and the saffron being annually picked the root is still preserved. The total annual produce is worth not more than 50,000 Hari Singhi or Kashmiri rupees and the general rate is 20 rupees a seer.

On our arrival a salute was fired from Sher Garhi, the residence of the Subah or Viceroy, and also from the Hari Parbat Fort situated on an elevation near the town.

Third May, Sunday, Kashmir. The whole day was spent in seeing the Dal near the town and Hari Parbat and the different places in boats. Met Dewan Kishan Lal and Lala Jagan Nath, his son, and Mutaboji, his second son.

Fourth May, Monday, Kashmir. Went to see the town in the evening in boats.

Fifth May, Tuesday, Kashmir. Accepted an invitation from Dewan Kishan Lal. It was accompanied with a sort of local music which, however, did not seem to be so very inviting. In fact nothing was seen in the whole town to justify the immoderate celebrity it has so long enjoyed.

Sixth May, Wednesday. In company with all the gents we went to Shalamar garden. It has 7 storeys and must, in the time of its great founder, Emperor Jahangir, have been a paradise as it is called and much superior to the gardens at Lahore and Pinjore; but it has nothing now to recommend itself except its name. On our return we went to the shop of Mulla Ahmad Khan an Haji Mohammad Sadiq, the famous merchants, for shawls.

Seventh May, Thursday, Kashmir. At night all the gentlemen were invited to a feast by Sheikh Imam-ud-din, Nazim of Kashmir, which was accompanied by music; but no illuminations took place on account of the wind.

Eighth May, Friday. Embarking in boats the whole of our party arrived at Manasbal and the Noor Jahan garden, 7 coss. Manasbal is a "Dal" or lake. The water of several nullahs and from the hills and issues accumulates in a wide and extensive plain and makes a large unfathomable sheet. Its original name in books is Mansrover. It produces immense quantities of Singhara (waternut) and Lily. A sacred reservoir containing bad stinking water, called Kheer Bhawani, is near the place. It is consecrated to Devi and is said to change several colours as a foreboding for coming event. The blackening of its colour is supposed to be demonstrative of the wrath of the goddess and to bespeak some misfortune for the country. Such times are called Maha Mai. According to Brahmans it is the same Devi as secretly escaped from "Ravana" and took shelter there in the form of water and had blessed "Ravan" that his reign will last for ever.

Ninth May, Saturday. The whole day spent at Hajin on the bank of the famous "Dal", called Wullur, in company with Sheikh Shah-ud-din and Lala Jagan Nath and it afforded the best opportunity for swimming in the lake. It is a large lake occupying a circumference of about 7 coss. Unfathomable in many places and formed by the accumulation of the waters of the Bitustha and many other streams from the hills, the fomer river thence flowing towards Baramula. In the midst of the lake stand the Baradurri and mosque of Badshah Zain-ul-Abdin, now in ruinous condition, and on one of its black-stones the inscription, not properly legible, is engraved in Arabic. The last line of the couplets gives the date 1211 Hijra (1796 A.D.). This is also called Lanek or Lanka. The lake produces waternut and lotus and is very dangerous to boats when a strong wind blows.

Tenth May, Sunday. From Hajin we returned by boats to Kashmir and, borrowing horse from Dewan Kishan Lal, went to see the famous Hari Parbat fort. It is situated on a small hill, commanding a pleasing view of the whole town, the Dal and the Shalamar. Four of its bastions are very strong. It has in it the reservoir of water, a store of provisions and 4 guns. It is in every way a commodious place capable of affording convenient accommodation to a garrison of 1,000 men. At present the strength of the Jammu garrison in it is only 500 men under Vazir Lakhpat Rai. The fort is said to have been erected in the time of the (Moghal) Kings, but subsequently strengthened by Ata Mohd Khan, Governor from Kabul. From this as well as from Shergurhee a cannon shot could be thrown to the town with great effect and advantage. Having seen the temple of Sharka Devi and having visited the shop of Moollan Khan, we returned to our Camp in the Sheikh's garden.

Eleventh May, Monday. The Sheikh ordered an illumination yesterday and took leave from our camp.

Twelfth May, Tuesday. It was decided that Lord Elphinstone, the Hon'ble Captain Hardinge and Captain Bates should stay at Kashmir for some longer period while the Hon'ble Charles Hardinge and Dr. Walker proposed to return to Simla. Consequently the latter gentlemen took leave of the former and returned to Khanpore in the Nagam Prgannah, 7 coss. Here a Pukka serai stands built by Delhi Kings and affords accommodation to large parties of travellers from Lahore and Amritsar, who generally frequent this road. About 400 Byragees were encamped here an route to the holy temple of Amar Nath. Rations were served to such medicants on pilgrimage by the Lahore Durbar accompained with a donation of 2 rupees per man in cash on his return. The number of these fellows amounted to no less than 6,000 men. Consequently the annual expenditure to the State on this item was about 15,000 rupees. But Raja Gulab Singh has now put a stop' to it. Our course, about 3 coss, lay on the bank of Doodh Ganga which issues forth from the white stone hills and empties itself into the Bitustha near Kashmir.

Thirteenth May, Wednesday. Passing by Ramoon and Durbagaum villages; crossing the Ramushee river thence by Buthupura and Shahjee Mung, where another Pukka serai stands and again crossing the Rambeara river, we arrived at Shoopun, 10 coss. This is a pretty large town in the Pargannah called Shoopoor Summbatoo. In Sambat 1869 (1813 A.D.) Maharaja Ranjit Singh sent his troops under Dewan Jeewan Mal and Ramdial to this place while himself followed as far as Rajauri; but a battle having taken place with Azim Khan, the Mohammadan ruler of Kashmir, Jiwan Mal was killed with great loss and the Maharaja and his troops were obliged to return. The expedition was renewed in 1874 (1817 A.D.) B.E. Ranjit headed the troops himself with his several Generals—Missar Dewan Chand, Sardar Hari Singh Nalwa, Mehan Singh, the present Maharaja of Jammu (Gulab Singh), Dewan Moti Ram, Jamadar Khushal Singh and Pandit Bir Dhar, father of Raja Kak, and undertook another expedition. Mohd Azim Khan was at Kabul and his brother Jabbar Khan, then in charge, offered resistance, but was defeated, and thenceforth Kashmir became a province of Lahore, destined at the present day to be added to the possessions of the rising family of Jammu through the interference of the British since 1903 (B.E.) (1846 A.D.), on payment of Rs. 75 lakhs as indemnity for Kashmir and Hazara.

The extensive valley of the snowy mountains of Peer, in which the province of Cashmeer is situated, is richly covered with villages and towns and intersected by various small streams formed from the several issues, fountains and rivulets descending from the hills. The Vyreenag in the Shahbad Purguneh being joined by it several tributary Nullahs, swells into a river which becomes navigable as it passes the Srinagar or the modern Cashmere, the Wulur Dul and the Baramoola. This is called the Vith or the Bitushtha throughout the hills, but descending into the plains of the Punjab it is denominated as Jehlum.

There are four Duls or lakes, viz., the one near Shalamar, the Aujar, the Manas Bal and the Wulur; the last is the largest lake said to be 8 coss long and 5 broad and supposed to be in many places unfathomable.

These lakes are formed by the accumulation of the waters of the many springs and streams in the extensive plain under the hills. They produce an immense quantity of waternuts and lotus. More than 2,000 boats are used by the natives on the water in their various pursuits of life and also pleasure boats on the banks and in the middle of these Duls stand some of the ancient buildings, which are really very imposing in appearance.

The people are generally very poor owing to the oppressions and extortions of their rulers and are, as poor people may be expected to be, very unclean in dress, diet and habits. They are for the most part immoral, avaricious, self interested and intriguing, but among the redeeming features of their character may be reckoned their diligence and unparalleled expertness and skill in handicraft works. The chief revenue and judicial functions of the province are administered by a set of native Pundits who have grown rich at the expense of the Mohamedans and the people at large. At present Pandit Tilak is the treasurer and Mohan Kaul is in charge of the Revenue and Excise Departments. Pandit Raja Kak and Lachhman Dhar are rich people and are engaged in contracts and commerce and derive large profits. The only Hindus are Pundits; but very little distinction seems to exist between them and the Mohamedans who are permitted to touch their drink and diet without objection. Their staple food is rice or flesh, their luxury tea, but the poorer classes live cheifly on vegetables. The productions are rice of various kinds, wheat, maize, til seed etc. Rice is so cheap that one 'Kharwar', about two and half maunds in weight can be purchased for one Hari Singhi rupee. At Pampura and its 12 villages saffron is cultivated while the iron mine forms an exclusive item of income to the Government. The houses in the towns and villages are built of wood and also of stone and mortar but they are very unclean and filthy. The principal manufacture is that of shawl, but the art of painting is also cultivated to some extent. The whole neighbourhood abounds with gardens and the best fruits, such as apples, pears, locouts, chest-nuts, almonds, Bahee, Butang, Subza and grapes are produced in large quantities. Rain showers are almost of daily occurrence in August and there are constant falls of snow from December to February. At this time of the inclement season people hide themselves in baths and other safe places heated by fire. A multiplicity of Chonar and Rittan trees may be observed in every quarter, while the Bedmushk, from which the best water is distilled, forms another important means of the luxury of the people.

The plains of Kashmir, being surrounded by the Peer range, only 4 or 5 passages are left by which ingress or egress could be effected and even these are covered with snow during the winter, at which time the Rajauree is the only pass which remains open. The people of this country are kept in a kind of Involuntary prison, none being allowed to go to or fro without a passport from authorities.

Shawl Dagh or receipts on account of shawl manufacture. This is the most important item of receipt to the State. The commodity produced is the best that could be found in the world, yet the manufacture is capable of further improvement in quality and income. The heavy taxes levied by the Government are the greatest drawback on the trade having a tendency daily to thin the number of the workmen in the country. It is probably due to the indiscretion of the Kardars. The manufacturers could be relieved of the burden if it was levied on the buyers at the time of sale. The quantity of wool exported to other places is also produced here. Many raw hands are engaged in the trade. There are two kinds of Shawl manufacturers. The method of imposition of tax is as follows.

One class is that of financiers, that is to say of those who have necessary resources to supply silk thread, pay for its dyeing and duties from their own pockets. They manufacture Doshalas, Shawls, Jamawar and Gabbas. A rich merchant starts a factory and opens shops according to his means, some lay out ten or twenty shops while others about one hundred. He would supply thread, dyes and duties himself and pay for the labour of Shawl manufacturers. The wages of the Shawl manufacturers are calculated according to the number of sticks of silk thread prepared by each. One who can work the stick in the woof and warp one thousand times is reckoned as one stick. Some manufacturers can work during the whole day fifty thousand times the stick up and down. According to the number of sticks daily wages of the manufacturers average between two and six annas, in the case of each according to the skill and expertness he displays in his work.

Rupees one hundred and seventeen is not fixed but is charged a rupee or two more or less. A piece or pair of Shawl having been thus prepared is carried to Chabutaras or customs houses to be stamped and the prices are fixed by the agents appointed for the purpose. On the articles estimated at Rs. 100, a surcharge of Rs. 40 is levied by Kardars, thereby raising it to Rs. 140. Annas six per rupee on the rough price is charged and credited to Government and a seal is affixed on the goods. The total of all the dues comes to Rs. 148-2-0 in Hari Singh coinage. In addition Rs. 5 or Rs. 6 are imposed on every shop of Shawl manufactures and two shops are reckoned according to five labourers. Thus 2 1/2 labourers make one shop. The annual average tax on each labourer is thus nearly Rs. 49-10-0. The total number of these capitalists is 3,500 and the proceeds therefrom at Rs. 148-2-0 per shop amount to Rs. 6,07,500. The cost of rice contributed by Government, excepting loss on deduction on the same, comes to Rs. 5,082.

The other class of Shawl traders consists of those who have no capital of their own to employ and, therefore, depend upon Government for money. These are comparatively few, about 2,000 in all, their production of an inferior quality and the Government income from them not exceeding 2 lacs. Pair Shawls, Square Shawls, Alwans, single and double threaded, Jamawar of the best sort may be found at the shops, but a still higher quality may be produced by commission and the advance of money. Nothing seems exempt from the payment of duties.

Thread weaving. The shop of such weavers is reckoned per one labourer and Rs. 11,000 are realized as tax from them.

Jewellers. Tax is levied on all kinds of articles brought into the city. Like Shawl cess it is collected on cash (Kabul or Qandhar currency) or on currency minted at the state mint at Re. 1 per thousand and on gold at Rs. 2 per metal worth Rs. 1,000. Tax on copper, zinc, precious stones or metal wares amounts to Rs. 12,000.

Permit Fees. Tax is charged on all goods and grains imported into and exported from Kashmir. Their details are as under: Rs. 1,04,000.

Articles of Exports:-

Shawls.
Saffron.
Kullumdans or Inkstands.
Paper.
Silk.
Cloth
Tobacco.
The distilled Bedmushk water.
Woollen cloth.
Black Zeerah.
Hill pony.

Articles of Import:-

Shawl wool from Tibet.
Tea.
Salt.
European cloth.
Sugar.
Goor.
Spices.
Medicines and groceries.
Brass and copper plates.
Indigo.
Iron and Steel.
Snuff from Peshawar.
Silk cloth, "Kinkhabs".
Chintzes.
Coconuts and other fruits.
Colours for painting.
Quick silver.
Arsenic, etc., etc.

Not only metals, the precious stones and all articles. including the necessaries of life, are subject to such a payment; but a tax averaging from one to two rupees per mensem per head is levied on all the classes of inhabitants (mentioned below) except on barbers and tailors:-

Dyer.
Cloth Merchant.
Banker.
Buneea.
Baker.
Wood seller.
Boatman.
Goldsmith.
Blacksmith.
Carpenter.
Potters.
Saddle Maker.
Corngrinders.
Inkstandmakers.
Paper Sellers.
Butchers and fishermen.
Masons.
Diggers of wells.
Seal engravers.
Plate sellers.
Silk traders.
Coolies.
Fruit sellers.
Uttars.
Confectioners.
Weavers.
Procuresses.
Prostitutes.
Dancing Girls.
Leechmen.

Leather merchants.
Servants.
Gun makers.
Beaters, etc., etc., etc.

All the classes pay taxes on them through their Moocudams appointed by the Government for the purpose.

The mint is the department in which the greatest abuse prevails. Five rupees per 100 rupees coined is the Government duty. Half the quantity of alloy is mixed with pure silver to coin the Huree Singhi rupees. Total annual income from the mine is Rs. 6,000

Water cess. Around Shalamar Dal vegetables are grown at the foot of the hills and Rs. 2,000 are collected as Government share therefrom.

The production of silk is not so much taken care of as towards Hindoostan and Bengal; the worms being kept generally on "Toot" (mulberry) leaves but a proper food to silk worms might (it is surmised) improve this article to a great extent. Rs. 1,00,000 annually are received as duty on silk trade.

Cattle cess. During summer cattle and goats of the whole valley proceed to the hills for grazing. Government agents go there and count the heads and duty of Rs. 20 is charged per head, the total proceeds per annum amounting to Rs. 45,000.

Waternut Mahal. Waternut is a mushroom growth in Wooller Lake. The inhabitants of the neighbourhood collect it first in boats and then bring it out of water. One part of the produce is taken by the collectors and two parts are delivered to Government. From the sale of the article Rs. 25,000 are annually contributed to Government Revenues.

Pure Honey. Whosoever keeps a bee-hive in a village has to pay half the quantity of honey to Government and thereby Rs. 2,000 are collected annually.

The following is a list of the Rajas of the country who are nothing more than Zamindars and pay in about a third of their revenues (about Rs. 60,000).

Raja of Moozuffrabad.
Rajah of Doputta (Attaoolla Khan).
Rajah of Kuthaee (Ruhmutoolla Khan).
Rajah of Uree (Moozuffer Khan).
Rajah of Chikar (lately deceased).
Rajah of Buttiar.
Rajah of Kuriani (Sher Ahmed Khan).
Rajah of Khouri (Nujjuf Khan).
The Jageerdars of Dhoond.

Aujar Dal. A small Dal near the city is used for the cultivation of vegetable and yields Rs. 5,000 to Government.

Charas and Bhang. Grows in mushroom form in villages along the rivers. At present Gurdial Singh Log is the contractor and Rs. 11,500 are received from the excise of the articles.

Agricultural Produce. The following articles are produced:-

Spring harvest	*Autumn harvest*
Wheat, barley, peas, tobacco.	Rice, Mung, Mash, Moth, cotton, red chillies, maize, china, Kangani, Kottu, jute.

The system of revenue assessment. Except wheat, barley, Mung, etc., out of 50 Kharwars produced by a person 23 are received in kind and for 8 "Kharwars" price is calculated at Rs. 1-6- 0 per "Karwar", thereby the Government gets 31 "Kharwars" as its share in cash and kind and 19 "Kharwars" are left with the cultivator, out of which he has to pay octroi and presentation fees. For the other products Government share is fixed at 50 per cent. The State share is sold to the cultivator at the rate of Rs. 1-6-0 per 'Kharwar' and the cost is realized in cash. Thus the cultivator is sometimes put to loss and at others equalises, but gets any profit very rarely. In the village one rupee annually is payable for every tree of "Charmagz". For other fruit bearing trees and grazing nine or ten rupees per hundred in addition to revenue are realized. From 4 or 5 paraganas revenues are realized in cash only. In the case of outlying parganas 1/4 of the cost of grain or 1/3 share of the produce is charged and the produce is contributed to Shawl manufacturers. The entire revenue for the year amounted to Rs. 12,00,000.

Saffron. In Bahu Pargana, also known as Pampur, about 5 coss from the city which contains 25 villages, saffron is grown in 15. In the month of May cultivation is taken up on high mountains. The fields are not watered with any stream or rivulet and are dependent or rain water alone. Otherwise the crop is ruined. In case of heavy rainfall the cultivation is abundant. In a year it is grown about 2,000 "Manuta", i.e., about 1 1/2 seer. Half is taken by Government and half left with the cultivator. Its average price is Rs. 15 per "Manuta". Thus Rs. 25,000 are realized from the produce of saffron. Once cultivated the crop is continued for 15—20 years. Every year the earth around the plant is loosened. The cultivation does not require much labour or cost. The proceeds for the year were Rs. 15,000.

The several purgunahs of Cashmeer are here subjoined:-

On the West Bank of the Bitushtha (Jhelum).

Shahbad.	Sukoudah.
Banihal.	Sayer of Moola.
Deosur.	Puch.
Brushpore.	Deo.

Adwun.	Bundwah.
Shahdrah.	Manjhania.
Rembpore.	Pangul.
Maloo Soomer Somun.	Kurdah Bun.
Kohu.	Sayer Mahme.

On the East Bank of the Bitushtha (Jhelum).

Karmog.	Pampoora or Vohoo.
Balut.	Wullur.
Vithur.	Duchun Para.
Mucherpoora.	Ghoorpara.
Chokul.	Nanat Nag or Islamabad.
Vithkur.	Kollur.
Kah Harnah.	Muttun.
Lar.	Burnug.
Phag.	

The system of measurement. Measurement of land is reckoned according to the quantity of seed used in it. The area in which one plant can be grown is, therefore, known accordingly. Land wherein one 'Kharwar' of seed may be used is counted as 'Kharwar'. The measurements are thus taken according to the quantity of grain grown in it. The method of land measurements in Bighas, Biswas, Ghumaon or Kanals is not prevalent. In fact one 'Bigha' Kashmiri is equal to four ordinary Bighas. Residential land is sold and bought according to area.

The total items of recepits from the Cashmere Province to the Supreme Government, therefore, are detailed in the subjoined statement called the Goshwara of the annual receipts, viz:-

		Rs.
Duties of Shawl looms	..	8,07,500
Border Makers	..	11,000
Jowahir Bazar	..	12,000

Sayer Permits	..	14,000
Tayufehdars or Professionals	..	1,10,000
The Mint	..	60,000
Mur Bahru or Produce of Dul	..	20,000
Silk	..	22,000
Shakh Shoomaree or grazing cattle	..	45,000
Waternuts	..	25,000
Honey	..	2,000
The Hill Rajahs	..	60,000
Dul called Aujar	..	5,000
Abkaree	..	11,500
Land Revenue	..	12,00,000
Saffron	..	25,000
Total Hari Singhi Rupees	..	24,30,000

A march of about 6 coss across the Soongloo River brought us to Mohandpura in the Arvund or Advund Pargannah. This was a very populous tract in the times of prosperity of Kashmir. An issue of water at this place is considered equally sacred by the Hindus and Muhammadans, the former calling it the feet of Vishnu, the latter those of Rasul or Prophet.

Fifteenth May, Friday. Travelling from Mohandpura reached Islamabad, alias, Anantnag, 7 coss.

Sixteenth May, Saturday. Leaving Anantnag reached Durroo in the Shahabad Pargannah, 7 coss.

Seventeenth May, Sunday. Passing through Chohun and under the snowy range of Pir in the Burraree Pargannah of Kashmir, we encamped in the extensive plain, 7-8 coss, called "Holul mundoo", deriving this name from a particular drug which abounds in this ground. It resembles the tobacco leaves but is of no use. This ground is generally the halting place for travellers owing to strong wind and fall of rain. The weather continued intensely cold.

Eighteenth May Monday. During the first two coss traversed a plain; but the rest of the march, 8 coss, we had to travel on nothing but snow. On the Pir range the whole of this tract was a continued sheet of white, even the trees were entirely covered with snow. No traces of villages or water to be seen, and, after experiencing the most tiresome difficulties scarcely to be paralleled in the whole of the journey, we reached safe at Chuppanee, 11 coss, in the Desa Pargannah of Kishtwar State. This pass is called Guzuri Bhuraree by some and Gurkhun Peerwalla by others. It is generally covered with snow except in July and August. The wind here is generally strong and dangerous and the fall of snow sudden and abundant. It has only fallen yesterday.

Nineteenth May, Tuesday. Passing via Chunee, Puttan, Goorkhun and Gyee we reached Mujmee, 6 cos, in the Kishtwar State. This tract is inhabited by a race of Hindoo Thakurs. The River Lidder, which, descending from the snowy range, falls into the Chandar Bhaga near Muddoul was crossed by a small bridge near Gyee. The country between the Pir Hill and the Chandar Bhaga is called Siraj. The people of the area are called "Khussi". The language is a mixture of the Kashmiri with the hill dialect. The dress of the females is long coats and caps with tails.

Twentieth May Wednesday. A route by Dhurous, Bumna, Pahna, Thunot, Pimasa and Khimont, all belonging to Kishtwar, we encamped at Bhagoo on the Peprun range, 6 coss. It is huge village inhabited by the Hindu Thakurs, yielding rupees 500 per annum. The chief production is opium. Its headman, Nunda, is in prison at Jammu owing to an insurrection against that State.

Twenty-first May, Thursday. A march by the villages noted in the margin over the Piprun Range and thence along the Lidder brought us, 6 coss, to Dodah, a town of the Kishtwar District, consisting of about 100 shops of the Muhammedan Kashmiris and a few of the Hindus, all speaking the Kashmiri language. Many of them manufacture Shawls. A 'Kacha' fort erected by Raja Gulab Singh with four strong bastions stands 1/2 mile to the east of the town and contains a large reservoir of water, 2 guns, stores and 350 men of garrison, 200 of whom are now detailed to Kashmir. Last year when Jammu was attacked by the Sikhs, the people of this unfortunate country had made a strong effort to throw off the oppressive yoke of Gulab Singh and had actually brought Jaimal Singh, son of Raja Tegh Singh of Kashtwar (the extinction of which family we have already noticed) to resume the reins of the Government of his ancestor's country. His arrival was effected through the Goorkhun Pass, and a large militia assembled to defend his claims. The fight lasted 7 days at Dodah, but the insurgents were at last routed by the superior forces of Jammu, who made Jaimal a prisoner and inflicted fines in money on every individual in the country. The old Rajas of Kishtwar seem to have descended from a race of Gorkha Rajputs and to have migrated to these hills from Bengal. The pedigree of the Rajas could not be known before Mehar Singh, who got the Kingdom from his father. He was succeeded by his son, Sujan Singh, who in turn handed it over to Tola Singh. But Raja Tola Singh, one of the line, became a convert to the faith of Muhammad in the time of the Kings. The family seems, however, to have retained a Hindu appellation. He had two sons, Tegh Singh and Bakhtawar Singh, who died issueless. Tegh Singh ruled for about twenty years until conquered by Raja Gulab Singh. Tegh Singh and his heirs died at Lahore and other places. Of his two sons, Zorawar Singh and Jaimal Singh, the latter died at Jammu last year while the former became a Christian at the Ludhiana American Misson. The total annual revenue of this once flourishing country is rupees 1,00,000. It produces saffron, apples, 'Bahee' and other fruits and, though populous enough even at the present day, the people generally groan under the oppressive rule of Jammu and like to have the old line of their rulers restored.

Twenty-second May, Friday. The Kishtwar country ends at the Chandar Bhaga, where we arrived after a march of 3/4 loss and crossed the river on swings as before in the Khussal country and encamped at Junot on the skirt of the Chattan Hill. The whole day was rainy and the weather cold.

Khussal had always belonged to the Gulian Rajpoots called Ranas, tributaries to Chamba, their annual tribute was a pair of Shawls of rupees 150 cash Down to the times of Jaswant Singh the tribute was regularly paid to Chamba; but about 20 years ago the petty State was alienated from it and Fatteh Singh was made to pay rupees 800 a year to Jammu. But this was only a preliminary arrangement of the ambitious chief of Jammu, who in Sambat 1895 (1838 A.D.), took possession of the whole country under pretence of disobedience, assigning a few acres of land to Fatteh and Chuppa. The annual revenue of this small tract was rupees 1,000, but recently it has been raised to rupees 1,600; but extortion is the chief feature of the Jammu Government and the people are dissatisfied. At Dudhnoo on the Chattan Range there is a sacred temple of the Devi. This tract skirts on Bahadarwah in the east and on Murmat on the west.

Murmut is another petty tract which belonged to a family of Hindu Rajputs of "Ramsian" denomination, tributaries to Bhadarwah; but was about 25 years back absorbed by the extending principality of Jammu while its original proprietors were obliged to support themselves by serving their oppressors.

The tract is inhabited by Hindu and Mohammadan population, but quite unlike the rest of the Kashtwar people the latter have no connection with the former. The Chostan Range abounds with hawks and other birds of prey as also with partridges. Opium is one of the products of the soil, the currency Nanak Sahai rupees and the language a hill dialect.

Twenty-third May, Saturday. Halted at Junot, awaiting our horses.

Twenty-fourth May, Sunday. Our road this morning lay along the village of Naldanagur Puranee in the Turwan Parganah, Malnee in the Barosoo Parganah of Bhadarwah, Khumbee in Koolar and on the Neeroo River and we halted at Khuram, 6 coss. Turwan, a small Parganah belonging to the undermentioned family of the Hindu Thakoors yields only a revenue of rupees 700/800 per annum and has, like the other neighbouring States, been incorporated in Jammu.

Twenty-fifth May, Monday. A march of about 6 coss, brought us by Durmga, Tatha and Kothi to the town of Bhadarwah. The road was good and lay along the bank of the Neeroo River. Near Gatha a temple consecrated to Vasdeo or Vishnu stands greatly venerated by the people. The town is pretty large, situate on a fine level plain and consists of many Shawl-looms and more than 800 houses and 300 shops of Hindus and Mohammedans. A river descending from snowy range flows into the town adding considerably to the beauty of the place and towards the north a 'pukka' fort overlooks the town from an elevation. The country is populous, fruit of every kind is produced in abundance. The old and now almost extinct family of this place claimed their descent from the lunar race of the olden times and were called the "Som Vanishies".

After the death of Daya Pal, Pahar Chand had succeeded to the 'Masand' in 1898 (B.E.) (1841 A.D.) ; but the Chamba Raja, who always looked upon this State as his tributary, expelled him, while in return Chamba has been deprived of it by Jammu. Since three moths the Rajah's nephew, Parkaram Singh, sent as Governor from Chamba, has been carried to the new Maharaja. The total annual revenue of this petty State does not exceed rupees 20,000 but it is considered be the most fertile and productive tract.

Twenty-sixth May, Tuesday. Via Bhajee, Tenall and the Pudhree Range we reached Limgeera, 11 coss, belonging to Chamba. This was the most tedious and difficult road ever travelled, a greater part of it is generally covered with snow and about 8 coss beyond Limgeera the country is a regular waste. Near this last-named village flows the stream from the snowy range. The Chamba "Kardars" or local authorities, attended and, owing to the fall of rain, the weather remained cold.

Twenty-seventh May, Wednesday. By the route mentioned in the margin we reached Surog in the Chamba State, 8 coss, and encamped on the bank of Luwal, near Jullaree. An iron mine is said to exist, but the ore produced from it is is said to exist, but the ore produced from it is neither good nor abundant. Beyond Surog the road is bad and the country waste; but farther on both begin to improve.

Twenty-eighth May, Thursday. Reached Sundla, 7 coss, by the following route. It rained a little.

Sundla.
Cross the Seerul at Duddur.
Slenree.
The Lullen Range.
Recross the Seerul on skins.

Twenty-ninth May, Friday—

Route:
Iminmeel.
Bhuree.
Kiaree.

Phoolghut.
Thodopur.
Bhudrum.
Cross the Sal, 7 coss.

The camp reached Chamba this morning and the gents were honourably received by the young Raja Siri Singh, Chief of the place. The Raja is a smart, handsome boy of about 7 years of age. He is fond of riding, shooting and archery and much liked by the people. The town of Chamba is a nice, clean and well-built place, the streets are wide and the temples numerous. The Hindus form a greater proportion of the population than the Mohammadans. For a quarter hour it rained heavily at Chamba. In the evening they went to visit Lakshmi Narain Temple, a beautiful and clean place. In the middle of bazar is a vast open space known as "Chaugan". The people are generally fair and very handsome. The temples are numerous in which about 2 maunds of perfume are burnt every day. The people are given to religious habits as well as faithfully devoted to their sovereign. The hills in the neighbourhood of Chamba are generally dry, while on each side of it flow the Ravi and the Sal Rivers. Vizir Bugga and his brother Mugna are the Ministers. The whole dominion of Chamba consisted of 84 Parganahs, but the Rehloo District having been lately dismembered. The present revenue of the State amounts to nearly a lakh of rupees. Lands are assigned to servants for support instead of cash, while collections from the Zamindars are made not in cash but in kind. This territory, though extensive, is chiefly rugged, barren and unproductive. The neighbouring Chiefship of Basohli was also an old principality belonging since immemorial time to a family of Rajputs called "Somurs". It was also called "Billawur" from the name of its former Capital. The Raja used to pay rupees 5,000 as tribute to Lahore; but about 9 years ago the country was annexed to Jammu and its real owner, the Raja, driven out without even any maintenance. It yields about rupees 40,000 per annum and is bounded on the north by Bhadarwah, on the south by Shahpore and on the east by the Bhudo country. The family—

Raja Medni Pal (1725 A.D.)
Anant Pal (Amrit Pal, 1757 A.D.)
Brij Pal (Bijai Pal, 1776 A.D.)
Mahinder Pal (1806 A.D.)
Bhopinder Pal (1813 A.D.)
Kullian Pal (deposed and now living at Jammu).

Thirtieth May, Saturday. We crossed the river by a bridge near Chamba and via Kurber and across the high range of hills at Jawanee, 12 coss. These hills are all dry ad beyond Kurber few traces of population or water occur along the road.

Thirty-first May, Sunday,—

Mohkulia ki Khut.
Rund.
Indur.
Raipore.
Selwun.
Dhudroh.
Atunnutoh.
Seenul ki Khut.
Khuneera.
Summoti.
Dothur.
Kumlah.
Sehota—10 coss.

We encamped at Sehota, situate in the midst of barren hills. The climate here is comparatively warm.

First June, Monday. Passing by Bhakkuni, Motla, Kukroti, Tholel and Bulleta, we arrived at Bhimnala—7 coss, in the Rehloo District now attached to British Government. Between

Sehota Tholel, a distance of 5 coss, no water is procurable, while the heat of the climate is intense. Rehloo, with six parganahs, belonged formerly to Chamba; but had lapsed to Lahore Government about 25 years ago. After the late prostration of Lahore before the British power an opportunity was afforded to Chamba authorities to put their Thana into it again, but timely notice having been taken, the district has come under the British management. Lala Salamat Rai of Panipat is the Pulasdar at the place. Rehloo is a pretty little town, consisting of about 300 houses and shops, beautified by thick groves of trees and intersected with artificial rivulets called "Kools". Towards the north, on an elevation, stands a fort not very strong and at present garrisoned by only 20 men in the Ahloowalia's service on behalf of British Government. The chief product is rice of the best description. The road is bad, if not difficult. Raja Gulab Singh's agents got leave today from our Camp.

Second June, Tuesday. A march of 7 coss by the route mentioned in the margin brought us to Kot-Kangra, where we joined the camp of Major Lawrence, Agent to the Governor-General in the Punjab and Captain E. Lake, the Political Assistant for Kangra and Nurpur Hills. The town of Kangra consists of two separate parts known as Kangra and Nagarkot, containing numerous shops and houses and a temple also called the Malkhana, all round the temple of Devi. Houses are erected by the various Chiefs for the accommodation of themselves and the pilgrims resorting to the place at the annual fairs or other occasions.

Third June, Wednesday. In the morning met Moulvi Rajab Ali, Ali Raza Khan and Balo Sahib. The confluence of Banganga and Patalganga under the Kangra fort is supposed by the Hindus to be the most sacred place and to unite in it the waters not only of the above two rivers but of 360 others equally holy. The place abounds with fish. The fort of Kangra is a strong place, said to have been founded in olden times of the Kurus and

Pandus, and contains in it the temples of Ambaka Devi, and of Bhyron and a tank called Kapur Sagar and supposed to be unfathomable. The fort and the whole country formerly belonged to an old family called "Kuttoch".

Originally these territories were under the control of Katoch Rajas. In the year 1863 (B.E.)—(1806 A.D.) the Gurkhas of Nepal intruded into the region and allied the Rajas of Jaswan, Seba, Datarpur Guler, Suket Mandi, Khalur, Kutlahar, Nurpur and Jhibba, who were in a way subordinate to Raja Sansar Chand, with themselves. Forr four years continuously a siege was laid was laid to the fort of Kangra; but Raja Sansar Chand successfully resisted them. He sought help from Maharaja Ranjit 1867-68 (B.E.)— (1810-11 A.D.) Maharaja Ranjit Singh proceeded to Kangra with his army. The Gurkhas fled before him after a brief skirmish. Thereupon Maharaja Ranjit Singh with the consent of Raja Sansar Chand took possession of the fort at Kangra and Sandhta Pargana and also acquired the country of Dandrana with the approval of Raja Sansar Chand and other Rajas who had joined hands with the Gurkhas. The rest of the area was left with Sansar Chand as before and he was treated with great respect and honour, was granted presents worth rupees 1,000, and an additional Jagir worth rupees 21,000 from Lahore territories. After Sansar Chand's death his son, Anrudh Chand, ruled for 4 years. But at the instance of Jammu Rajas, who had acquired great influence at the Lahore Court Maharaja Ranjit Singh sought the hands of two daughters of Raja Sansar Chand. Anrudh Chand declined the offer and was proceeded against under orders of Maharaja Ranjit Singh. Anrudh Chand repaired towards the Hardwar along with his sisters and married them to the Raja of Garhwal and himself died at the same place. On the recommendation of the British Maharaja Ranjit Singh conferred a jagir worth rupees 60,000 on Parmod Chand and Ranbir Chand in Parganah Mehalpuree, rupees 30,000 worth on Jodhbir Singh in Nadaun, who are in their occupation at present.

The principality which was absorbed by the rising power of Lahore now forms a part of the extended British frontiers in the Punjab. Our camp this day reached Rani Ka Tal, 7 coss, via Daulatpur, crossing Banganga and another known as Kathu Pathu. The place had only a few shops used for halting by people going to the mela at Kangra and Jawala Mukhi.

Fourth June, Thursday. Reached the famous town of Jawala Ji, 7 coss. The famous temple of Jawala Mukhi is an old building of which the upper storey and the dome was gilded by orders of Ranjit Singh. Inside it is seen that curious phenomenon of nature, called the "Jawala Mukhi". In more than 12 places spontaneous fire springs constantly from the walls in the form of so many torches and is the chief object of Hindu worship. The system of income and expenditure since the time of Maharaja Ranjit Singh was that the entire proceeds were collected by the agents of the Sarkar out of which rupees 5-4-0 were spent on 'Bhog' for Maha Mai and the rest was assigned to a number of houses. The same practice prevailed at the time. A small reservoir of water covered by a dome called "Gorakh Tibbi" also produces a flame. The devoted pilgrim creeps into it by a small flight of stairs while the greedy "Gosain" follows him with a light in his hand, which being brought close to or in contact with the issue of water the air immediately catches the flame which spreads in a beautiful blue purple and red all over the surface and soon disappears. No smell of saltpetre or sulphur can be perceived and it may probably require a close scientific examination before the nature and cause of this wonder of nature can be ascertained. Many houses and Dharamsalas erected by the Rajas and Sardars are there for the accommodation of pilgrims.

Fifth June, Friday. After seeing the Amkeisur Mahadeo, the small artificial canal said to have been cut in the time of Emperor Akbar, and other curiosities we crossed the Beas and encamped at Nadaun, 5 coss. This is an old populous hill town consisting of about 250 shops and many houses, chiefly of the

Hindus and a few of the Mohammadans. This was the Capital of Raja Sansar Chand Katoch and in his time more populous; but has suffered considerably under the Sikh Rule. Just under the town there is a ferry of the Beas on which a boat and skins are used for the passage across.

Sixth June, Saturday. Via Huthee Khel, Fattehpore and the Jambaree Devi, we reached the Hamirpur Hatee, 10 coss. This place belongs to Katoch and was given by the recommendation of the British Government to Ranbir Chand by Ranjit Singh as a part of his jagir of rupees 60,000 per annum. Long after his exile from the country Ranbir Chand bestowed it upon Raja Sochet Singh, who had negotiated the grant for him, and it is now in the hands of Maharaja Gulab Singh. Our camp here fell in with that of Lords Browne and Hay, proceeding from Simla to Jammu. It rained in the morning.

Seventh June Sunday. Arrived at Meeran, 7 coss, Ranbir Chand and Parmodh Chand, owners of the place, paid their visit to the chiefs of our party.

Eighth June, Monday. Passing by Tourha, Hurne, Devi and Patta, we reached Kumharhati, 8 coss, in the Khalur principality. The famous Malloun Fort, the chief retreat of Nurmur Singh Thapa, who played so conspicuous a part in the Gurkha Wars, stands on an elevation in this vicinity. We crossed the Sutlej in the evening and encamped at Bilaspur in a garden.

Ninth June, Tuesday. We halted at the Capital of Khalur and received the visit of Jagat Chand, Chief of the place. In the afternoon the exalted one (Captain Hardinge) and Dr. Walker left for Simla by Dak. The town of Bilaspur is situated on a fine level plain on the banks of the Sutlej with beautiful buildings belonging to the Raja. Khalur is an old principality. Raja Bhim Chand of the Chandella denomination, the founder of the family and a descendant from the line of Sishupal, the hero of Mahabharata, first migrated from Chanderi some hundred years ago, and built a fort in these hills bearing the name of Khalur, an appellation which became general for the whole country before the capital was transferred to the place.

The following is a genealogical table:-

Bhim Chand.
Abhey Chand.
Kabul Chand.
Syal Chand.
Mayal Chand.

Raja Kharak Singh died of his excesses in the prime of his youth and his posthumous child, Garabh Chand, now about 8 years of age, being in the neighbourhood of Subathu, was not acknowledged by Mr. Clerk, then the British Political Agent, under the suspicion of his spurious birth. The succession, therefore, devolved on Mian Jangee, who assumed the title of Raja Jagat Chand.

The territory yields about a lakh of rupees annually; but the ruling Chief is a regular miserly fellow and anxious to store out every penny he can from the people. A kind of labourers called "Niariahs" wash the sand of the several nullahs that pour themselves into the Sutlej and produce gold, 23 tolas of which are paid to the State for the use of the Ranis. The following is a list of forts in the country—

Seewan, Teewan, Buchurhoo, Bisbak, Kote, Kuhloor, Satgurh, Rathinghour and Bahadurgarh.

With reference to the famous principality of Mandi it was ascertained that it was governed by an old family of Rajputs since hundreds of years. Its revenue exceeded seven lakhs of rupees per annum. The famous fort of Kamalagarh and the iron and salt mines are the peculiar boasts of the Chiefship. The

Rajahs are called Mundials from the name of the Capital Mandi.

Raja Balbir Sain is the offspring of a concubine, and the three sons of Teigha, therefore, claim the Chiefship even to the present day on the basis of the purity of their blood. Balbir was created Raja by Maharaja Ranjit Singh after the death of Zalim Sain, whose two sons from a concubine were not acknowledged.

Tenth June, Wednesday. After a long march of 14 coss, via Bhajjaoon, we reached Sai Hatee in the Baghal District. This is the most fertile and flourishing territory in the immediate neighbourhood of Simla. It is famous for its verdant rice fields, for its abundance of water and the general luxuriance of climate. The wheat, tumeric and the ginger form no small parts of its productions. The inhabitants are for the most part Kunsit Rajputs, thriving and happy under their present ruler. This petty Chiefship yields a revenue of rupees 20,000 a year, having been bound to supply the Supreme Government with 82 coolies since the Gurkha War. Cash at the rate of rupees 4 per man is annually paid to the British authorities. The Capital is Arki; but the State is called Baghal from the circumstances of its formerly abounding in "Bhags" or tigers.

Eleventh June, Thursday. Crossing the streams of Jool and Kooni in the Kunehar, a petty State, yielding rupees 1,000 annually, we reached Sasree, 15 coss. Koonehar belongs to Rana Kishan Singh, who is said to be of a distant branch of the Saree belongs to the Raja of Patiala and Simla, which we reached the following morning, is 7 coss from there.

The writer took leave from Charles Hardinge, returned to Ludhiana and resumed his duties.

Postscript. The present copy of the journal was prepared by Shambhu Nath, son of Budh Singh, Qanungo of Parganas in the neighbourhood of Hissar, at the instance of Lala Ganeshi Lal, Tehsildar of Ludhiana, under whom he was privileged to have worked, on the 17th April, 1847, at eleven hours of the day at the house of late Sardar Megha Singh, which has since been occupied by Mr. Andrews Malcolm, Deputy Collector, Ludhiana District, for rupees 50 per mensem. The writer has committed the account to writing because he can hardly be sure that he would live till tomorrow. At the time Captain William Henry Lawrence was the Deputy Commissioner (II Class). Mr. Henry Robert Davies, the Assistant Superintendent and Commissioner and Mr. Andrews Malcolm the Deputy Collector of Ludhiana District. Indulgence of the readers is craved for any inadvertant addition or alteration of the original text.

CHAPTER 3

THE GOVERNMENT OF INDIA AND THE MAHARAJA OF KASHMIR

By

William Digby

GOVERNMENT PAPERS
EAST INDIES
PAPERS RELATING TO KASHMIR

No.1
THE GOVERNMENT OF INDIA to the SECRETARY OF STATE FOR INDIA (EARL OF KIMBERLEY), dated Simla, April 7, 1884

EXTRACT

We have the honour to address your Lordship on the subject of the Kashmir State.

The three principal facts which it is necessary to notice are that the death of the Maharaja Ranbir Singh is apparently near at hand; that the administration of the Kashmir State is so thoroughly disorganised as to threaten a complete breakdown; and that the heir-apparent to the Chiefship is said to be unfitted in character and habits to govern the State. The first two of these facts we have unfortunately been in a position to anticipate for a long time past. The Maharaja has been suffering for years from a mortal disease; while the recent famine afforded convincing proof of the corruptness and inefficiency of the administration of Kashmir. We have also heard from time to time unsatisfactory accounts of the heir-apparent, and it has of late been reported that his father entertained some idea of setting him aside by a testamentary disposition. In our judgement, the time has now come for determining the course which the British Government should adopt on the death of the Maharaja; and we therefore proceed to lay our views before your Lordship.

Turning first to the question of the succession to the present Chief, we are of opinion that the eldest son, Mian Pertab Singh, should be proclaimed at once when his father dies. We do not consider that we can take cognizance of the vices attributed to Pertab Singh unless they have reduced him to a condition of actual incapacity, which does not appear to be the case; nor do we think that in this matter we should be justified in attaching any weight even to the wishes of His Highness Ranbir Singh. For the general interests of peace and good order among the Native States, no encouragement should be given to the idea that an eldest son can be set aside at the will of his father; and we hold that in practice nothing but the clearest evidence of actual incapacity to rule should be allowed to stand in the way of a regular succession by order of primogeniture. Further, we are entirely opposed to permitting any partition of the Kashmir State, by will or otherwise, among the three sons of the present Chief.

Feeling confident that our opinion upon these points are in accord with established policy, we have anticipated your Lordship's orders by issuing the instructions necessary for the guidance of Lieutenant-Colonel Sir Oliver St. John, K.C.S.I., the Officer on Special Duty, in case of an emergency arising. In the meanwhile we do not think it desirable formally to announce to the Maharaja that a will affecting the succession could not be recognised, because this course might raise unpleasant discussions. But the Officer on Special Duty will avail himself of any good opportunity for intimating to His Highness that such a will would not be expedient.

On the succession of the new Chief, it will not, in our opinion, be proper to postpone any longer a representation of our views upon the necessity for introducing substantial reforms into the administration of Kashmir. The misgovernment to which the people of that country have long been subjected was some time since prominently brought to our notice by Mr. Henvey. We did not take action at once, conceiving that a more favourable opportunity would present itself on the occurrence of a fresh succession—an event which seemed unlikely to be long postponed. When that event takes place, we consider that it will be our duty to impress upon the Kashmir Government its obligations to its own subjects, and to see that the reforms which are so urgently needed are no longer postponed. With this view we would propose, immediately on the occurrence of the next succession, to inform the Maharaja that we regard the present state of affairs as most unsatisfactory, and that substantial reforms are required. We would if possible lead the new Government to propose the measures necessary to give effect to this altered policy, but we should require that their execution should be entrusted to competent hands. While firmly insisting upon the necessity for a Change, we should avoid any direct interference with administrative details.

We are however, sensible that, if our advice is to be effectual, it may be necessary to alter the present arrangement under which our representative remains in the Maharaja's territory for a portion only of the year. Such a change would probably be welcomed by the people of Kashmir; and as it would not be introduced until after the death of Maharaja Ranbir Singh, his feelings in the matter would be fully respected. It is a measure which may be called for, not merely by the need for assisting and supervising administrative reforms, but also by the increasing importance to the Government of India of watching events beyond the North-Western frontier of Kashmir. Any disturbances which continued misgovernment might create in Kashmir would be acutely felt on the frontiers of Afghanistan; the connection between Kashmir and its dependent Chiefships would in all probability be severed; and grave political complications might easily ensue. We have therefore to consider the necessity for providing for efficient political supervision not merely in the interests of the people of Kashmir, but also in the interests of the people of India. Under these circumstances we are anxious to obtain from Her Majesty's Government authority to appoint, if it should appear to us necessary, at any time after the death of the present Maharaja, a Resident Political Officer, who will exercise a general supervision over the affairs of the Kashmir State. We do not propose that this officer, if appointed by us, should hold any actual position in the government of the State, nor do we think that it would be necessary to give him special powers in the Province of Kashmir. It will suffice if he occupies, with regard to Jammu and Kashmir, the position and powers ordinarily given to a British Resident in a feudatory State.

The British Government are not debarred by any engagement, express or tacit, from posting a Political Officer permanently in Kashmir; and we see no reason why an arrangement which has been accepted without demur by such a State as Hyderabad should not be adopted in regard to the Kashmir State. If this view is correct, the only question which arises is, whether existing circumstances do not render it desirable to give us the authority we seek.

No.2

THE SECRETARY OF STATE FOR INDIA to the GOVERNMENT OF INDIA

MY LORD MARQUIS, India Office, May 23, 1884.

I have to acknowledge the receipt of the letter of your Excellency's Government, dated the 7th April, relating to Kashmir affairs.

2. In anticipation of the death of Maharaja Ranbir Singh, which is believed to be near at hand, your Excellency in Council has had under consideration (1) the course to be adopted in regard to the succession; (2) the measures which should be taken on the commencement of a new reign, in order to secure reforms in the administration of the State; and (3) the expediency of a change in the existing arrangements for the representation of the British Government at the Maharaja's Court.

3. Your Excellency in Council is of opinion that any attempt on the part of the Maharaja to exclude his eldest son from the succession should be discouraged, and that Mian Pertab Singh should be proclaimed immediately on his father's death; you propose to require from the new ruler substantial reforms in the administration, and to insist upon their execution being entrusted to competent hands; and you request from Her Majesty's Government discretionary authority to appoint, at any time after the death of Maharaja Ranbir Singh, a British Resident in Kashmir, with the position and powers ordinarily given to such an officer in a feudatory State.

4. While I regret to receive so unfavourable an account of the character of the Maharaja's heir, I agree with your Excellency's Government in regarding as inexpedient any deviation in the case of Kashmir from the regular succession by order of primogeniture, or any partition of the State, by will or otherwise, among the three sons of the present Chief. I approve, therefore, of the instructions in accordance with this view, which I understand to have been sent to the Officer on Special Duty in Kashmir.

5. As to the urgent need of reforms in the administration of the State, there is, unfortunately, no room for doubt. It may, in-

deed, be a question whether, having regard to the circumstances under which the sovereignty of the country was entrusted to the present Hindu ruling family, the intervention of the British Government on behalf of the Muhammadan population has not already been too long delayed; but, however this may be, Her Majesty's Government are satisfied that, upon a fresh succession, no time should be lost in taking whatever steps may be requisite in order to place the administration upon a sound footing.

6. The same occasion would, in the opinion of Her Majesty's Government, be a suitable one for introducing a change in the present arrangement under which your Excellency's representative remains in Kashmir for a portion only of the year.

7. In 1846 it was decided not to appoint a political officer to reside permanently at the Maharaja's Court, whilst in 1873, when the measure was recommended by Lord Northbrook's Government, the necessity for it did not seem to Her Majesty's Government to be so clearly established as to justify them in disregarding objections which were expressed by authorities entitled to respect. But in the interval which has since elapsed, circumstances have greatly changed; and whether regard be had to the condition of the country, to the character of the Prince into whose hands the Government will shortly pass, or to the course of events beyond the border, which has materially increased the political importance of Kashmir, the appointment which you request a discretionary authority to make appears to be not only desirable but necessary. Your Excellency in Council is, therefore, at liberty to proceed in the matter as you may think proper at any time after the death of Maharaja Ranbir Singh, taking care meanwhile that strict secrecy is observed as to your intentions.

I have, & c.,
(Signed) KIMBERLEY.

No.3

The GOVERNMENT OF INDIA to the SECRETARY OF STATE FOR INDIA (LORD RANDOLPH CHURCHILL), dated Simla, October 19, 1885

EXTRACT

We have the honour to forward correspondence relative to affairs in the Kashmir State.

The demise of the late Maharaja Ranbir Singh was announced to your Lordship by telegram on the 12th September; and the papers now enclosed will acquaint Her Majesty's Government with the steps we have taken to carry out the policy approved by Lord Kimberley's despatch, dated the 23rd May, 1884. The succession of Pertab Singh, the eldest son of the deceased Maharaja, to the undivided Chiefship of Jammu and Kashmir has been recognised and confirmed. The position of the Political Officer in Kashmir has been placed on the same footing with that of Residents in other Indian States in subordinate alliance with the British Government. The attention of the new ruler has been drawn to certain measures of reform which we consider essential to remedy the long-standing misrule in His Highness's territories. At the same time the Maharaja has been assured that we desire to leave the initiation of these measures in his hands, to abstain from unnecessary interference in his affairs, and to allow him all legitimate discretion and a liberal period of time for the execution of a work which is as difficult as it is necessary.

Your Lordship will perceive that the change in the Political Officer's appointment has evoked a remonstrance from the Maharaja Pertab Singh. We were prepared for some opposition in this matter on the part of the Durbar, and, as the question has been fully considered and finally settled, we have declined to enter into any further discussion on the subject.

We trust that our proceedings may meet with the approval of Her Majesty's Government.

Enclosure 1 in No.3
From the SECRETARY TO THE GOVERNMENT OF INDIA, Foreign Department, to the OFFICER ON SPECIAL DUTY IN KASHMIR, dated Simla, August, 1, 1884
EXTRACT

I am directed to convey to you the instructions of the Governor-General in Council upon the condition of affairs in Kashmir.

In case of Maharaja Ranbir Singh's death, his eldest son, Mian Pertab Singh, will succeed to the undivided Chiefship; the new Maharaja will be called upon to introduce such reforms as may seem to be necessary; and a Resident political officer will be stationed in Kashmir. It remains to inform you of the precise steps which the Governor-General in Council desires you to adopt for carrying out these arrangements.

So long as Maharaja Ranbir Singh is alive, the Government of India do not propose to make any change in their existing policy. His Highness should be quietly dissuaded, if he refers to you on the subject, from executing any testament in favour of the partition of his territories; but it will not be necessary for you to make any formal communication to His Highness upon this matter; or to travel beyond existing practice in recommending to him administrative reforms, or other desirable measures. You should abstain from any allusions to the subject of changes in the existing position of the Officer on Special Duty in Kashmir, and you should avoid as much as possible anything which is calculated in the Maharaja's present state of health unnecessarily to disturb his mind. It is of course desirable that you should use your influence, as far as you can, even during the life of the Maharaja, for the improvement of the condition of Kashmir; but the Governor-General in Council wishes to treat

His Highness with the utmost consideration; and, as any substantial reform would probably involve a very unpalatable degree of interference with his proceedings, it will be sufficient if, during the remainder of his life, you can preserve the administration of the State from any material change for the worse.

If at any time the Maharaja's death should appear to be very near at hand, you should make arrangements to join His Highness at Jammu, or wherever he may then be, and to prevent any disorder occurring. If his illness should unfortunately terminate fatally, you should take the earliest opportunity of announcing that the Viceroy is pleased to recognize the succession of Mian Pertab Singh to the Chiefship, and you should formally instal the new Chief on the gaddi of Jammu and Kashmir.

At the same time you should inform His Highness, and the members of his Durbar, of the views and intentions of the British Government in regard to the future administration of the State. You should give them clearly to understand that His Excellency the Viceroy regards the existing condition of affairs in Kashmir as most unsatisfactory; and you should warn His Highness and those about him that substantial reforms must be introduced without delay. You should then announce that, with the view of aiding His Highness in the introduction and maintenance of those reforms, the Viceroy has decided to give His Highness the assistance of a resident English officer, and that for the future the British representative in Kashmir will have the same status and duties as the Political Residents in other Indian States in subordinate alliance with the British Government.

It is important, in order to avoid uncertainty and the risk of disorder, that this announcement of the intentions of the Government should take place without delay, and that they should be clearly and fully understood both by the Maharaja and by all others concerned when he is installed. The recognition and installation of the new Chief should be as prompt and formal as possible, and nothing should be omitted that can have the effect of assuring His Highness of the good-will of the British Government; but, while treating the Maharaja with the utmost friendliness and courtesy, you cannot speak too plainly in regard to the Viceroy's views and intentions.

Immediately after the news of Maharaja Ranbir Singh's death reaches the Government of India, a letter addressed by His Excellency the Viceroy to the new chief will be sent to you for delivery. A draft of this letter is enclosed for your information. When you receive the signed copy of this draft or before you receive it, if the ceremonies connected with the change of rulers should afford you an opportunity of speaking earlier, you should invite the Maharaja to indicate the reforms which he may consider it necessary or desirable to introduce; and you should ask His Highness to inform you of his views with regard to the persons whom he would propose to place in charge of the administration. It will not be expedient to bring in a Minister from elsewhere if a sufficiently well qualified local candidate can be found; and as far as possible the Governor-General in Council would wish to leave the Maharaja free to form his own Government. Any proposals, therefore, which His Highness may put forward on this subject will be tentatively accepted, unless you should see decided reason to object to them as holding out no prospect of success.

You will notice that the draft letter to the Maharaja impresses upon him the necessity for consulting you fully at all times, and following your advice. You should therefore not hesitate to offer your advice freely whenever you may think it desirable to do so; the more particularly because, owing to the peculiar conditions under which the Maharaja will succeed to the Chiefship, it will be necessary that his administration should for a time at least be closely supervised; the condition of Kashmir must be thoroughly reformed; and the Governor-General in Council cannot allow this object to be frustrated by any obstruction or procrastination on the part of the Durbar.

I am now to enumerate, for your information and guidance, the principal measures of reform which appear to the Governor-General in Council to be necessary after any arrangements required for the immediate alleviation of distress, it distress exist, have been adopted and carried out. In the opinion of the Governor-General in Council those measures are: the introduction of a reasonably light assessment of land revenue, collections being made in cash if on examination this seems to be a suitable arrangement; the construction of good roads; the cessation of State monopolies; the revision of existing taxes and dues, especially transit dues and the numerous taxes upon trades and professions; the abolition of the system of farming the revenue, wherever this system is in force; regular payment in coin; the establishment of a careful system of financial control; the removal of all restrictions upon emigration; the reorganisation and regular payment of the army; and the improvement of the judicial administration. In order to afford the Maharaja all possible help in the introduction of such reforms, the Governor-General in Council will if necessary grant His Highness a loan from Imperial revenues, and will also be willing to place at his disposal, for a time, the services of any officers of the British Government who may seem specially qualified to assist the new administration in carrying out the measures contemplated. Such assistance seems to be more particularly required with regard to the revision of the settlement and the construction of roads. The pay of any officers transferred must, however, be found by the Kashmir State.

With reference to the relations existing between Kashmir and the States upon her northern border, the Governor-General in Council does not think it necessary at present to issue any detailed instructions. The question is an important one, and will require your close and constant attention. You should be kept accurately informed of all movements of troops and other noteworthy occurrences in the direction of the frontier; and you should be prepared to advise Maharaja Pertab Singh freely on all matters of frontier policy. But at present the Governor-General in Council has no special instructions to give you on this subject.

I am to add that if the death of Maharaja Ranbir Singh occurs during the Kashmir season, and you find yourself obliged in consequence to leave Srinagar for Jammu, you should on starting hand over the charge of your current duties to the Agency Surgeon or other qualified officer. The Governor-General in Council is willing to leave to your discretion the question of the route by which you should go to Jammu; but he desires me to suggest to you that your passing down by the direct route through Kashmir territory might have a good effect in maintaining quiet and order. And I am to say that it is very desirable not to move any British troops across the border if this can possibly be avoided. If it becomes absolutely necessary to do so, the special sanction of the Government of India should be obtained before any movement is made.

I have only to remark in conclusion that circumstances may evidently occur to which the terms of this letter will not be strictly applicable. The Maharaja Ranbir Singh may die suddenly in your absence, or his life may be unexpectedly prolonged. Mian Pertab Singh may be absent from Jammu at the time of his father's decease, and it is even possible that before that event occurs he may become actually incapacitated for rule. These or similar circumstances may render some departure necessary from the letter of the instructions now given to you. But the Governor-General in Council relies with confidence upon your judgment in the event of any such contingency, and has no doubt that the instructions now given to you will suffice for your guidance in all matters of practical importance. If necessity arises they can hereafter be modified.

Enclosure 2 in No. 3
FROM RESIDENT in Kashmir to SECRETARY TO THE GOVERNMENT OF INDIA, Foreign Department. Jammu, 16 September, 1885
EXTRACT

I have the honour to report my arrival here yesterday morning, my journey having been much delayed by the bad state of the road. At Vernag, late at night on the 12th, I received a telegram from Mian Pertab Singh, the heir-apparent, informing me of the death of his father, Maharaja Ranbir Singh, at 4.30 p.m. that day.

From conversation with Dr. Gopal Chander, His Highness's medical attendant, and others, I learn that, about the 29th August, the Maharaja, who was still weak from the effects of the fever from which he had suffered two months ago, had an attack of dysentery, which the medicines given him failed to relieve. He grew rapidly worse, but was under no apprehension of a fatal result till 24 hours before his death, when, finding that the forgiveness and return of a Brahmin whom he had exiled many years ago, and under whose curse he was persuaded by a seer he was labouring, failed to give him any relief, he made up his mind that his end was at hand. He then enjoined his sons to live in peace with one another, and told Pertab Singh, the eldest, to complete the good works he had begun. He also ordered that the contract for the sale of liquor in Jammu, recently sold for 40,000 rupees, should be cancelled and the sale of spirits forbidden as heretofore; and further directed that the toll levied on persons crossing the Tavi river by ford should be discontinued, and that fire-wood and vegetables should for the future be allowed to enter Jammu free of duty. At four in the afternoon he became insensible, and according to Hindu custom was removed from his bed to the floor, where he breathed his last shortly afterwards.

The next day, the 13th, the Maharaja's body was burned on the bank of the Tavi river with great ceremony in the presence of a large multitude. The corpse is said to have been enveloped originally in forty coverings of shawl and other rich stuffs, interspersed with gold coins and jewels of great value placed there by the women of his harem; but I am told that all but thirteen of the wrappers were taken off by the attendant Brahmins before the body was placed on the pile. The whole of the Maharaja's ward-robe, jewels, riding horses, with seven elephants, and a number of cattle, besides a very large sum in cash, the whole estimated at from five to ten lakhs of rupees, were set aside for distribution among the Brahmins or to be sent to holy men in the neighbourhood. All business was suspended, and all shops ordered to be closed; but the next day this order was so far relaxed as to allow provision dealers to carry on their trade through one leaf of their shop doors. All Government employees, including the soldiers, shaved their heads and faces, excepting only Sikhs, Mussulmans, Brahmins, and those Rajputs connected with the Maharaja by marriage. White garments are worn by all, and ornaments of every description laid aside.

The period of mourning extends over thirteen days, and the Minister, Diwan Anant Ram, whom I saw immediately after my arrival, made some difficulty about my seeing the new Maharaja Pertab Singh before its expiry. The duties of religion, he declared, absolutely debarred the chief mourner from touching or even sitting on the same carpet with any other human being, till its close. Thus my reception in Durbar would be impossible. Under these circumstances it became impracticable to carry out to the letter the instructions conveyed in your letter of the 1st August, 1884, a formal installation of the new Maharaja on the gaddi being incompatible with the earliest possible announcement of his recognition, and the delivery of his Excellency's message as to the views and intentions of the British Government. It seemed to me, however, all-important that there should be no delay in these last, and I therefore told the Diwan that it was imperatively necessary that I should see the Maharaja at once. He replied that if I would consent to forego the usual ceremonies of reception, and had no objection to sitting on the floor (it being impossible to admit any article of furniture into the room with the Maharaja), His Highness would be glad to see me.

Accordingly, at five in the afternoon I went to the Palace, where I was received by Mian Amar Sing, the late Maharaja's youngest son. In an inner room opening from the Durbar Hall I found the Maharaja sitting on a small square carpet covered with white cotton. A similar one was placed by its side for my accommodation. After I was seated all present left the room, entirely contrary to custom (I have never had an interview with the late Maharaja without two at least of his Council being present). After a few sentences of compliment and condolence, I told Pertab Singh that I had a message for him from the Viceroy, to be delivered in the presence of his Council. He replied that he had not yet appointed a Council, to which I answered that it was to the members of late Maharaja's Council that I referred. He then called in Diwan Anant Ram alone. It was clear that an unpalatable communication was anticipated, and that it was hoped to confine it to as small a circle of hearers as possible. I therefore said that the message I had to deliver was not private and confidential though very important. On the contrary I had hoped to deliver it to His Highness in Durbar, but this being impossible I begged that he would call in at least Babu Nilambar and Diwan Gobind Sahai, who I knew were waiting outside. On this Pertab Singh ordered them to come in. On their seating themselves I told His Highness that His Excellency the Viceroy had ordered me in the first place to lose no time in announcing that His Excellency is pleased to recognise his succession to the Chiefship. This was received with expressions of gratitude and loyalty, the Maharaja rising and bowing his thanks. I then gave him the message contained in your letter, translating it sentence by sentence into Hindustani, only using the words "Kashmir and

Jammu" instead of "Kashmir" only, as it might have been asserted afterwards that the message referred to Kashmir only, and not to the whole State.

The first part of the message referring to the introduction of reforms was received without any mark of surprise by my auditors, but the announcement of the immediate appointment of a Resident was evidently an unexpected blow.

I then took leave of the Maharaja. In the evening Babu Nilambar called on me with reference to another subject, and asked that I would explain, for the Maharaja's information, what was meant by the 'assistance of a Resident'. Did it imply that the Resident would take an active part in the administration of the country? I told him that I could not undertake to define the exact duties of a Resident, but that he would certainly leave all the active work of administration to the Durbar, while claiming the right to be made acquainted, should he require it, with all its details. He would give advice if asked for, and on any point he thought proper unasked; and in this latter case would expect his advice to be followed.

To-day Babu Nilambar called on me again, accompanied by Diwan Anant Ram. They brought a message from the Maharaja, begging me to use my influence to obtain for him a short delay before the appointment of a Resident, in order that he might get the credit for the reforms he had long made up his mind to introduce if ever he got the opportunity. It is unnecessary to detail the long conversation that ensued. Babu Nilambar finally acknowledged that the main objection was to the name 'Resident'. To this I replied that at the present juncture putting aside other arguments, the name was all-important. The Maharaja and his councillors appeared to me to underrate vastly the difficulty of the task before them. It was one thing to order reforms and another to carry them out. In remedying the abuses which were ruining the country, they would have opposed to them the entire army of employees, high and low, who had been fattening on the land for years. The public appointment of a Resident would show these officials that there was something beyond caprice or the zeal of a new ruler in the reforms initiated at Jammu, and they would soon recognise that they must be carried out. As the same time the people at large would welcome the appointment of a Resident as an assurance of substantial reforms to come. Under these circumstances, while anxious to do all in my power to meet the Maharaja's wishes, I regretted that I could not recommend to his Excellency any delay in the formal appointment of a Resident.

The state of affairs seems to be somewhat as follows:- The death of Wazir Punnu (who fell down dead in Durbar on the 6th instant) was a stroke of extraordinary good fortune for the opposite party, represented by Diwan Anant Ram and Babu Nilambar. It not only removed their most powerful adversary, and the man who had the greatest influence with the present as with the late Maharaja, but it also keeps the country quiet without any effort on their part. The name of Punnu was a byeword and a reproach among the people, and all the tyranny and oppression from which they suffered was invariably laid to his door, not always with justice. Had he survived his old master, he would have been the leading spirit in the Councils of the new Chief, and the people, hopeless of improvement, would probably have made rebellious demonstrations, which, with an army eighteen months in arrears of pay, would not have been easy to suppress. But Punnu died six days before Pertab Singh succeeded to the Chiefship, and the people, overjoyed at their deliverance from the man whom they believed their sole tyrant, are probably indifferent to the change of rulers, and will remain quite in confident anticipation of early relief from their burdens.

Another fortunate circumstance for the new Chief is the general prosperity of the Country, as far as it can be prosperous under such a Government. The late spring rains caused some loss in the low country and the outer hills, as did the summer floods in Kashmir, but the agricultural out-turn for the last year has everywhere been exceptionally high, and the prospects of the crops now in the ground are excellent. Commerce is shown by the Punjab trade reports to be steadily improving in spite of the vexatious restrictions placed on it. Thus, as far as the country itself is concerned, Maharaja Pertab Singh and his councillors have everything in their favour. At present he is looking for advice to Babu Nilambar and Diwan Anant Ram. The first is clever and well-intetioned, but without practical experience of administration and deficient in force of character. The Diwan is perhaps well meaning, but his bringing up inclines him to lean to the old way of managing the country, and he is weak and cunning. They are, I fear, wholly unable to cope with the difficulties which will meet them in improving the administration, should they make any real effort to do so. Certain simple reforms, such as the abolition of obnoxious imposts and export dues and the more regular payment of officials, they may effect, but it will, I fear, be hopeless to look for any serious improvement in the administration generally, without constant and heavy pressure, and material interference in details.

A probable early source of trouble will be the influence possessed over the new Maharaja by his personal followers. These, who are mostly men of the lowest class, are already beginning to assert themselves, and to offer to help their friends to lucrative employment. It can hardly be long before they and the party of Nilambar and Anant Ram come into conflict. The latter will not have to courage to lean on the Resident, and govern as Salar Jang did in Hyderabad in spite of the Chief, but will try to trim with the usual consequences. On these points I will write more fully as the situation develops itself. For the present I have only pointed out to Anant Ram and Nilambar the urgent necessity for paying the troops, and for relieving the export trade of the country from its burdens. They will not, or cannot, give me any information of the actual state of the finances, except that the public treasury is practically empty. I have every reason to believe, however, that the late Maharaja regularly diverted the revenue of certain districts to his private chest. Some of this was devoted to religious purposes, but popular report has it that he has left large sums hoarded in obscure forts in different parts of the country. It is also said that he solemnly enjoined that this money should never be used to meet the current expenditure of the State, and no doubt, if it exists, every effort will be made to keep it intact, or at all events to spend it on no useful object. The annual customs contract expires in the course of a month or two, and this will be a favourable opportunity for a revision of the tariff, which should entirely free the woollen and metal trades of Kashmir from the heavy export duties to which they are now subject. This will give an impulse to production in Srinagar, which should tide the artisan class over the winter, of which the prospects are exceptionally bad owing to the final collapse of the shawl trade in Europe, and the paucity of visitors in the valley this year.

The Maharaja ends his mourning on the 26th when he will take his seat in the Durbar. This will be the proper opportunity for the delivery of the kharita from his Excellency the Viceroy, of which a copy was enclosed with your letter of the 1st August, 1884.

KHARITA, dated Simla, the 14th September 1885, referred to in last paragraph of above Enclosure

From His Excellency the VICEROY AND GOVERNOR-GENERAL OF INDIA to the MAHARAJA OF JAMMU AND KASHMIR

I have received with deep regret the news of the death of your father, Maharaja Ranbir Sing: and I wish to assure you without delay of my most sincere sympathy.

Maharaja Ranbir Sing rendered valuable service to the British Government. I feel that his loss is the loss of a friend; and I wish that it had not fallen to me, during the period of my

Viceroyalty, to consider the measures rendered necessary by this unfortunate event.

It is now my duty to inform you, on behalf of the Queen-Empress of India, that I recognise and confirm your succession to the Chiefship of Jammu and Kashmir. I trust that Your Highness's life may be long and prosperous; and that, in all difficulties, of whatsoever kind, you will rely with confidence upon the good-will of the British Government, which will never fail you so long as you are loyal to the Crown and earnest in the desire to rule your State with justice and moderation.

Your Highness has before you a difficult task. During the illness of your father the administration of the State became seriously disorganised, and it will be necessary for you to introduce many reforms. But my Agent, Sir Oliver St. John, will remain with you and help you to the utmost of his ability; and I feel confident that with his aid all your difficulties will be successfully met and overcome. I request your Highness to refer to him for a more detailed explanation of my views regarding the future administration of the Kashmir State; and I hope that your Highness will not fail to consult him freely at all times, and to be guided by his advice in carrying those views into execution.

Enclosure 3 in No. 3
From MIAN PERTAB SINGH to His Excellency the VICEROY AND GOVERNOR-GENERAL OF INDIA

Jammu, September 18, 1885.

Your most esteemed Excellency,

I beg to offer my heartfelt thanks for your Excellency's kind message of condolence on the demise of my father, whose devoted loyalty to the British Crown won for him those assurances of personal friendship from your Excellency which he valued so highly, and of which he felt so very proud.

I have also to present my grateful thanks to your Excellency for the most welcome message conveyed to me on the 15th instant by Colonel Sir Oliver St. John, the officer on Special Duty in Kashmir, that your Excellency has been pleased to recognise my succession to the gaddi of this State, and I hope by the blessing of God to let your Excellency have the satisfaction of learning before long that I am as fully alive to the undoubted and immense importance of conscientiously discharging my duties towards my subjects by doing all in my power to secure their best happiness, as I am awake to the supremely important duty of giving renewed proofs of loyalty to the British Government by following in the footsteps of my father and grandfather.

I do not hesitate to admit that the existing state of affairs in Kashmir and Jammu urgently requires immediate introduction of substantial reforms into the administration of the country, and now that I have power commensurate with my responsibilities, I beg to assure your Excellency that nothing shall be spared on my part, and no time will be lost to prove beyond any possibility of doubt that it is my ambition to succeed in making my country a model of a well-governed State in alliance with the Government of India.

It has, however, pained me extremely to learn that exactly at the time when I have made up my mind to deserve and win your Excellency's approbation and encouragement by proving myself equal to the onerous and responsible duties of a good ruler, your Excellency has been thinking of changing the status of the British Officer on Special Duty in Kashmir to that of a Political Resident, and thus lowering me in the eyes of my subjects and in the estimation of the public. It is fully known to your Excellency that I have only just now acquired the power of showing to the world that, without any interference from any quarter or any, the smallest, diminution of long-enjoyed rights and dignity of this State, I am able and willing of my own accord to introduce and maintain such reforms as are calculated to entitle a ruler to the lasting gratitude of his subjects, and encouraging approbation of the paramount power as well as the public at large.

I may submit to your Excellency that I am fully aware of the wise and benevolent principles which guide the Supreme Government of India in its relations with the Native States, and I have not the least doubt that your Excellency will estimate me not by the splendour of my Court, nor by the pomp of my retinue, but by my conduct towards my subjects and by the only standard of good government combined with sincere and active loyalty.

I am confident, also, that I have only to convince your Excellency of the purity of my intentions, the earnestness of my purpose, and the firmness of my determination to govern well, to win your Excellency's sympathy with me in my desire to see the position of the Officer on Special Duty in Kashmir unaltered in his relations with this State.

I have sufficient confidence in the unbiassed justice of your Excellency's Government to hope that your Excellency will not form any unfavourable opinion of my abilities, intentions, and character, till the result of my administration for a sufficient length of time should justify a definite conclusion, and that your Excellency will see no necessity for altering the status of the Officer on Special Duty in Kashmir, and that, therefore, there will be no occasion now for my waiting personally on your Excellency at Simla, to give your Excellency the trouble of taking into serious consideration the sanads of Her Imperial Majesty's Government, securing to the Chiefship the full enjoyment of all the rights of my father and grandfather, and to submit to your Excellency the grounds on which I attach so much importance to the credit of earning the reputation of a just and benevolent ruler without any meddling from any quarter, and of preserving intact in all its relations the integrity of the State as inherited from my father as well as of endeavouring to exalt its dignity in the estimation of the paramount power by doing exactly what the ruler of a large and important State should do.

Requesting your Excellency to excuse the trouble I have given you, I beg to subscribe myself, etc.

Enclosure 4 in No. 3
From PRESIDENT IN KASHMIR, to SECRETARY TO THE GOVERNMENT OF INDIA, Foreign Department, dated Jammu, Sept. 27, 1885
EXTRACT

In continuation of my letter of the 16th, I have the honour to report that Mian Pertab Singh, eldest son of the late Maharaja Ranbir Singh, formally took his seat in the Durbar on the afternoon of the 25th instant.

The previous day and the morning of the 25th had been occupied in distributing gifts to Brahmins by the river side, at the place where the late Maharaja's body was burnt. In addition to a large sum of money, these gifts consisted of 13 sets of everything that had been used by the Maharaja in this world, including horses, cows, and other domestic animals, but only one elephant. The total value is estimated by public opinion at two lakhs of rupees, but was probably less. The remainder of the Maharaja's effects, with a sum of five lakhs from his private treasury, are retained to be added to the fund consecrated by him to the perpetual use of the temples, which fund last year already amounted to 15 lakhs.

On concluding the distribution of the gifts destined to facilitate his father's passage to Paradise, Maharaja Pertab Singh returned to the Palace, and performed the ceremony of "dastarbandi," i.e., tying on of the turban, which marks the close of the period of acute grief.

At 5 p.m. I paid the Maharaja a formal visit to congratulate him on his accession. The kharita of his Excellency the Viceroy had already been delivered to him privately, to put an end to further useless argument on the question of the "Resident," and to avoid mention of the topic in Durbar, which would have been very distasteful to the Chief. Instead therefore of reading the kharita, I made a short speech in Urdu, of which a translation is attached (Enclosure A.).

Babu Nilambara Mukerji then read a manifesto in English, a translation of which in Urdu was subsequently read by Diwan Anant Ram, followed by the proclamation alluded to.

The imposts and customs mitigated or abolished are as follows:-

(1) The custom of "khodkasht." This is a system by which the State farms a part of the village lands itself. Advances are annually made to the persons employed for the purpose, but it is notorious they they embezzle the money, and cultivate the land with forced labour, and seed extorted from the villagers.

(2) The custom of "leri". This is a system of paying sepoys and others by remission of rent, instead of in coin, and, for some reason not easily explained, is much disliked.

(3) Each group of ten houses in Jammu territory will no longer, as before, be obliged to supply one Sepoy or other Government servant; forcible enlistment generally is abolished; and the rule of obliging families to provide substitutes for deserters is done away with.

(4) The customs duty on rice and other provisions brought into Srinagar for sale is reduced from two annas in the rupee to half an anna, in other words from 12 1/2 to 3 1/8 per cent.

To understand the severity of this tax is must be explained that Government itself is the principal grain dealer, and fixes a permanent rate at which grain is sold. Thus the rate for unhusked rice is Rs. 1-4 (English) per kharwar, equivalent to about 10 annas a man. If a Zemindar sends rice to market, he can ask no more for it than 10 annas a man, and has in addition to pay the customs contractor 1 1/4 anna before he can offer it for sale. Under these conditions it is clear that the remission of three-fourths of this tax will benefit the producer, and not the consumer, who will pay the same price for his rice as before.

(5) The next impost remitted is also in favour of the Zemindar. Every large village community in Kashmir comprises a "Zillahdah," or "Harkara,", whose business it is to report the misdeeds of his fellows. The Durbar affect to look on these officials as rural police; but as they are occasionally women, and have no powers beyond reporting, spies would be a better name for them. They are paid by a cess of 1 1/2 per cent on the gross produce of the land. Some years ago it occurred to Wazir Punnu that the Zillahdars were making too much money, and he therefore made their chief, the Harkara-Bashi (head-bringer of news) pay an annual sum to the treasury. This has been raised till it now amounts to 60,000 Chilki rupees (37,500 English), a great deal more than the estimated total value of the cess from which it is supposed to be paid. This most obnoxious impost is now abolished, but the Zillahdars are warned that they must continue to send in reports, and that if found extorting anything beyond the legitimate 1 1/2 per cent they will be punished.

(6) The tax on the sale of horses in Kashmir, called "Zar-i-nakas", which at one time amounted to 50 per cent of the purchase money, is abolished.

(7) The tax on "Ekhas" plying for hire to Sialkot, which amounted to Rs. 1-11 on a total of Rs. 2-10, is abolished, and some other minor dues are remitted.

On the whole the above constitute a valuable boon to the people, especially to the cultivating classes of Jammu, whose main grievances are now removed. Sensible relief is also given to the Kashmir peasant; but the artizan of the towns, whose needs are greater, gets nothing but a slight possible reduction in the price of fruit and vegetables.

Yesterday afternoon I had a private interview with the Maharaja, at which only Diwan Anant Ram and Babu Nilambara Mukerji were present. According to my instructions I asked him to let me know what reforms he proposed to initiate, and to what persons he proposed to entrust their execution. As regards reforms he would only refer me to the manifesto (Enclosure B), repeatedly declaring with reference to both reforms and ministers that he required time to reflect. At last he said that he entrusted Babu Nilambara with all business connected with finance, while Diwan Anant Ram would continue as before to conduct foreign affairs, which he defined to be those of Ladak and Leh, and correspondence with myself. I told the Maharaja that I was going back to Kashmir for the present, but that I should return before long, and hoped that by that time he would have matured his schemes for reform. I could not, however, leave without doing my utmost to impress on him the imperative necessity of relieving the manufacturing classes of Kashmir from the present burdens on trade. I then tried to explain the question to him, but the only answer to be obtained was that he would think it over. I should here remark that I had previously discussed the question with Babu Nilambara, who tried to argue that the Government of India should do something in return for concessions on this point. Of course I replied that our only object was to benefit the Kashmir Government and the people, who are the only sufferers from the insane policy of imposing crushing duties on their own manufactures. I fear that much pressure will be required to bring about this most essential reform.

As mentioned in my former letter, Maharaja Ranbir Singh is said to have left considerable private wealth. Babu Nilambara tells me that this is certain, but that neither he nor anyone outside the household have any idea of the amount. The public treasury, or rather treasuries, for there are many in Jammu itself, are empty, but money has been produced from the Palace (2 3/4 lakhs) to pay the troops up to the end of the last Hindu year, for which they had as yet received nothing. This leaves them only five months in arrear. The troops in Kashmir have already been paid.

My impression as regards the new Maharaja is that, though entirely wanting in the quick wit of his father, he has inherited a full share of his obstinacy and cunning. He will consent to certain surface reforms, but on the cardinal points of delegating real power to his ministers, freeing trade, improving communications, and making a proper land settlement, he will, I fear, offer as much opposition as he dares.

Babu Nilambara and Diwan Anant Ram, freed from the fear of Wazir Punnu, seem to think themselves strong enough to go on alone without the support of a Resident, which they formerly declared to be essentially necessary. They will soon find themselves mistaken, but in the meantime had better be left to themselves. On this account I am glad to return to Kashmir, for which I start to-morrow, inspecting the cart-road en route. On this work, the completion of which is an essential preliminary to the greatest of the reforms required in Kashmir, a proper land revenue settlement, I will submit a full report at the earliest opportunity. I will also, while in Kashmir, ascertain the exact burdens now imposed on the export trade which are constantly varying

I have seen with regret that His Highness keeps his younger brothers, Ram Singh and Amar Singh, and his cousin, Raja Moti Singh, of Poonal, at a distance. I have let him know that I think this a mistake, and have exchanged visits with them for the first time. During the late Maharaja's reign overtures to this effect met with no response.

ENCLOSURE A

Your Highness! I beg to offer you my congratulations on your accession to the place occupied by your father and grandfather, whose loyalty and devotion to the British Crown you will, I feel sure, do your utmost emulate.

No Chief in India has ever succeeded to the gaddi with more opportunities for doing good. The State of Jammu and Kashmir has fallen behind the majority of the States of India in that progress which is necessary to the welfare of the people and the good name of their rulers.

It is Your Highness' good fortune to have it in your power to remedy these shortcomings; and, though the task will be a difficult one, I feel assured that you will address all your energies to it. The Government of India will take the warmest interests in your efforts to improve the administration of your State and the condition of your subjects of every class; and the eyes of all enlightened persons in India will be fixed on you to see how you perform the duties for which you are now responsible.

It is my earnest hope to be able before long to congratulate you on ruling over a country foremost in India for good government and happy subjects as it is for loyalty and devotion. May your Highness' reign be long and prosperous, and may your name be handed down to posterity as the Nowshirwan of Jammu and Kashmir.

ENCLOSURE B

Sir Oliver St. John Sardars, and Gentlemen,

My heart and cordial thanks are due to His Excellency the Viceroy, and his worthy representative and my sincere friend,

Sir Oliver St. John, for the kharita, recognising my succession to the Chiefship of this large and important State, and I take this fitting opportunity to declare publicly, that of the many arduous and responsible duties which I shall have to perform as the ruler of this State, the foremost under all circumstances will be the duty of following in the footsteps of my illustrious grandfather and his lamented Highness, in giving substantial proofs of unswerving and devoted loyalty to Her Imperial Majesty's Government, and, when the necessity will arise, of placing all the resources of my country at the disposal of his Excellency the Viceroy, and of personally joining the British army with the whole of my military force.

2. Next in importance to my obligations to the paramount power, but next to those only, will be the duty of governing my country with justice and moderation. The responsibilities which I am going to undertake will be high and heavy indeed, but I believe God will grant me firmness and strength enough to discharge them with credit to the family of my renowned ancestors, and benefit to the lakhs of subjects, whom it has pleased Providence to place under my care.

3. I have before me the difficult task of introducing substantial reforms in the administration of the country, but I believe I have only to look the difficulties boldly in the face and show a determined front, to achieve complete success and earn the reputation of a just and good ruler. Armed with purity of intentions and firmness of purpose, I may reasonably entertain the hope of being able to clear the administrative agency of all corruption and incompetency, and impart to it the maximum of honesty and efficiency. I now warn my officials of all ranks that I have fully made up my mind to put down corruption and intrigue wherever they may be found, and I hope they will do all in their power to help me in making my administration a blessing and a source of unmixed good to my people.

4. I know that the paramount power as well as the public will watch with interest the progress and development of my measures of reform, and I am fully alive to the fact that they will estimate me not by the pomp and splendour of my court and retinue, but by the amount of happiness that I may secure to my subjects.

5. I need not trouble you now with minute details of what I intend to do, but I think I can declare without committing myself to any particular measure the policy and the general principles that will guide me in the conduct of my affairs. I shall adopt such measures only as are calculated to secure to my subjects their greatest good and the fullest enjoyment of their rights and privileges, and shall conduct my administration so that the tiller of the soil will enjoy a fair share of the produce of his labour, and the manufacturer the fruit of his skill and industry, that every facility will be given to commerce by improving the means of communication and removing unnecessary and vexatious restrictions, that every encouragement will be offered to get all the resources of the country properly developed, that adequate measures will be taken to give my subjects the benefits of sound and useful education, that ample provision will be made for the relief of the sick and the suffering, and that real merit and worth in my subjects will be recognised and fostered without any distinction of race or rank, creed or colour.

6. To commemorate this auspicious accession with a few acts pointing to the character of the policy I am going to follow, I do now abolish and reduce certain duties and taxes, and remove certain restrictions detailed in the proclamation which my Diwan will read out to you.

No.4

The SECRETARY OF STATE FOR INDIA to the GOVERNMENT OF INDIA

India Office, London, 27th November, 1885.

My Lord,

Para. 1. I have to acknowledge of the receipt of the letter of Your Excellency's Government, dated the 19th ultimo, reporting the measures which have been taken in reference to the State of Kashmir, in consequence of the death of Maharaja Ranbir Singh on the 12th September.

2. When in the spring of the year 1884 the death of the Maharaja was supposed to be imminent, Her Majesty's Government, in accordance with recommendations submitted by the Government of your Excellency's predecessor, decided that, upon the occurrence of that event, His Highness's eldest son should be recognised as successor to the undivided State, but that he should be required to introduce substantial reforms into the administration, and to entrust their execution to competent hands. The Government of India was also authorised, at its discretion, to substitute for an Officer on Special Duty in Kashmir a Resident with the same position and duties as Political Residents in other Native States in subordinate alliance with the British Government.

3. The papers now received from Your Excellency's Government show that, the contingency contemplated in 1884 having arisen, the utmost consideration has been shown to the susceptibilities of Maharaja Pertab Singh in giving effect to the policy then determined upon. His Highness has been informed that, within reasonable limits, he will be allowed full scope and ample time to introduce the requisite administrative reforms, and will get the full credit for initiating them, while it has properly been pointed out to him,in reply to his objections to the proposed change in the status of the representative of the

Government of India at his court, that an arrangement, which is considered suitable in the cases of the other great Princes and Chiefs of India, cannot be regarded either as derogatory to the dignity of the Kashmir State, or as indicating a desire on the part of the paramount power to interfere unnecessarily in its internal affairs.

4. I have to express my full approval of the proceedings of Your Excellency's Government in this matter. Having regard to the condition of the country, to the character of the new ruler, and to the aspect of affairs beyond the frontier, in reference to which Kashmir occupies so important a position, I entertain no doubt as to the necessity for the measures now reported, which will, I trust, conduce to the material well-being of the people of the State, and tend to the better security of imperial interests.

I have, etc.,
(Signed) RANDOLPH S. CHURCHILL.

No.5
The GOVERNMENT OF INDIA to the SECRETARY OF STATE, dated Simla, August 18, 1888
EXTRACT

In March last Mr. Plowden thought the time had come when, for the sake of the State, it was essential to effect some reduction of the Maharaja's authority. There is no doubt some justification for Mr. Plowden's estimate of His Highness's capacity for rule; but, on the other hand, the condition of the State does not seem to demand at present such decided action as Mr. Plowden has suggested. We have, therefore, determined not to resort to measures which would have the effect, directly or indirectly, of taking the power out of the Maharaja's hands, and His Highness will now have another opportunity of showing under favourable circumstances whether he is capable of carrying on the administration.

Enclosure 1 in No.5
REPORT on the Affairs of the STATE of JAMMU and KASHMIR by the RESIDENT in KASHMIR, dated Sialkot, March 5, 1888
EXTRACT

I have had more opportunities of studying the Maharaja's character than perhaps any other officer in the country. My intercourse with him, official, private, and social, has been frequent; my relations with him have been always friendly; there has never been any friction or tension between us. He has never failed in personal courtesy to me, nor ever refused to see me at any time or on any occasion; therefore, I can fairly say that I am not actuated by any feelings of personal dislike towards His Highness.

I think, however, that the Government of India should be under no illusion as regards Maharaja Pertab Singh. From first to last I have failed to discover in him any sustained capacity for governing his country, or any genuine desire to ameliorate its condition, or to introduce those reforms which he has acknowledged to be necessary. More than two years have passed since his accession, but not only has he achieved nothing, but he has opposed beneficial measures proposed by others. The progress made has been in spite of him. I do not believe he is loyal, but fortunately he is powerless to carry his country with him. And I am convinced that the Government will commit a serious mistake if it believes that the reforms which the country urgently needs will ever be effected by Maharaja Pertab Singh. He will never, of his own free will, establish a capable and honest administration; nor, if any power of interference is left him, will he permit any administration appointed by the Government of India to carry on the business of the country. He will thwart and oppose in it every way he dares; the only restraint will be the limit of his powers and his fears; therefore I do most earnestly advise that the Maharaja be made plainly to understand that he has had his chance, and that he will not be allowed any longer to stand in the way. I would assign him a liberal income, to be placed at his absolute disposal, and treat him with full honour as titular Chief; but I would exclude him from all real power. He may reign, but not govern. A great danger with the Maharaja is that his notorious weakness of character and purpose render him an easy tool in the hands of an unscrupulous adviser, and therefore it is essential that he should be controlled by some agency upon which the Government of India can place confidence. I consider that a reduction of the Maharaja's authority on these lines is an essential condition precedent to all other necessary measures.

Next, as to the form of Government. One plan is to appoint Raja Amar Singh Prime Minister, on condition of his undertaking to carry out in all respects the policy of the Government of India. He has not got sufficient experience or solidity of character to execute a task of this magnitude without the aid of a resolute and experienced adviser, and it would be necessary to constitute some such office as "Secretary to Government," and to nominate to it a suitable British Officer—Native or European. I have great doubts whether Raja Amar Singh can be trusted, and, unless he has a strong officer at his elbow to keep him straight, I do not think it would be safe to employ him. He has never forgotten his father's intentions on his behalf, and the object he is working for is to become Maharaja of Kashmir. Once he gets power into his own hands, he will use it without scruple to attain this end. At present the Maharaja is friendly to Raja Amar Singh, because he wishes to break the bond which unites the two younger brothers and Diwan Lachman Das, but there is no genuine affection or confidence between them; and the well-known fact that the late Maharaja would have liked to supersede Pertab Singh in favour of his youngest brother is a special cause of jealousy. And I should expect that, after a short time, all the influence which the Maharaja possesses, especially Zenana influence, would be brought to bear again Amar Singh. Another probable result of his elevation would be a feud between him and his brother Ram Singh, thereby raising against him another hostile party.

Another plan is to bring a Prime Minister from elsewhere. There is no one in the Maharaja's employees fit for the post, and the selection would need particular care. The situation is this: no Native could administer the affairs of Jammu and Kashmir unless he is not only of exceptionally strong character but also exceptionally honest; and, in any case, he would require besides the full support of the Government of India. If a weak man is chosen he will succumb to local intrigue, notwithstanding all the support which the Government may give him; and, if he is not honest, he will yield to the temptations with which the place abounds, and go with the swim. But, if a Native Minister is brought in from outside, I recommend precautionary measures being adopted with the young Rajas. I should order each of them to take up his residence in his own jagir, and so occupy the same position as Raja Moti Singh, of Punch. It is not right that these young men should be given large jagirs which they never visit. It ought to be a condition of the grant that they reside on their property and be personally responsible for its administration. They might pay yearly visits to Jammu just as Moti Singh does. Another good result of this measure would be to lay the foundation of a class of Sardars such as exist in the Rajput States. As long as Raja Ram Singh continues to command the State Army there is no hope of any serious re-organisation; and, if Raja Amar Singh were to remain at Jammu, he would not leave a stone unturned to render the Prime Minister's position untenable.

A third plan is to continue the existing Council, making the Resident its temporary head, and strengthening it by the addition of two selected Natives. An administration so constituted would probably be strong enough to introduce all needful reforms, and to set the country in order. Three years would suffice to set things straight, and the Resident might then withdraw from the headship of the Council, and an administration be established on ordinary Native lines.

I believe that, sooner or later, the Government will have to choose one or other of these three plans or some modification of them. But, whatever plan is adopted, there is one measure which must under any circumstances be prescribed. This is, first, the immediate removal of the band of incompetent, corrupt, and mischievous men who are at the bottom of most of the intrigues by which this unfortunate State is torn; and, secondly, the appointment of an adequate number of trained native officials on reasonable salaries who can be trusted to carry out the orders given to them. Until the entire Kashmir establishment has been recast, and honest and competent servants substituted for the fraudulent and incapable men now employed, no reforms can be carried out, nor can any mere alteration of the form of Government be of any use.

I will endeavour to anticipate an objection which I foresee is likely to be raised. The action suggested in this report brings forward the question of the amount of interference in the affairs of a Native State which may be rightfully and expediently exercised by the paramount Power. It is the settled purpose of the British Government to avoid unnecessary and improper interference in the affairs of Native States. And the basis of this policy is respect for the rights of others, because our treaties with the principal Native States are founded upon their general independence in internal affairs. But, notwithstanding these treaties, cases must from time to time occur in which the Government of India as paramount power is forced to interfere in a radical manner, and it does habitually interfere in a lesser degree. A reluctant interference which circumstances have rendered unavoidable does not, however, infringe the general principle of non-intervention. The question is whether in the case of Kashmir an instance of unavoidable interference has arisen. I submit it has. First, because mis-government producing evil consequences to the people has admittedly existed for many years, and, though a wide margin of time and opportunity has been allowed, there seems no hope whatever that the State, unaided, will be able to settle its own affairs. Secondly, the condition of Kashmir affects countries on its northern border beyond its limits, and thus becomes an injurious and disturbing element in the Imperial scheme of frontier defence. I advocate interference only so far as is indispensable for the accomplishment of the object aimed at, but I would interfere decidedly and effectually for this purpose. A strict adherence to the principle of non-interference implies that Government must also tolerate the local disorder and mal-administration which are bound to ensue.

Enclosure 2 in No. 5
From RESIDENT IN KASHMIR to the SECRETARY TO THE GOVERNMENT OF INDIA, Foreign Department, dated April 21, 1888
EXTRACT

I have the honour to enclose a kharita from His Highness the Maharaja to the address of His Excellency the Viceroy. I am not aware of the contents of the kharita, but I understand that it gives cover to a scheme for the reorganisation of the State Council.

I should be glad to be informed what is the rule in other native States in respect to the transmission of kharitas, i.e., whether or not the Resident is entitled to be furnished with a copy of the kharita or to be informed of its contents. The precedents in this State appear to show that the Resident is not informed in the first instance, but that the Government of India furnishes him with a copy together with the reply. But so short a time has elapsed since a Resident was first appointed in Kashmir that it can hardly be said that any binding usage has yet been established.

In the present instance I have asked His Highness to give me a copy of the kharita not only because the Maharaja expressed his intention of informing me of his proposals and of availing himself of my assistance, but because that both under the instructions of August 1884 and under subsequent instructions the Resident is bound to offer his advice on all important matters, while on his part the Maharaja is required (kharita of 14th September, 1885) "to consult the Resident freely at all times and to be guided by his advice in carrying his views into execution".

KHARITA, dated Srinagar, the 13th April 1888 From His Highness PERTAB SINGH, Maharaja of Jammu and Kashmir, to his Excellency the VICEROY AND GOVERNOR-GENERAL OF INDIA

Your Excellency is already aware that circumstances obliged me to dismiss Diwan Lachman Das, Prime Minister and President of the Council. As I think that the Council which was formed with your kind advice should be continued, I have prepared a scheme for its reorganisation which I beg to forward herewith to your Excellency.

I beg to express the high consideration and esteem I entertain for your Excellency and to subscribe myself, etc.

JAMMU AND KASHMIR COUNCIL
Constitution

1. The Council shall consist of a President, a Vice-President, three Members, and a Secretary.

2. His Highness the Maharaja shall be the President.

3. His Highness shall appoint a Vice-President, Members, and a Secretary.

4. Three shall form a quorum.

5. The Vice-President, Members, and the Secretary may be removed and substituted by majority of votes of the Members of the Council, for reasons to be recorded.

6. The Council shall be a consultative one.

APPOINTMENT OF MEMBERS

7. Raja Amar Singh is hereby appointed Vice-President, and Raja Ram Singh and Babu Nilambar Mukerji, Members, with Diwan Janki Prasad, Member and Secretary.

8. The Members shall represent the following branches of administration:-

1. Military.—Raja Ram Singh.

2. Judicial and Foreign Department.—Raja Amar Singh.

3. Revenue.—Babu Nilambar Mukerji.

4. Miscellaneous.—Diwan Janki Prasad.

9. The Vice-President shall also be the Prime Minister with executive powers.

10. The Vice-President and Members shall take the following oath:-

"I solemnly declare that in giving my opinion as a Member of Council, I shall keep in view the best interests of the State, and shall freely express my honest convictions, without fear or favour, and I shall not divulge any secrets of the State."

BUSINESS

11. The Council shall sit three days in the week, authorised holidays excepted, and any extraordinary meeting shall be held, on the requisition of the Prime Minister.

12. It shall be the duty of the Council to legislate and hear and pass opinion on all subjects that may be brought forward by the Members.

13. The Council shall, on meeting, frame rules for its guidance, which may be removed or modified by it only.

14. All matters shall be decided on majority of votes.

15. Besides the matters which may be brought forward in the Council by the Members, the Prime Minister, who is the head of the Executive Government under His Highness, may refer to the Council for opinion all important questions affecting the administration in all its branches.

16. The respective opinions of the several Members shall be recorded and signed.

17. When a Member brings forward, or the Prime Minister refers, any special matter to the Council, it shall be the duty of the Secretary to furnish all the Members with a written statement of the subject-matter.

18. The office establishment shall be considered and settled by the Council or meeting.

Enclosure 3 in No.5
From the SECRETARY TO THE GOVERNMENT OF INDIA to the PRESIDENT IN KASHMIR, dated Simla, July 25, 1888
EXTRACT

The Government of India have decided to accept in principle the scheme which His Highness has put forward, and your own alternative proposals have for the present been set aside. In coming to this conclusion the Governor-General in Council has not overlooked the fact that the Maharaja's scheme is open to many objections, and that partly on account of His Highness's personal character and partly for other reasons, it is not unlikely to prove a failure. But before sanctioning any measures which would have the effect, directly or indirectly, of taking all power out of the Maharaja's hands, the Government of India have felt that it would be just and right to allow the

Maharaja a further opportunity of showing whether he is competent to discharge the duties of a responsible ruler. If after full and fair trial it becomes evident that he is wholly incapable of conducting the administration of the State the proposals which you have submitted will be reconsidered.

In the meantime I am to ask you to afford the Maharaja every assistance in your power with regard to the reorganisation of his Council and all other matters upon which he may consult you. The Governor-General in Council does not desire you to press upon him your own views as to these matters. You should understand that the responsibility for the success or failure of the present experiment will rest upon the Maharaja; and your aim should be to meet his wishes in every possible manner, not refusing your advice when His Highness asks for it, but avoiding any course of action which might prevent him from feeling that the Government of India desire to allow him the fullest opportunity of proving his fitness. You should help His Highness as much as possible in doing this, but you should not insist upon the advantage of any measure which he disapproves, however desirable it may seem to be in his own interests.

You will notice that the Government of India have declined to permit the employment of Babu Nilambar Mukerji as member of council incharge of the revenue administration. If the Maharaja should raise the question of employing him in any other capacity, you may inform His Highness that the Government of India do not consider it desirable that the Babu should return to Kashmir. With reference to the question of principle whether the Maharaja is at liberty to employ Native British subjects without the consent of the British Government, you should give His Highness to understand that the interpretation of the treaty of 1846 with regard to this point is no longer open to discussion. The Government of India desire to give the Maharaja all possible assistance, and he will always find them willing to place at his disposal the services of competent British officials; but they must maintain their right to be consulted before any British subjects receive employment within the State.

The enclosed kharita points out to the Maharaja the urgent necessity for a thorough examination into the condition of the Kashmir finances. This is evidently a point of the greatest importance, and you should use your influence to bring it to the special notice of His Highness and his advisers.

The Governor-General in Council does not consider it necessary to give you more detailed instructions with regard to the course which you should pursue. He has no doubt that a consideration of this letter, and of the terms of the enclosed kharita, will suffice to show you the principles upon which he desires you to act, and he hopes that with the aid of judicious and sympathetic advice on your part the Maharaja may, before you leave Kashmir, have succeeded at least in laying the foundations of an efficient scheme of Government.

KHARITA, dated SIMLA, the 25th July, 1888, enclosed in above

From His Excellency the VICEROY AND GOVERNOR-GENERAL OF INDIA to His Highness the MAHARAJA OF KASHMIR

I HAVE received your Highness's letter of the 13th of April, informing me of the dismissal of Diwan Lachman Das, and forwarding, for my consideration, a scheme which you have prepared for the re-organisation of your Council.

Your Highness's letter has received my most careful attention, and I have now to inform you of the conclusions at which I have arrived with regard to the very important questions which you have been good enough to refer to me.

In the first place, I cannot avoid informing your Highness that the news of the sudden removal of Diwan Lachman Das was received by me with some surprise. Your Highness appointed him to your council after consulting me, and I hoped that your Highness would, before making another change of Government, give me some previous intimation of your views. However, this point has already been brought to your notice by Mr. Plowden, and I do not now desire to dwell upon it any further.

With regard to your Highness's scheme for the future administration of Kashmir, I would ask you to consider the following observations.

Your Highness proposes that the administration should be conducted or assisted by a council consisting of a president, a vice-president, three other members, and a secretary. The presidency you would retain in your own hands. You would appoint your brother Raja Amar Singh to be vice-president, and you would also make him Prime Minister with executive powers. The other three members of the Council would be Raja Rama Singh, Babu Nilambar Mukerji, and Diwan Janki Prasad; and they would be charged respectively with the control of affairs in the millitary, revenue, and miscellaneous departments. The Prime Minister would have special charge of the judicial and foreign departments. Diwan Janki Prasad would be secretary in addition to his other duties. It is proposed that the Council should be consultative.

It appears to me that a Government constituted in this manner is open to some criticism. In the first place, I am inclined to doubt whether it is altogether in accordance with your Highness's dignity to be president of the Council. Secondly, your Highness's brothers are still young, and have had little opportunity of acquiring practical experience in administrative work. Babu Nilambar Mukerji has no knowledge of revenue matters, and is altogether unfit to take charge of so important a department of the administration. Of Diwan Janki Prasad I know little, but I understand that he is not a man of marked character and ability. Under these circumstances your

Highness's scheme does not appear to me to hold out any certain promise success.

Nevertheless, I do not desire to raise any objection to the principle of the proposed arrangements. I regard your Highness as the responsible ruler of the State, and I wish to meet your views as far as possible, and to afford you every assistance in carrying them out. If, therefore, your Highness prefers to maintain a Council and to assume the presidency yourself, I am ready to assent to your vies in this matter, and also with regard to the nomination of your brothers and Dewan Janki Prasad. On one point only I feel that in your Highness's interests I must ask you to modify your proposals. I cannot think that the appointment of Babu Nilambar Mukerji as revenue minister would be desirable. I am of opinion that for the charge of revenue affairs, your Highness should secure the services of some thoroughly competent official with practical experience of administration. I also think that at least one other official of similar qualifications should be appointed to direct, either as member of Council or in some other capacity, the judicial and executive branches of your Government. If your Highness can name any Native officials in the British service who seem to me to possess the requisite qualifications I shall be glad to place them at your disposal. If your Highness cannot suggest any names I shall be ready and willing to make inquiries, and to supply you with the best men available either in the Punjab or elsewhere. I have learnt with pleasure that your Highness has already asked for the services of some four or five officers to be employed in the accounts and forest departments. But your Highness's government seems to require something more than the loan of a few subordinate officials. What is wanted is that you should associate with your principle officers two or three thoroughly trained and capable persons, who will be able to give your Highness effective aid in directing and controlling to main branches of the administration. I trust that your Highness will consider these suggestions and will take such steps as may have the effect of view. I need hardly add that, with regard to this question and to all other questions of importance, Your Highness should freely consult the Resident, who will give you every assistance in his power.

In making these observations I do not overlook the fact that, since the appointment of the Council of which Diwan Lachman Das was a member, considerable progress has been made in the direction of reform; useful work has been done with regard to the revenue administration, and in the reorganization of the Public Works and Medical Departments. But much remains to be done, and it is because I am deeply conscious of the importance of the Kashmir State, and of the responsibilities of the British Government in regard to it, that I have so carefully examined the proposals which your Highness has put forward.

I would particularly urge upon your Highness's attention the necessity for a careful investigation into the condition of your Highness's finances, and of the executive and judicial services. Until these are placed upon a thoroughly sound footing it will be impossible to hope for any material increase in the prosperity of the State. I desire to express the high consideration which I entertain for your Highness, and to subscribe myself your Highness's sincere friend.

(Signed) DUFFERIN,
Viceroy and Governor-General of India.

No. 6
The SECRETARY of STATE to the GOVERNMENT of INDIA

India Office, London, October 12, 1888.

My Lord,

I have perused with deep interest the papers regarding Kashmir affair which accompanied your Excellency's letter of the 18th August, 1888. From them I learn that the instability of the several administrations to which Maharaja Pertab Singh had entrusted the management of the affairs of his State since his accession in 1885 has much retarded the execution of the various reforms which have been repeatedly pressed on the attention of the Maharaja, and that, after the abrupt dismissal of the President of the Council, Diwan Lachman Das, in March last, by the Maharaja, His Highness submitted for the consideration of your Excellency a scheme for there constitution of the State Council, in which the Maharaja proposed to assume the post of President.

2. Though this scheme of administration is open to many objections, partly on account of the Maharaja's personal character, and for other reasons, and is not unlikely to prove a failure, your Excellency's Government have determined to allow His Highness a further opportunity of showing whether he is competent to discharge the duties of a responsible ruler.

3. Judging from the reports of the Residents in Kashmir, I can have little expectation myself that the experiment of a Council presided over by the Maharaja will be successful; but, on the other hand, the objections to any radical change in the government of the province at the present juncture are such that I am willing to sanction your proposal to give the Maharaja another occasion of proving whether His Highness possesses either the capacity or the will to introduce and carry into effect those administrative measures which are essential to the prosperity and security of the Kashmir State.

I have, &c.,
(Signed) CROSS.

No. 7

The GOVERNMENT OF INDIA to the SECRETARY OF STATE FOR INDIA, dated Fort William, April 3, 1889

EXTRACT

In 1888 the condition of Kashmir was by no means satisfactory; and the Resident, Mr. Plowden, had come to the conclusion that so long as the present Maharaja was maintained the power there could be no hope of better things. He therefore urged the Government of India to interfere and exclude His Highness from all concern with the administration. There was much to support Mr. Plowden's view, and we were by no means confident as to the result of any further abstention from interference; but on the whole we decided that the Maharaja should have another opportunity of showing, under favourable circumstances, whether he was capable of ruling the State. He was accordingly continued in power; and Mr. Plowden, who soon afterwards left Kashmir on promotion, was succeeded by Colonel Parry Nisbet, C.I.E., a personal friend of the Maharaja, and an officer of large administrative experience. It was hoped that Colonel Nisbet might succeed in establishing a strong influence over His Highness's mind, in freeing him from the domination of certain unprincipled persons about him, who took advantage of his timidity and superstition, and in gradually bringing him to a proper sense of his position and its responsibilities.

This hope was disappointed, and, after four months in the Kashmir Residency, Colonel Nisbet has come to the same conclusion as his predecessor. The immediate cause which led him to re-submit the matter for our orders was the discovery of some letters, said to have been written by the Maharaja, which were of such a nature as to present his character and conduct in a very unfavourable light. We were not disposed to attach my excessive importance to these letters, because we had received a number of very similar documents a year before, and were not ignorant of the Maharaja's failings. But in this instance the discovery of the letters was immediately followed by a voluntary resignation of power on the part of the Maharaja; and, taking into consideration this and all the other circumstances of the case, we felt that the time had come when some measure of interference could be no longer deferred. We have, therefore, determined that the Maharaja's resignation shall be accepted, and that we should avail ourselves of the opportunity in order to effect a thorough re-organisation of the Kashmir Government.

The form in which our interference is to be exercised will be seen from the terms of our instructions to Colonel Nesbit. To sum these up in a few words, the administration of the State will be handed over to a Council, consisting of the Maharaja's brothers and certain selected officials in the British service. This Council will have full powers, subject to the condition that they will take no important step without consulting the Resident, and that they will act upon the Resident's advice whenever it may be offered. This is the arrangement established in Gwalior, where it is working well. The Maharaja will be excluded from all interference with public affairs, but will retain his rank and dignity as Chief of the State, and will receive from the State revenue an adequate, but not extravagant, allowance for the maintenance of his household and any other necessary expenditure.

These arrangements will not be exclusively based upon the Maharaja's edict of resignation, which was an attempt to save his dignity and secure better terms than he could otherwise expect. This edict contains some inconvenient stipulations, and it would be embarrassing to agree to it as it stands We prefer to treat it as a confession of incapacity for the rule of the State, and to base our further proceedings upon general grounds.

Your Lordship will observe that our instructions to Colonel Nesbit deprecate any interference in the affairs of the State beyond what is necessary for the reform of the administration. We greatly regret the necessity for any interference at all. But we are now convinced that in the interests of the people of Kashmir, and of the ruling family itself, it is no longer right or possible to leave the affairs in the hands of the Maharaja; and we trust that Her Majesty's Government will concur in this opinion.

Enclosure 1 in No. 7
From Colonel R. PARRY NISBET to Sir H.M. DURAND,
dated Sialkot, February 27, 1889
EXTRACT

The day before yesterday I had placed in my hands such reliable evidence as I have said invariably to those who have talked to me, would alone satisfy me of the disloyalty or utter imbecility of the present Ruler of Jammu.

This consists of a batch of thirty-four letters, in the Maharaja's own handwriting, some of which are so compromising as to leave, I submit, no course open-save his removal from the State, unless the alternative theory be accepted of his being a half-witted individual, irresponsible for his own acts.

Of their authenticity I have, myself, no doubt, and they are admitted to be in the Maharaja's own handwriting by his brother, Raja Amar Singh; besides, a mass of letters like this are not likely to be forgeries in the way one or two might be.

But, side by side with these treasonable letter in this packet, there are others in an utterly foolish strain, thereby confirming me in the conclusion I have unwillingly come to, that, though with lucid intervals of good sense and propriety, the Maharaja is utterly incapable of being left in charge of his own affairs. The gist of these other letters is that the Maharaja offers large sums of money to certain individuals on condition that they will murder, or cause to be removed, Plowden, the late Resident, his own two brothers, Ram Singh and Amar Singh, and one of the Maharanis, who, for some reason, is personally objectionable to him.

These acts are not those of a man in such possession of his intellect as would justify Government in leaving him in uncontrolled charge of the most important frontier State.

The conclusions the letters lead me to are confirmed by certain rather extraordinary acts of the Maharaja in oppointing unworthy and incapable persons to important offices of the State, even since I took over charge, without consulting the proper counsellor, or, infact, any one at all. The thing is the Maharaja is a timid and very superstitious man at the entire mercy of a set of unscrupulous scoundrels who take advantage of his fears and imbecility to plunder the State to any extent, and there appear to me weighty reasons for advising the practical setting aside of the Maharaja's authority.

It surely is politically dangerous to leave the actual administration of this great State in the hands of an individual who may play us false at any moment, without, perhaps, appreciating the disaster that would follow, and, I believe, any steps Government may take short of annexation will be right and necessary, and generally approved by the Princes and Chiefs of India.

Under the circumstances stated I think it is necessary for me to come to Calcutta at once on hearing from you, to talk the matter fully over with you, so that you may be in a position definitely to settle the future policy of Government towards the State.

Enclosure 2 in No. 7
From the RESIDENT IN KASHMIR, Sialkot, to the FOREIGN SECRETARY, Calcutta

Telegram March 8, 1889.

I start to-morrow for Calcutta. I have been last two days at Jammu, and Maharaja has himself proposed what will, I think, solve the difficulty of the existing situation of affairs. He asked to be allowed to form a new Council of State, constituted of his two brothers, with Pandits Suraj Kaul and Bhag Ram, and an English officer selected by the Government of India, the

Maharaja surrendering entire control of public affairs to such Council for five years.

Enclosure 3 in No. 7

From Colonel R. PARRY NISBET to Sir H.M. DURAND

Kashmir, March 13, 1889.

I send you the original edict (with translation) and the official letter handed to me by the Maharaja of Kashmir containing His Highness's application to be relieved of the management for a time of State affairs in order to redeem the past.

I trust this voluntary offer on his part may afford, with perhaps further conditions, an acceptable way out of no doubt a very acute difficulty.

As the Government of India have carefully refrained as long as was possible from any sort of interference in the direct management in the affairs of the Kashmir State, so I think now a direct appeal to do so cannot be ignored, and that there should be no hesitation in adopting the best and most complete measure likely to bring about the reforms necessary.

Sub-enclosure

From RAJA AMAR SINGH, President of Council and Prime Minister to His Highness the Maharaja of Jammu and Kashmir, to Colonel R. PARRY NISBET, C.I.E., Resident in Kashmir, Jammu

March 8, 1889.

I have the honour to submit, for information of yourself and the Government of India, the original Irshad of His Highness the Maharaja by which he abandons his direct management of the Jammu and Kashmir State for a term of five years, and desires that it may be performed by a Council of State consisting of his brothers, Raja Ram Singh and Raja Amar Singh, and three other members, one of whom to whom to be an

English officer of special experience and qualifications selected by the Government, and other two members will be

Pandit Suraj Kaul and Pandit Bhag Ram

2. I am directed to request that you will kindly furnish me with a certified copy of the Irshad, if you want to keep the original in your office.

3. I am further directed to request that you will move the Government of India for early nomination of an English officer to serve on the Council of State as proposed in the Irshad.

Sub-enclosure

My Dear Brother Raja Amar Singh,

In the interests of the 'State' and for better administration of the country, and with a view to remodel it, as near as possible on the English system, I hereby authorise a Council, the members of which, for period of five years, will conduct all the public affairs of the State as they think best. The members will be as follows:-

Raja Ram Singh and Raja Amar Singh,

An English member, specially selected by the Government of India on a salary Rs. 2,000 or 3,000 per month.

Rai Bahadur Suraj Kaul and Rai Bahadur Bhag Ram.

This Council will have full and sole powers in all in Public Departments of the State for a period of five years.

In the event of a vacancy occurring among the three last members during the prescribed period of five years, the Government of India will be asked to nominate a new member.

After the expiration of the said period of five years the Maharaja will have the power of re-organising the administration if he finds it necessary to do so.

This period of five years will count from the date of this edict.

The Council will not interfere in any way with the private affairs of the Maharaja.

The Maharaja will continue to draw his monthly allowance for his privy purse as hitherto, no change whatever being made.

The jagirs and other grants of immovable, movable property hitherto made by the Maharaja will hold good and the Council will not interfere.

All usual expenses connected with marriages and other family customs will be provided by the 'State'.

Of my two brothers I will myself appoint one as President of the Council.

During the said period of five years the Maharaja will not interfere and will have no voice in the administration of the public affairs of the State, but he will continue to enjoy the honorary rights and position of Maharaja.

The Council have no power to alter existing treaties without the previous approval of the Maharaja.

The Council will have no power to assign jagirs or immovable property of the State or to make new rules on such subjects without the consent of the Maharaja.

Signed and sealed by
His Highness the Maharaja
on 27th Bhagan, 1945—8th March, 1889.
Seal of the 'State'.

Enclosure 4 in No. 7
INSTRUCTIONS from GOVERNMENT of INDIA to RESIDENT in KASHMIR, dated April 1, 1889
EXTRACT

I am to request you to inform the Maharaja that for a time at least he will be expected to refrain from all interference in the administration. He will retain his rank and dignity as Chief of the State; but full powers of government will be vested in a Council consisting of the Maharaja's brothers and three or four officials selected by the Government of India. It is not thought desirable that one of these officials should be an Englishman. The President of the Council will be Raja Amar Singh. Besides retaining his rank and dignity the Maharaja will receive from the revenues of the State an annual sum sufficient to maintain his household in due comfort, and to defray any expenditure which may rightly devolve upon him; but he will have no power of alienating the State revenues, and the sum placed at his disposal, though adequate, must not be extravagantly large.

I am further to request you to make the Maharaja and the Members of Council thoroughly understand that, although the Council will have full powers of administration, they will be expected to exercise those powers under the guidance of the Resident. They will taken steps of importance without consulting him, and they will follow his advice whenever it may be offered.

In communicating to the Maharaja and others concerned the decision of the Government of India, you should be careful to avoid basing that decision exclusively either upon the letters or upon the Maharaja's resignation. The letters are repudiated by the Maharaja, and as I have said before they are not of a very novel character; while on the other hand the Government of India are by no means prepared to make the present settlement a matter of compact with the Maharaja, and to accept all the conditions laid down by his edict of the 8th March, for example the five years' limit. You should therefore base the decision of the Government upon a full consideration of all the circumstances, the letters and the Maharaja's wish to retire from the control of affairs being considered amongst other things, but only as portions of a difficult and complicated case, which it has been necessary to settle on broader grounds of general policy.

You should now proceed to work out fresh proposals upon the lines I have indicated. It will be necessary in the first place to define exactly the future position of the Maharaja, the amount of his annual allowance, the expenses which it is intended to cover, the extent of his powers over his own household, and generally the conditions which he will have to conform. It will also be necessary to show the proposed constitution of the council, the duties falling upon each of its members, and the method of transacting business. You should also ascertain the requirements of the State in the manner of subordinate officials, and should submit for the approval of the Government your view as to the steps to be taken for re-organising the administrative services. In forming has no desire to turn Kashmir into the semblance of a British district, or to place all administrative posts in the hands of Punjabi foreigners. The want of good native officials makes it necessary to import some trained men from the outside, but the number so imported should be kept as low as possible, and your object should be to form with their help a class of Kashmiri officials who will be capable hereafter of administering the State themselves. It is altogether against the wishes and policy of the Government of interfere unnecessarily with the customs and traditions of a Native State, or to force upon it the precise methods of administration obtaining in British territory. Administrative efficiency is not the only object to be attained in such cases, nor, indeed, the principal object.

The Government of India will be glad to know, as soon as possible the true facts as to the financial position of Kashmir. A separate report should be submitted on this point, and in submitting it you should inquire into the question of the jagirs and allowances given by the Maharaja, and should make proposals as to the manner in which such grants should be treated.

Finally, I am to request that the new arrangements may be introduced as quietly as possible. There should be no ceremonial, and nothing that can be regarded as the public degradation of the Maharaja, who should simply retire from the conduct of affairs. It is desirable that the change should attract no more attention than necessary, and above all, that it should not be regarded as the punishment of a great native Chief for proved disloyalty to the Crown. Rumours to the effect that the Maharaja has been convicted of treasonable practices have already been in circulation, and such rumours do harm both in India and elsewhere.

No. 8

The SECRETARY OF STATE FOR INDIA to the GOVERNMENT OF INDIA

My Lord Marquis, India Office, London, May 24, 1889.

From the papers transmitted with your Excellency's letter, dated 3rd April, 1883, I learn that the further opportunity which was given to His Highness the Maharaja of Kashmir of proving whether he was capable of conducting the administration of his State has once more established his unfitness for the position of ruler.

2. You have, therefore, decided to accept the Maharaja's voluntary resignation, and to effect a thorough re-organisation of the Kashmir Government.

3. In accordance with this determination, the administration will be entrusted to a Council, consisting of the Maharaja's brothers and certain selected Native officials in the British service. This Council will have full powers, subject to the condition that they will take no important step without consulting the Resident, and that they will act upon the Resident's advice whenever it may be offered. The Maharaja will be excluded from all interference with public affairs, but will retain his rank and dignity as Chief of the State, and will receive from the State revenues an adequate, but not extravagant, allowance for the maintenance of his household and any other necessary expenditure.

4. Her Majesty's Government fully approve your proceedings, and share your conviction that in the interests of the people of Kashmir, and of the ruling family itself, it has become impossible to leave the control of affairs in the hands of the Maharaja.

I have, &c.,
(Signed) CROSS.

From the GOVERNMENT OF INDIA to the SECRETARY OF STATE FOR INDIA, dated Simla, July 26, 1889
EXTRACT

In continuation of our despatch of the 3rd April, and in further reference to the condition of affairs in Kashmir, we have the honour to enclose copies of the papers noted in the margin.

We take this opportunity of expressing the satisfaction which it has given to us to be made aware that the course which has been adopted in dealing with this question has met with your Lordship's approval. The events which have taken place since our decision was arrived at have not let us to modify in any way the opinions which we formed at the time. The Maharaja's allegation that the edict of the 8th March last was signed by him under compulsion is, we believe, entirely unjustified by the facts of the case. The circumstances under which His Highness requested that he might be relieved from active participation in the duties of government are set forth in detail in paragraph 8 of the Viceroy's letter of the 28th June, 1889.

We have, on the other hand, no doubt that His Highness's action in requesting the permission of the Resident to retire from the management of public affairs for a term of years, may have been due to fear of the consequences which he, at that time, apprehended from the discovery of the correspondence, of which copies have been already laid before your Lordship.

Now that His Highness has ascertained that the action of the Government of India has been justified upon other grounds, and that the correspondence in question has been treated with comparative indifference, it is quite possible that His Highness regrets the somewhat precipitate proposal which he made to the Resident. The fact that he should have preferred such a request, and immediately receded from it, affords, in our opinion, further proof of the slight amount of reliance which can be placed upon his character as a ruler.

We are glad to report that we are receiving from the Resident satisfactory accounts of the progress which is being made by the new Council in improving the administration of the State. A large portion of the arrears due to the army have already been paid. We need scarcely dwell on the danger which was likely to arise to the public safety from the existence of a large and ill- disciplined military force, which had, for some months past, been allowed to remain without the pay which was due to it.

We learn that, in the same way, heavy arrears of salaries have been made good in all the departments, a condition indispensable to honest and diligent service of a kind which for many years past has, we fear, been too rarely rendered by

Kashmir officials, Public works, the progress of which was seriously threatened owing to want of funds, are being actively pushed on. Much unnecessary expenditure has been curtailed, and the Resident expresses his belief that if the next harvest should prove to be a good one, and suitable measures be taken for the recovery of the land revenue, the close of the year will see the establishment of financial equilibrium in the accounts of the State.

It is in our opinion scarcely possible to overrate the importance of the results likely to be produced by a period of upright and efficient administration in a country circumstanced as is Kashmir, and with its antecedents. It has been the painful duty of the Government of India from time to time to call the attention of the Secretary of State to the Chronic misgovernment to which the people of Kashmir have been subjected by the present Maharaja and his predecessors. It had become evident before the accession of the present Maharaja that the only hope for the state lay in a vigorous attempt to remove the most flagrant of the abuses under which, in spite of the great natural resources of the country, its population had steadily dwindled, and its people had become impoverished to the point of chronic scarcity. At the time when the death of the late Maharaja was imminent, the Government of India entertained the gravest doubts whether the present Maharaja, then heir-apparent to the throne, was fit to succeed to it.

The circumstances under which it was determined to give him an opportunity of proving his fitness are within your Lordship's knowledge. Our experience of him has shown that neither his abilities nor his inclinations are likely to bring about any appreciable improvement in the condition of the people committed to his charge.

In this connection we may refer your Lordship to the report of the settlement Operations in Kashmir and Jammu, submitted by Mr. A. Wingate, C.I.E., C.S., Settlement Officer, to the

Maharaja in 1888. This report, of which a copy is attached to this despatch, contains abundant evidence to show that most of the abuses continued to prevail unchecked. Under the system of assessment in force the cultivator of the soil had, as Mr. Wingate points out, been pressed down to the condition of a coolie cultivating the State property at a bare subsistence allowance, while the population continued to diminish, and the former occupants of the land were being steadily ousted from its possession, which was passing into that of the official classes, who have been enriched at the public expense. This transference of the land from the cultivating to the non-cultivating classes had, in Mr. Wingate's opinion, been proceeding with increased rapidity since the death of the late Maharaja, from which date the central authority appears to have become weaker. The artisan classes, whose skill and industry are well known, appear to have shared the ruin of the cultivating classes.

We have thought it our duty to dwell briefly upon this subject, because the supersession of the Maharaja appears to have been regarded in many quarters as the result of a selfish desire on the part of the Government of India to extend its influence in Kashmir, and possibly to prepare the way for the ultimate annexation of the State. We have, we trust, said enough to satisfy your Lordship that the consideration which has had most weight with us has been the responsibility, from which we cannot divest ourselves, of securing for the people of Kashmir a form of government less intolerable than that to which they have been subjected for many years past. The circumstances under which the destinies of Kashmir were handed over by the British Government for political considerations to an alien dynasty, increase, in our opinion, our responsibility for the condition of the country, and impose upon us an obligation, which we cannot ignore, of taking effectual steps in order to terminate the long period of suffering, mismanagement, and wasted opportunities through which the State has passed.

Enclousre 1 in No.9
From Colonel PARRY NISBET to Sir H.M. DURAND

(Demi-Official.)

Kashmir Residency, Srinagar,
April 19, 1889.

After arrival here on the 13th, I paid a visit of ceremony on the 15th to His Highness the Maharaja, which he returned on the 16th, but I refrained from discussing any business at these interviews.

On the 17th instant, accompanied by Captain Ramsay, I proceeded to the palace at 11 a.m., and met His Highness the Maharaja in private Durbar. Those present besides the Maharaja were his brothers, Rajas Ram Singh and Amar Singh, the two members of Council, Pandit Suraj Kaul and Pandit Bhag Ram, Diwan Janki Prasad, an old official of the State, and Sardar Bup Singh, Governor of Kashmir. I informed His Highness the Maharaja without comment of the orders of the Government of India, dated 1st April, 1889, and that he might be under no misapprehension, I, at the same time, handed to his Prime Minister, Raja Amar Singh, these orders in writing in the form of a letter, copy of which is annexed, as an answer to his No. 159, dated 8th March, 1882, which is in the correspondence.

His Highness the Maharaja said—'I will consider the letter and return an answer'. After some few minutes conversation the interview closed. In leading me down the Durbar room the Maharaja again said—'I will think it over and give you an answer to what you have told me.' I replied kindly 'an answer is not required, as what I have communicated to you are the orders of the Government. I will always come and give you any further explanation you may wish,' and we parted. I subsequently repeated to the brothers of the Maharaja that they should let him thoroughly understand that the communications made to him were the definite orders of the Government of India, which it was not necessary for him to answer.

On the 18th instant there was a first meeting of the new Council.

Sub-enclosure
From the RESIDENT in Kashmir to RAJA AMAR SINGH, Prime Minister, Kashmir

April 17, 1889.

With reference to your No. 159, dated 8th March, 1889, I beg to inform you that the letter with its enclosure was laid before his Excellency the Viceroy and Governor-General in Council, who, after full consideration of the circumstances and the general condition of affairs in the Kashmir State for a long time past, has ordered me to inform His Highness the Maharaja that for a time at least he will be expected to refrain from all interference in the administration. He will retain his rank and dignity as Chief of the State, but full powers of government will be vested in a Council consisting of the Maharaja's brothers and three or four officials selected by the Government of India. It is not thought desirable that one of these officials should be an Englishman. Besides retaining his rank and dignity, the Maharaja will receive from the revenues of the State an annual sum sufficient to maintain his household in due comfort and to defray any expenditure that may rightly devolve upon him, but he will have no power of alienating the State revenues, and the sum placed at his disposal, though adequate, will not be extravagantly large.

His Highness the Maharaja and the Members of Council should thoroughly understand that, although the Council will have full powers of administration, they will be expected to exercise those powers under the guidance of the British Resident. They will take no step of importance without consulting him, and they will follow his advice whenever it may be offered.

Such are the orders of the Government of India, and, on my own part, I beg you will assure His Highness that it will be my endeavour to assist in carrying them out in the way I trust that may be most conducive to the happiness and benefit of His Highness and the State.

Enclosure 2 in No. 9
From His Highness the MAHARAJA OF KASHMIR to the MARQUESS OF LANDSDOWNE

Kashmir, May 14, 1889.

It is after great suffering and distress, and undergoing greatest contempt and taunt at the hands of my inferiors, that I have, with fear, decided to send the special message to your Excellency per bearer. Necessity and feelings of loyalty have obliged me to seek advice from your Excellency and take shelter under your Lordship's fatherly care. As advised by my late-lamented father from my very childhood, my heart is full of loyalty to the paramount power, and I am always ready to do all that can be desired by the blessed Government. Your Excellency is authorised to consider me as one of your Lordship's most faithful and humble servants. When my late father always considered it an honour to serve the Government loyally and faithfully, I should, and I do, consider it greater honour still to follow his example. All my country, treasury, army, even my life and blood, are at the disposal of the British Government and our Mother-Sovereign, the Queen-Empress.

I know very well that I have been extremely misrepresented before the Government of India through sources which had a show of reliableness, but this, alas! I have come too late to know, when my internal enemies, who are envious of my position, have succeeded to drive me to a very mean and pitiable position, and implore your Excellency to release and save me from it, taking me destitute position inconsideration. The recent allegations brought against me about secret correspondence with Russia, conspiring with Dalip Singh, attempt to poison the British Resident, Mr. T.C. Plowden, and lots of stupid stories, did not affect my mind in the least, for I was under the impression that some special officer will be deputed by your Excellency's Government to inquire fully into the false charges, and thus I shall get the best opportunity of disclosing everything fully, and, through his source, be able to bring all facts to the notice of your Excellency, and have my secret enemies brought to book through your Excellency's kind sympathy. But to my greatest pleasure no notice was taken of those false letters, and all other stupid stories were taken as nonsense by the supreme power. After this was over, the following communication was sent by Colonel R. Parry Nesbit, Resident in Kashmir, to Raja Amar Singh, Prime Minister:-

'From the RESIDENT in Kashmir to RAJA AMAR SINGH, 'Prime Minister

'Kashmir, April 17, 1889

'Sir,

'With reference to your number 159, dated 8th March, 1889, I beg to inform you that the letter, with its enclosure, was laid before his Excellency the Viceroy and Governor-General in Council, who, after full consideration of the circumstances and the general condition of affairs in the Kashmir State for a long time past, has ordered me to inform His Highness the Maharaja that, for a time at least, he will be expected to refrain from all interference in the administration. He will retain his rank and dignity as Chief of the State; but full powers of government will be vested in a Council consisting of the Maharaja's brothers and three or four officials selected by the Government of India. It is not thought desirable that one of these officials should be an Englishman. Besides retaining his rank and dignity, the Maharaja will receive from the revenue of the State an annual sum sufficient to maintain his household in due comfort and to defray any expenditure that may rightly devolve upon him, but he will have no power of alienating the State revenues, and the sum placed at his disposal, though adequate, will not be extravagantly large.

'2. His Highness the Maharaja and the Members 'of the Council should thoroughly understand that, although the Council will have full powers of administration, they will be expected to exercise these powers under the guidance of the British Resident. They will take no step of importance without consulting him; they will follow his advice whenever it may be offered.

'3. Such are the orders of the Government of India, and, on my own part, I beg you will assure His Highness that it will be my endeavour to assist in carrying them out in the way I trust that may be most conducive to the happiness and benefit of His Highness and the State.

'I remain,
'Yours truly,
'(Signed) R. PARRY NISBET.'

And now your Excellency can judge what my position at present is, and how much I am slighted in the Durbar, my enemies staring with pride and triumph into my eyes very often and showing all possible contempt.

My chief enemy, and in the present circumstances enemy of the State, who has taken a fancy to become the ruler of the Kashmir State, and who envies my position since long time, is, I am sorry to say, my own youngest brother, Raja Amar Singh. It is only now that I have found him out in his true colours, and all doubts as to his ill-motive have been removed. Since the very day I succeeded to the throne, he caused to set afloat all sorts of rumours against me about my incapacity, insanity, &c., &c.

Many a time he was directly caught in conspiring against me. He encouraged, pecuniarily and otherwise, people connected with the press with the only object of their writing against my person, vilifying me, and causing to circulate the worst rumours against me. Having convenient access to Europeans, &c., &c., and the Residents, to which I never objected, having no suspicion regarding his doings, he filled their ears, as often as possible, with such black stories about me, directly and indirectly, thinking very well that his doing so will, in the long run, set the Government of India against me, and he will be proclaimed Ruler of Jammu and Kashmir territories in that case. To almost every Resident, and specially to Colonel R. Parry Nisbet, he appeared to be the most reliable and intimately connected informant, and all should have believed in what he said; and I have every reason to believe that all rumours which reached the Government against me must have been through this, and this source alone.

Being disgusted with this unworthy conduct, and having ample proofs to silence him in his very face, I twice resolved to order him to remove himself to his jagir, and have nothing to do in the capital. On both these occasions, being informed of my resolution against him, he entered my room, where was no one except him and myself, shedding childish tears, throwing his turban on my feet, imploring for mercy, promising all good-will and hearty loyalty for the future, and asking for pardon as my dear brother, humblest slave. After all, he was my youngest brother, very dear to me; his lovely young face is still liked by me, and on both these occasions my blood was naturally warm for him, and I was completely moved by his entreaties, and pardoned him after all. To prove to him that my heart was quite in sympathy with him—and I truly loved him as my dear brother—I, at his request, bestowed upon him the rich jagir of Bhadderwa, in exchange to the comparatively poor Bisoli which he had got during the time of my late father, and again made him Prime Minister of all. But, as was known afterwards, he was never slow in conspiring against me, even then. Regaining my confidence twice, and knowing I was quite confident and entirely at ease from his side, he possessed redoubled power and influence in the State, which is natural, and every State official was made to believe and look upon him as my powerful assistant and adviser. All these advantages he brought in force against me for the gain of his one sole object in view above mentioned, and he was able enough to create a strong party of his own among my officials, giving them all hopes of future success and prosperity, in case they remained faithful only to him and join with him in overthrowing me and mine. This promise he has fulfilled now in promoting those who joined him, and degrading those, my sincerely faithful servants, who stood by me amidst all temptations.

Colonel R. Parry Nisbet, as soon as he was installed as British Resident at my Court, I looked upon him as my safe friend, and thought that my difficulties were at an end, because I knew him to be one of the sincere friends of my father and good supporter to myself. I must also confess that for some little time in the beginning he was my sympathiser to some extent, but it is very difficult to say what made him entirely change his motives towards me and to fall in the very clutches of the very same secret and powerful enemy of mine, Raja Amar Singh. This sudden change must be astonishing to all others as it was to me, so it is the most difficult task to investigate fully into the cause of this sudden change of his policy.

To overcome such difficulties as I was labouring under, at the hands of powerful intriguers who were using all sorts of influence within and without, I asked for the loan of two well-experienced officers from the Government of India to act as my councillors, and I must express my deep and heart-felt gratitude for the kindness with which the Government of India conceded to my request. But excellent men as these were, they also changed their former attitude at once as soon as the Resident changed his, and I believe that they must have done so naturally, as they are more dependent upon the good-will of the Representative of the British Government, under whose employment they have spent almost all their life, and to whom they owe all they have got, than myself, whom they are only lent to, so I was soon being made powerless.

At this juncture the brewing plot of the much-talked-of-letters, alleged to have been written by me, was brought into force. Almost all the rumours about the source from which they are purported to have reached the Resident are false, and without any foundation whatever. Solely Raja Amar Singh was at the bottom of the whole thing. These letters are nothing but most daring forgeries, and there was none more daring than my blood relation, the Raja Amar Singh. I have every reason to thank heartily your Excellency's Government for considering and treating them beneath notice, &c. This news, when it reached Jammu, gave much joy to all but to my brother Raja Amar Singh, and his party fellows, as, for instance, Sardar Roop Singh, the present Governor of Hakim-ila of Kashmir, Diwan Janki Prasad, his Secretary, ex-Governor of Hakimala, Wazir Shibsaran, and Diwan Shibsaran, his own Prime Minister, and who has full power to do anything in the State, and many others to whom it gave excessive pain. I am sure, if the Government of India would have required witnesses, Raja Amar Singh had been the first to swear against me. He was even ready to accompany Colonel Nisbet to Calcutta to complete my disaster for ever. When he came to inform me of his intention, made according to order of Colonel Nisbet, to leave for Calcutta with the Resident at his desire, I questioned him as to what opinion he expressed about the letters before the Resident. In reply he admitted to have said only that the etymological letters resemble those of the Maharaja's handwriting, but the signatures are not quite so. Being startled and heartily pained at this his reply, I simply told him, "All right, Raja Amar Singhjee. You can go to Calcutta with the Resident, if you like, but this was not expected from you. In your admitted deposition you have left nothing to destroy me." On the other day he, I believe, with the consultation of the Resident, decided not to go, and told me—"As your Highness is not favourable to the proposal I won't go, not to displease your Highness".

With the information of these letters, and with the full confidence and strength of being supported by my own brother and his now strong party, Colonel R. Parry Nisbet dashed into my room at a fixed time and brought such a great and many sided pressure in all solemnity and seriousness that I was obliged to write what was desired, rather demanded by him, in order to relieve myself for the moment, having full faith that your Excellency's Government will not accept such a one sided view of the case, and that full opportunity will be given to me of defending myself. I never admitted the genuineness of these letters, and even an ordinary sense can find out that I could never write such nonsense as the letters are purported to contain. Do I not know the dangers of the change of Government? Do I not understand the value of a peaceful Government presiding over us all? Do I not know what security all the Native Princes of India now are enjoying from internal and external dangers? Do I not understand that my dominions are most safe under the benign British Government? Do I not understand that what them on earth can induce me to correspond with Russia? Who is in Russia to read Dogra Vernacular? Having been in possession of high honours and all regards from the British Government, and having got everything from being loyal to it, what more can I expect, or aspire to get, from a foreign power, where tyranny and despotism are well known to all? As to Dalip Singh (God forbid), if he ever happens to come here, who is in a more dangerous position to suffer from his wrath? That I would conspire with him, is to hit the axe at the very foot of my own existence. About the attempt to poison Mr. T.C. Plowden, I think Mr. Plowden himself must be the best witness. My administration in those days was vested in the Council composed of Diwan Lachman Das, President, Raja Ram Singh, Military Member, Raja Amar Singh, member of all the civil affairs; and let them all sincerely say if they know anything about it. Raja Amar Singh, who was the chief adviser and general controller of all affairs, and under whose cunning guidance Diwan Lachman Das used to act unknowingly, may support this charge—I cannot say but none other, not even one single soul in the whole State will ever stand a witness to this charge. Moreover, who is the fool in the world to commit such base conspiracies to writing? Suppose there was such foul conspiracy on my part, would not the whole thing have been managed orally? But I assure your Excellency with all sacredness that such an idea never occurred to me, in dream even. Although your Excellency's Government treated the letters as beneath notice, my cruel enemies have got the fullest advantage that they expected. They are now full conquerors over my head and under their feet trample me. What is my position now? Simply that of a dead body: even worse than that, for I am taunted every moment by some sort of disgrace and disregard or other. These inferiors and traitors, who only yesterday showed me every respect and bowed down before me, pass me now with contemptuous smile, and I constantly bear the destruction and degradation of all those, my faithful old hereditary servants, who stood by me. Of course a dead body is unconscious of all these troubles, of which I am unfortunately not.

In his communication, dated 17th April, 1889, to Raja Amar Singh, above quoted in full, the Resident says: "His Excellency the Viceroy and Governor-General in Council, after full consideration of the circumstances and the general condition of affairs in the Kashmir State for a long time past, has ordered me to inform His Highness the Maharaja that, for a time at least, he will be expected to refrain from all interference in the administration. He will retain his rank and dignity as Chief of the State, &c., &c." Now, to put it very plainly, I have never, up to this time, enjoyed complete independence of action in State affairs. Under such circumstances it has been very cruel indeed to hold me personally responsible for any maladministration and to punish me severely as a criminal. By the above order of your Excellency it is plain enough to understand that matters have been so represented as to prove that only my interference has brought about the state of affairs for which the Government of India has been obliged to pass such strictures upon me;whereas the case is quite the contrary. The man whose disloyal interference is the chief cause of all mismanagement, and who should have been severely punished, has got not only scot-free, but has been placed over my head, enjoying perfect satisfaction of having been successful in his wicked design. Had there been any other loyal and faithful Prime Minister of mine than Raja Amar Sigh, he would have been expected to send in a suitable reply to the Resident's communication and saved me from the deadly disgrace which I have been subjected to; but my brother, Raja Amar Singh, quitely submitted to it, and was extremely satisfied to see me thus disgraced, as it was really his own heartly intention to see me so.

What rank and dignity can I retain under such circumstances? My condition is worse than a deposed ruler, inasmuch as he is taken out to some other place where he does not witness the most insulting scenes. And as regards the stipend that I am allowed at the mercy of the Council and the Resident, such is given even to the treacherous enemies of the British, who massacred their regiments and are now imprisoned or kept safe as political prisoners in the hills. Certainly, if the alleged letters had been proved genuine still no worse fate would have befallen me. The present Council, not content with reducing me to such a state of distress, have now fallen upon all those who remained faithful to me. Not to go into a full details, I will only say that Pandit Mahanandjee, Governor of Jammu, Pundit Zankak, Assistant Governor of Kashmir, Pundit Shibak, Officer of Timber Department, Dussoundhiram, an honest Chief Judge of Jammu, and Pundit Paralal, office of deciding the old balance accounts, and many others, have all been dismissed, with exception of Dussoundhiram, by one stroke of pen, on one plea and pretence or other, but really simple because they were sore in the eyes of Raja Amar Singh, and did not hear to his illegal recommendation and stood on my side. Their places are now being filled with such men who are notorious for their show of contempt to me.

If your Excellency really wants to make me responsible for the administration of the State (and I am very glad and quite ready to take such responsibility over my head), I would ask to be made responsible ruler. In spite of what has been represented against me about my incapacity, etc., etc., I would ask your Excellency to give me a fair trial in order to see what I am capable of doing for the furtherance of the interests of the Supreme Government and prosperity of my State. From three to five years' time, as I think it quite sufficient for me to put everything into order from the date of holding responsibility, provided I am allowed full strength and independence to choose my own councillors and ministers, and British Resident, instead of throwing obstacles in my way like Colonel R. Parry Nisbet, supports and strengthens my hands. This just Resident should be chosen by the Government of India. I shall always be glad and ready to seek his advice and sympathy, but in all matters concerning the State, &c., the Resident will have to consult me solely. For the present I would like to take Raja Ram Singh, Pundit Suraj Kaul, and Pundit Bhag Ram as my councillors (and remove Raja Amar Singh to his jagir), with full powers to add or diminish any one.

If after a fair trial being given to me, I do not set everything (excepting the Settlement Department, which is under the guidance of Mr. Lawrence, and which will not be settled within five years) right, and am found not to rule to the satisfaction of the Supreme Government, and my people within the prescribed time, your Excellency's Government is at liberty to do anything that may be considered advisable. In case this liberty is not allowed to me by the Supreme Government, and I have to remain in my present most miserable condition, I would most humbly ask your Excellency to summon me before you—and I will be most happy to obey such summons—and shoot me through the heart with your Excellency's hands, and thus at once relieve an unfortunate prince from unbearable misery, contempt, and disgrace for ever.

Awaiting your Excellency's commands, &c.

P.S.—The papers on which I write do not bear my official seal, and the reason is that my English Office is in the hands of the Prime Minister, Raja Amar Singh. The English clerks have been detained by him, by the advice of the Resident, to write for me, and thus I write in my own handwriting, and do not think it advisable to use the sealed papers. I hope your Excellency will excuse me for my bad handwriting. The bearer of this petition is authorized to answer any inquiries or refer them to me.

Enclosure 3 in No. 9

From His Excellency the VICEROY AND GOVERNOR-GENERAL OF INDIA to His Highness the MAHARAJA OF KASHMIR

Simla, June 28, 1889

I have received your Highness's letter of the 14th May. It was brought to Simla by a person, deputed by your Highness for that purpose, who appears to have taken advantage of your confidence in order to publish in the newspapers part of a confidential document which should not have been made known to the public at such a moment. I shall always be glad to hear from you should you desire to make me aware of your views, and I hope that you will, in future, forward your letters to me by the ordinary post, through which they will be safely delivered without the risk of any such indiscretion as that which has taken place in the present instance.

It is satisfactory to me to learn from your Highness that you are loyally disposed towards the paramount power, and that it is your desire to be guided by my advice. I shall give it to you frankly, and without any attempt to conceal my thoughts.

Your Highness has stated in your letter that your conduct has lately been completely misrepresented by your secret enemies; that Colonel Parry Nisbet, the British Resident in Kashmir, has dealt unjustly with you, and that your chief enemy has been your youngest brother, Raja Amar Singh. You suggest that the letter to Raja Amar Singh, signed and sealed by your Highness on the 8th March of this year, was written without due consideration, and in consequence of pressure put upon you by the Resident; you urge that you have never enjoyed sufficient independence of action in regard to the affairs of your State to enable you to give satisfactory evidence of your ability as a ruler; you beg that you may now be given a further trial, and, with this object, you virtually recede from the proposals contained in the letter to Raja Amar Singh, of which I have just spoken; and, in conclusion, you express, in the strongest language, your inability to submit patiently to the position in which you now find yourself.

I must point out to your Highness that the decision of the Government of India to relieve you of an active share in the government of your State was arrived at not only in consequence of recent events, but of circumstances which must be within your Highness's recollection, and which occurred some time before my arrival in this country. During the last years of the administration of my predecessor, the Marquis of Dufferin and Ava, extremely unfavourable reports had been received by the Government of India of the manner in which the affairs of Kashmir were administered by your Highness. The finances of the State were in disorder, a disorder which, there could be little doubt, was increased by your own extravagance, while your Highness had surrounded yourself by persons of the worst reputation, whose influence over you had produced the most unfortunate results. These complaints, which were made not only by the then Resident, but also by certain of the Princes and

Sardars of the Kashmir State, were borne out by papers which were placed in the hands of the Government of India. These contained, amongst other matters, ample evidence to show that you were squandering the resources of your State in a most reckless and improvident manner, and in the encouragement of the most unworthy persons.

At this time the Government of India anxiously considered the course which it should adopt in reference to your Highness, and its decision was conveyed to you in the kharita of the Marquis of Dufferin and Ava, dated the 25th July of last year. In this letter Lord Dufferin pointed out to you the impropriety of your dismissal of your Prime Minister, Diwan Lachman Das, who had been appointed after consultation with the Government of India without reference to that Government. He strongly urged upon your Highness the necessity of a careful investigation of the condition of the finances of Kashmir, and of the executive and judicial services, and he intimated to you that he was prepared to accept, with certain modifications, a scheme which had been proposed on behalf of your Highness for the formation of a reformed Council, of which you were to be the President. The constitution of this Council appeared to Lord Dufferin to be open to certain objections, but, in deference to your Highness's wishes, he determined not to press these. He, moreover, expressed his readiness to supply you with a certain number of trained native officials who might be of assistance to you in strengthening your administration.

About this time, in order to meet your Highness's wishes, advantage was taken of the appointment of Mr. Plowden to another post, in order to appoint, as Resident in Kashmir, a gentlemen well known to you, and regarded by you with feelings of friendship and confidence.

Looking back at these events, it is surely not too much to say that the result of the action of the Government of India in 1888 was to give your Highness, in the fullest sense of the term, a fair trial, such as that for which you now so earnestly ask. I am, however, constrained to tell your Highness distinctly that the results of that trial appear to have been of a most unsatisfactory kind. In the spring of this year my attention was called to the documents referred to in your Highness's letter; many of these had every appearance of being genuine, and they have, moreover, a striking resemblance to those other papers, of which I have already spoken, and which came into the possession of the Government of India at a previous time. Your Highness is correct in expressing your belief that the action subsequently taken by my Government was not justified merely by the disclosures contained in these letters. Even if the whole of these had been unquestionably genuine, I could not bring myself to believe that they had been written deliberately, or with a full appreciation of their meaning. There were, however, other circumstances which the Government of India could not do otherwise than take into consideration. The reports from the new Resident of the manner in which your Highness had administered the State had been not less unfavourable than those submitted, from time to time, by Mr. Plowden. Notwithstanding the ample resources of your State, your treasury was empty; corruption and disorder prevailed in every department and every office; your Highness was still surrounded by low and unworthy favourites, and the continued misgovernment of your State was becoming, every day, a more serious of anxiety.

This however was not all. A meeting had taken place between your Highness and Colonel Parry Nisbet at Jammu on the 7th March, and upon that occasion your Highness had distinctly stated that it was your wish to have no more to do with public affairs, and had asked the Resident whether he was prepared to assume, in conjuction with a Council, the management of the State. You repeated several times to the Resident that you were tired of the trouble which had been occasioned to you by official affairs, and that you would prefer to go away and to live in peace privately. At the termination of the interview you stated that you would send your brother, the Prime

Minister, Raja Amar Singh, to discuss the matter further with Colonel Parry Nisbet, and Raja Amar Singh, on the following morning, assured the Resident that you had made up your mind to give up interference with public affairs during the next few years. A further conference between yourself and the Resident took place on the following day. You still adhered to the language which you had used on the previous day, only stipulating that the Council was not to interfere with your private affairs. In the afternoon the Prime Minister brought to Colonel Parry Nesbit your edict constituting a Council of State, which was to include an English member, and which was to have 'full and sole powers in all the public departments of the State for a period of five years,' during which it was provided that 'the Maharaja will not interfere, and will have no voice in the administration of the public affairs of the State, but he will continue to enjoy the honorary rights and position of Maharaja.' This proposal, emanating directly from your Highness, could not be treated by my Government otherwise than as embodying your deliberate intentions and wishes; nor can I admit that you are now justified in describing the edict to which I have referred as having been hurriedly written under pressure from Colonel Parry Nisbet, who, your Highness will remember, throughout these conversations, expressly pointed out to you that it would not be practicable for him to undertake the management of the State in the manner which you had suggested.

When your letter to Raja Amar Singh was laid before the Government of India, I felt that, in view of the circumstances which I have recapitulated, no other course was open to me than to accept in substance the proposal which you had made. In so doing, however, some important modifications were made in the original scheme. Amongst these I may mention my refusal to take advantage of your suggestion that an Englishman should be appointed to serve upon the new Council; such a step seemed to me to be unnecessary, and I determined not to take it. Again, instead of requiring that the new arrangement should last for at least five years, it was stipulated that it should continue for a time, of which the length was not specified. I may also remind you of the consideration shown to your Highness by the stipulation that your Highness should receive a suitable income from the State revenues, and that your rank and dignity should be reserved to you. That this has been done, has been amply proved by the respect shown to you by His Excellency the Commander-in- Chief on the occasion of his recent visit to your State.

What I have written will show to your Highness how it has come to pass that the Government of India felt itself obliged to introduce these changes for a time into the Government of Kashmir. The arrangement was arrived at after careful consideration, and with a full knowledge of facts, of which your Highness is well aware. I may add that, by last week's mail from England, I have received a letter from the Secretary of State for India, informing me that Her Majesty's Government fully approve the measures taken by the Government of India in April last, and share their conviction that, in the interests of the people of Kashmir, and of the ruling a family itself, it has become impossible to leave the control of affairs in your Highness's hands.

It is idle to contend that all this has been the result of a conspiracy against you, in which the Resident, your brother, and the officials of the State, have all had a part. In your letter to me, you admit that you knew the Resident to be "one of the sincere friends of my father, and a good supporter of myself". You had yourself designated your brother, Raja Amar Singh, towards whom you felt the greatest affection, for the office of Prime Minister. The officers lent to you by the Government of India were, you tell me, excellent men, and they were supplied to you at your own request. If, however, I am to accept the statements now made by your Highness, it would be necessary for me to believe that Colonel Parry Nisbet, Raja Amar Singh, and the officers referred to, must all of them have changed their nature as well as their disposition towards your Highness within a few months. All these men were, I believe, ready to be your friends, but they have found that your conduct in public and private life was such as to render it impossible for them to co-operate cordially with you.

What I have said has reference to the past. For the future, let me earnestly entreat your Highness to show to the people of Kashmir, as well as to the Government of India, by bearing in a dignified manner the loss of power which you have sustained, and above all, by not associating yourself with local intrigues and conspiracies, or attempts to obstruct the Government, that you have not entirely lost the qualities of a wise and prudent ruler. The settlement announced in Colonel Parry Nisbet's letter of the 17th April to the Prime Minister is, as I have already pointed out to you, not necessarily a permanent one. Time will, however, be necessary if the finances of the State are to be restored to order, and the results of past maladministration effectually removed. Until this has been done, the present arrangement must certainly remain in force. When these good results have been achieved, it may be possible to give your Highness a larger share in the control of the public affairs of Kashmir. Much would, in such a case, depend upon your own conduct in the meanwhile. You cannot, therefore, govern yourself too cautiously, or be too careful in selecting your associates and confidants.

I would also ask you to inform Raja Ram Singh, who has, I understand, accompanied your Highness to Jammu, that the Government of India cannot regard with indifference his continued absence from the Council of State. He holds the important post of Commander-in-Chief in charge of the Military Department, and his failure to attend to the business of this cannot do otherwise than produce the most serious results. Unless therefore, he returns shortly to Srinagar and resumes the discharge of his duties, it will be necessary to make some arrangement for the transfer of those duties to other hands.

I will add only one word to what I have said above. Should your Highness at any time desire to address me in connection with this, or other matters, it will always be agreeable to me to learn your wishes, or your opinions; and should you, at the present time, seek an opportunity of hearing from my own lips my views in regard to these questions, I shall at any convenient time be ready to receive you and to converse with you in a friendly and confidential spirit.

Enclosure 4 in No.9

PRELIMINARY REPORT of SETTLEMENT OPERATIONS in KASHMIR and JAMMU by A. WINGATE, Esq., C.S., SETTLEMENT OFFICER

From A. WINGATE, ESQ., C.S., Settlement Officer, Kashmir, to His Highness the MAHARAJA OF KASHMIR AND JAMMU

Srinagar, August 1, 1888.

Para. 1.—History of Appointment.

" 2.—Preliminary arrangements.

" 3.—Character of former survey.

" 4.—Rejection of the previous measurement.

" 5.—System of measurement adopted.

" 6.—Area measured in first month.

" 7.—Local Weights and measures.

" 8.—Forms of Settlement Records.

" 9.—Details of Establishment.

" 10.—" " Expenditure.

" 11.—Budget estimate of current season.

" 12.—Remarks on the above.

" 13.—Estimated cost of measuring the Kashmir Valley.

" 14.—Probable maximum area of Kashmir Valley.

" 15.—" minimum area of Kashmir Valley.

" 16.—" area of measurement.

" 17.—" average out-turn per measure.

" 18.—" out-turn and work each season.

" 19.—Estimated cost of the settlement.

" 20 and 21.—Classification of lands.

" 22.—Remarks on the grouping of villages.

" 23.—Difficulty of ascertaining current rates of assessment.

" 24.—Crop experiments.

" 25.—Rice cultivation.

" 26.—Famines, etc.—Variations in the season affect the harvest; for example, a wet spring would injure the young crop, or insufficient snows would diminish the water supply, but famine appears only to be caused by heavy rain and cold at the time of ripening or reaping, and fortunately this is a rare occurrence. It is, however, always important that the shali crop should be cut and garnered with the utmost expedition, and any revenue system which tends to delay that operation must in critical season seriously aggravate the disaster. The rabi crops not infrequently suffer from insufficient spring showers, but, from a famine standpoint, wheat, barley, and the like are of little importance, and therefore in the following history of the seasons only those calamities are noticed which seriously affect the population:-

A.D.	Samwat	
1815 ..	1872 ..	Population estimated at 8,00,000.
1824 ..	1881 ..	Severe earthquake, followed by
1828 ..	1885 ..	cholera.
1831 to .. 1833	1888 to .. 1890	Severe famine, caused by heavy rain in the autumn.
1835 ..	1892 ..	Population estimated at 2,00,000.
1838 ..	1895 ..	Floods.
1842 or .. 1843	1899 or .. 1900	Cholera.
1857 ..	1914 ..	Ditto.
1859 to .. 1860	1916 to .. 1917 ..	Scarcity owing to short water-supply.
1865 ..	1922 ..	Floods.
1869 ..	1926 ..	Ditto.
1871 ..	1928 ..	Ditto.
1872 ..	1929 ..	Cholera.
1873 ..	1930 ..	Population estimated at 5,00,000.
1875 ..	1932 ..	Poor harvest.
1877 to .. 1879	1934 to .. 1936	Severe famine, caused by heavy rain from the end of September, 1877, followed by cholera.
1879 ..	1936 ..	Good rich harvest.
1880 ..	1937 ..	Very good ditto.
1881 ..	1938 ..	Good harvest.
1882 ..	1939 ..	Good ditto.
1883 ..	1940 ..	Poor ditto, too little rain.

1884 ..	1941 ..	Very good harvest.
1885 ..	1942 ..	Poor harvest, spring rains too heavy, and sowings retarded.
		Severe earthquake.
1886 ..	1943 ..	Fairly good harvest.
1887 ..	1944 ..	Good harvest.

Population estimated at 3,00,000 to 4,00,000.

Para. 27.—Decrease of Population (See p. 67)

" 28.—Chronic Scarcity of Food (See p. 68)

" 29.—Profits on the sale of Cleaned Rice.

" 30.—System of Revenue Collection under the Sikhs.—Coming now to the mode of collecting the shali and the revenue generally, I premise that my remarks are based on inquiries made in two tehsils only. The tehsils of Phak and Lal are called cash- assessed, and that was one of the reasons why I commenced there. Under the Sikhs the State took a half-share of the kharif crop, and in addition four traks per kharwar, and on account of the rice straw and the vegetable-produce of the "Sagasar" plots, the whole of which were kept by the Asami and were supposed to be free of assessment, Rs. 1-9-0 per cent. was added to the total. The patwari and kanungo got 1/2 a trak per kharwar between them. Inferior village servants got something. Nazarana was levied four times a year, and "tambol" (about two per cent.) was taken on occasions of marriages in the ruler's family, &c., &c. The villagers had also to feed the State watchers of the grain, called "Shakdar". Non-resident cultivators paid a little less, and Pandits and Pirzadas only paid two extra traks instead of four. For the rabi and kimiti crops all classes of cultivators were taxed alike, and in addition to the half-share, three traks per kharwar were taken under the names of extra cesses. the "kimiti" crops appear to be those that have always had a money-value and are til-gogal, sarson, tobacco, cotton, linseed, saffron, and the like. The distinction is said to date back to the time of Todar Mal, and for these crops money was always required, the assessment being calculated in rupees after division of the produce and the produce being returned to the cultivator. For other crops, whether kharif or rabi, the collection might be in kind, or the villages might be farmed out. But I can find no trace so far of any crop rates. Walnut oil, fruit trees, and honey, have also always been taxed. Under the above the State share was not less than three-fifths of the gross produce, and what the cultivator actually retained was certainly less than two-fifths and probably only about one-third. The abundance of fruits, berries, and nuts, the extensive grazing area, and forest produce, enabled the cultivators to live, but an assessment so heavy as this would extinguish all rights in land, would render land valueless, and would reduce a population forcibly confined within the valley to the condition of tenants-at-will.

Para. 31.—Effects of a Crushing Assessment.—Accordingly, we find that pressure has from time to time been exercised to keep the land in cultivation, and to such an abject condition have the cultivators—naturally a fine race—been reduced that I have been told by the highest and most trusted officials in Srinagar that the Kashmiri cannot be trusted with shali because he would eat the whole of it, that he will not plough unless the tehsildar gives him the seed and makes him, and that without this fostering care of Government he would become extinct. The truth being that he has been pressed down to the condition of a coolie cultivating at subsistence allowance the State property. The Kashmiris are called cowardly, because they have lost the rights belonging to the peasantry elsewhere and tamely submit to be driven like sheep before a sepoy. But it is useless to expect that a small population forming an isolated state that looked only to its hills for protection could withstand powerful neighbours like Afghans or Sikhs, or that so distant and inaccessible a province would not be ruthlessly ground down under the endless succession of governors that have enriched themselves in this valley. The Kashmiri is strong and hardworking, but his spirit is dormant; and he is grudged the quantity of food the climate makes necessary, but which a short- sighted policy considers gluttonous; and consequently he is being closer pressed every harvest. With fair treatment the peasantry would make a great advance in numbers and in prosperity; and if their claim to consideration, which I am now advancing, is met, the happy days when Zain-ul-abdin passed his jubilee among a contented people may be repeated. If that claim is denied, the State, as I shall presently show, will soon have no land left to legislate for, and will have to beg for its revenue from its present servants. These servants foresee that a land settlement must come some day, and meanwhile they are buying up or otherwise getting possession of the land, and to secure a little temporary rest the cultivators are only too ready to take shelter behind any sufficiently influential pandit.

Para. 32.—Revenue Management since A.D. 1846.—Since the times of the Sikhs, the pressure has been undoubtedly relaxed; but it must still be pretty severe when cultivators are found ready to sell whole villages for no other equivalent than the protection of a powerful name. Many of the Mukaddams, or heads of the villages, are very intelligent, but when it comes to seeing their children stinted of food, with hearts sickened by deferred hope, they sign away fatuitously day by day such rights as they possess. During Maharaja Golab Singh's rule (A.D. 1846 to 1857) the Sikh procedure was followed, but some slight relaxations were made in favour of land newly cultivated, for large areas were lying waste. His Highness was fond of horses, and a number of grass-rakhs were reserved from cultivation. Under Maharaja Ranbhir Singh, circles of villages were annually farmed out to contractors called kardars. About 1865 (S. 1922) the extra traks per kharwar were reduced for all Pandits and Pirzadas for a time to only one trak. From about 1869 (S. 1926) the practice of contracting with the Mukaddams or with the Zemindars gradually established itself in place of the farming system, and only two extra traks came to be levied instead of four. In 1873-4 (S. 1930-1) the village contracts seem to have been divided up into "asamiwar khewats", or cultivators' accounts, and either produce or cash was taken from each man. In 1875 (S. 1932) the harvest was a bad one, and the State took two shares of the produce and left one only to the cultivators. Next year fresh contracts were entered into either with Mukaddams, Kardars, or cultivators, and two traks per kharwar were again added to the assessment, besides an aggregate tax of Rs. 9-12-0 per cent. if paid in cash, or 9 kharwars 12 traks per 100 kharwars if paid in kind. This tax included a number of items, such as support of the palace-temple, the abolished kanungo's share, and so on. In 1877 (S.1934) the scarcity began, and the new contracts broke down, and so the State collected in kind only; and this practically continued till 1880 (S.1937), when a new "asamiwar khewat" was made, based upon previous years' collections, as estimated in cash, but payable either in produce or cash as the cultivator was able. This "khewat" or cash settlement is supposed still to be valid, but after the good harvest of S. 1937 and 1938 the settlement was thought to have been too easy, and so it was raised by Rs. 8-9-0 per cent., the chief item of the increment being Rs. 6-13-0 for a pony tax, which might be paid in ponies instead of money, and in place of the Rs. 1-9-0 per cent. formerly levied for fodder, the cultivators were required to give five kurus of rice straw per 100 threshed. This settlement includes all cesses except the "tambol" and "nazarana". In 1885 (S.1942) the Rs. 8-9-0 per cent. tax was remitted, and so now the "khewat" of S. 1937 is supposed to have been reverted to, with the exception of the five kurus of rice straw, which are still taken. In 1886 (S.1943) one seer per kharwar, formerly payable to the zillahdars, was made payable to the State, who appointed paid chowkidars. If this revenue history is not very correct, it must be remembered that access to the revenue records has been denied me.

Para 33.—The so-called Cash Settlement of 1880.

" 34.—Hap-hazard way in which the Settlement was immediately increased.—To find out the mechanism of the winding-up process would be tedious if not impossible, but as an example I cite another village. In S. 1937, the "khewat" was fixed at Rs. 617-12-0. In S. 1939, when the villages were practically going by auction, a bidder offered Rs.107-4-0 increase, and this village was knocked down to him at Rs. 725 per annum.

To this extra taxes, namely:-

	Rs.	A.	P.
Dharmarth ..	3	10	0
Shafakhana ..	7	4	0
Nazarana ..	0	14	6
Palace Temple ..	0	14	6
Pony-tax ..	69	5	0
Tambol ..	2	0	0
	84	0	0
Outstanding balance	1	2	0
Total ..	85	2	0

were added, making the total Rs. 810-2-0 for S. 1941. In S.1942, the extra taxes were remitted, as already stated, and so the account stands—

	Rs.	A.	P.
Assessment ..	725	0	0
Add for cotton supplied for spinning and weaving soldiers' clothing— 2 Kharwars at Rs. 14 = Rs. 28 + a fine of Rs. 4 for failing to supply the clothing within the year..	32	0	0
Outstanding balance ..	39	3	0
Total ..	796	3	0

For S. 1943 the assessment is Rs. 725, and with outstanding balance the total is Rs. 741-11-9.

These are the village accounts showing collections. The tehsil accounts showing demands, give for S. 1941 Rs. 787, for S. 1942 Rs. 752, and for S. 1943 Rs. 733. It is difficult to deduce from accounts such as these what proportion of the gross produce the State takes, and more difficult still to find out what a village really does pay, as I have now to show. I enter into this detail because it is absolutely necessary it should be understood that any intelligible comparison between the results of the proposed settlement and either the previous khewat or the present demand, or the actual collections, will be impossible.

Para. 35.—How the Revenue is Collected.—It might be thought actual collections could be compared with the results of the settlement, but the custom of applying arbitrary prices to the portion of the revenue collected in kind, and which forms a large percentage of the whole, and the want of certainly either as to the proportion collected in kind or as to the share of each crop which is taken to make up that proportion, will effectually prevent any comparison with anything whatsoever. The khewat, or so-called cash settlement, so far from being a boon to the people, has been used as a means for getting rid of the restrictions which are imposed by a division of produce, and is accordingly equally detested by the villagers. This is how it is worked. An order is annually issued from Srinagar for the collection of a certain quantity, say nine lakhs of kharwars of shali, the demand being based upon the general aspect of the ripening crop, and pitched 20 to 30 per cent. above what there is a likelihood of getting. Each tehsildar is then informed of the amount he is expected to contribute to this total. He finds this amount, converted at Rs.2 chilki (Rs. 1¼ imperial) per kharwar, comes to, say, 10 annas in the rupees of his total revenue. He accordingly gives instructions to collect so many kharwars from each village, the total collections coming up to the amount named from headquarters, or probably rather more, but varying from 16 annas to nothing, according to the amount of shali he thinks can be secured from any particular village. As soon as the villagers learn they have to pay their khewat, say, 10 annas in shali, two annas in cotton, mung, &c., and four annas in cash, bargaining and bribery begin; the village, if a fairly well-to-do one, eventually securing enough shali to live upon; if a poor one, eventually securing enough shali to live upon; if a poor one, having to look forward to some other means of eking out a livelihood for the winter.

Perhaps an instance will make the system clearer. It is a village I happened to examine; the accounts are for the year S. 1939, and the rupees are chilki, or worth 10 annas each.

Amount of Demand.		Amount Collected.	
In cash...	Rs. 384-7-3	In Cash ..	Rs. 369-10-9
In Kind ..	Kh. 191-6¾	In Kind ..	Kh. 182-2-0

The meaning of the division of the demand into "cash" and "kind" merely signifies that there must be so much shali or makki, and that for the rest collections may be in cash or in any other produce. In the following details gross produce is shown for most things in 16-trak kharwars, and the Government share in 15-trak kharwars:-

Thus we have Rs. 369-10-9 set down as collected in cash, but which may have been paid partly in kind, and 174 kharwars 2 traks compulsorily levied in kind, which, at the standard price of Rs.2 per kharwar, would amount to Rs. 348-4-0. This account would show that the total collections were valued at Rs. 717-14-9.

The tehsil accounts state the demand was Rs. 699. This village rose from Rs. 449 in S. 1937, the year of the khewat. In S. 1940 and 1941 there was a further increase to Rs. 758, and notwithstanding the remission of taxes in S. 1942, the demand still is over Rs. 700. If it is asked why the district officers should maintain complicated weighments and accounts when the cash demand has been fixed at, say, Rs. 700 and they might take Rs. 350 in cash and 175 kharwars in shali, the answer is that no one can tell me.

Para. 36.—Fixed prices for produce enable a Tehsildar to manipulate the incident of the Assessment.

Para. 37.—Why the price of Shali is fixed so low.

" 38.—How Cotton is dealt with.

" 39.—Cost of Transport to Srinagar is borne by the Villagers.

Para. 40.—Introduction of a Landlord class.

" 41.—Chakdars.

" 42.—Mukarridars.

" 43.—Evasion of conditions on which Land was granted.

" 44.—Instances of Lands held in excess of the Grants.

" 45.—Chakdars ousting the old Cultivators.

" 46.—Clandestine possession of Villages.

" 47.—Instances of Villages ruined by Over-assessment.

" 48.—The Law Improvement Department.

" 49.—How Proprietary Titles are manufactured.

" 50.—Impossibility of annihilating all rights in Land.

" 51.—Official utterance differs from official practice.

" 52.—Proposals for dealing with the Land.

" 53.— " with regard to Cultivators.

" 54.— " " Chakdars, &c.

" 55.— " " Waste Lands.

" 56.—Importance of regulating the distribution of water for irrigation.

Para. 57.—Self-preservation required that the Darbar should confer rights upon the peasantry.

Para. 58.—Serious opposition anticipated.

" 59.—Outstanding Balances.

" 60.—Forced Labour.—Another matter urgently demanding attention is the manner in which begar, or forced labour, is managed. I am not prepared to say that it can be got rid of all at once. For example, for the Gilgit-expedition-transport resort to compulsion is probably necessary. But, were you Highness aware of how orders are carried out, many abuses might cease. At present chakdars' lands, jaghir and other specially assigned villages, villages secretly bought or in possession of officials or influential persons, are all exempt. I rode through a particularly nice village with a little bazaar, and the women and children looking to the trained observer in many little ways better off than the average. I said this village is doing very well, but was answered at once it belongs to so and so, mentioning a well-known official. No coolie can be seized in villages so protected, and that is one of the main reasons that the khalsa cultivators seek to transfer themselves to some nearer shelter. Consequently the whole burden of providing coolies falls upon the khalsa villages and mostly on those too small and poor to attract anybody's care. Further, the way of collecting coolies occasions more discontent than is necessary. A requisition is made, say, for 500 coolies. The tehsildar doubles the number. His emissaries quadruple it, and so a village that ought to supply, perhaps, five coolies, is asked for twenty. Fifteen men have to buy themselves off. It is notorious that this year large sums have been illegitimately collected in this way, to the prejudice of the good name of the Darbar. Just as I ventured to recommend that the amount of shali to be taken from each village should be fixed once for all and published, so I would suggest that one coolie per so many rupees of assessment be required to be furnished by each village. A roll would then be made showing how many coolies each village ought to furnish, and this simple expedient would in a great measure stop the oppression and bribery now going on. Eventually, in the Settlement Rules, I should propose to define for what purposes and to what extent, and by whose orders, begar, or forced labour, may be required, and to regulate its remuneration. At present an order to collect coolies sends most of the able-bodied population of a tehsil into hiding for a week or two, to the great detriment of agricultural operations, and a settlement could not exist side by side with such disorganization of revenue-paying families.

JAMMU

Para. 61.—Depredations of Game animals.

" 62.—Out-turn of Work.

" 63.—Classification of Lands and Soils.

" 64.— " " "

" 65.—Difficulty of getting Information.

" 66.—Land Tenure.

" 67.—Previous Settlements.

" 68.—Obstacles to increased Cultivation.

" 69.—Necessity of reorganizing the rights of Proprietors.

" 70.—Proposals for dealing with Cultivators.

" 71.—I have now laid before your Highness my proposals for dealing with the land in Kashmir and Jammu. Should these proposals meet with approval they will be embodied in a Code of Settlement Regulations and submitted for final sanction before the introduction of the settlement in the first tehsils. My account of what is in progress under your Highness's authority, but against your Highness's interests, has been long because I stand alone, and my mere assertion that the State treasury was being depleted, and the poor were being turned out of their lands, and the staple food of the people had become a monopoly of the officials, would not be believed. I appeal to your Highness with some confidence, because I have been impressed during my interviews with the belief that your Highness has a ready sympathy for the poor, a keen interest in land questions, and a determination to protect the cultivators against the officials. But my heart fails me when I think that there is no one among those who surround your Highness from whom I can venture to hope for a word in support of my prayer, that one and all will use every argument to persuade your Highness that my proposals will be detrimental to the traditions, the policy, or the dignity of the State; that they are impossible, and that neither the rice nor the land ought to be trusted out of officials custody. I remember how carefully your Highness had been prepared to be firm on two points, one, that the "Hak malikana", or proprietorship of the land in Kashmir, belonged to the Maharaja, and second, that no settlement should be announced till the whole country was measured and ready for settlement on one day or the Government could not be responsible for the rice supply. I remember also with what cordial approval your Highness's remarks on these points were invariably received by the high officials present. The first position, they well knew, secured to them the power of terrorizing over the defenceless cultivators, and, continuing their methods of acquiring the proprietorship of the lands for themselves. And the second position would keep my department from interfering with these practices for years, and as the first papers would grow obsolete before the last were prepared, they knew, that if that condition could only be maintained, the settlement would never come at all. Your Highness, however, was soon convinced that to indefinitely postpone the settlement, however desirable from the point of view of the officials, was a serious danger, and I have since been urged to prepare tehsils for settlement as soon as possible. But the first position is still preserved, and, though your Highness has listened with patience, I cannot hope I have prevailed. Yet, unless the cultivators are guaranteed possession of the lands they till, a cash, or partly cash and partly shali, settlement is impossible. If the cultivators are to work hard, pay punctually, and keep the treasury fuller than it has ever been before, they must not be the hopeless, discontented, depressed class they are now. The State cannot expect to get everything and give nothing. And behind a strong contented peasantry there must be persons ready to lay out capital when necessary. But who will lend money to a cultivator who may be turned out of his fields and day? Your Highness may think an order not to turn anybody out would suffice. It would be useless when the cultivators themselves are ready to transfer all and any rights they have, to accept any position, any field, so long as they get some shelter, and the officials are eager by every device known to educated and clever men in a position of untrammelled power, and all working with one object, to convert themselves into proprietors, to manufacture prescriptive rights to intervene between the State and the cultivator, to finally arrive at the coveted end when the pandits shall be landlords, the cultivators tenants-at-will, or, rather, coolies who cannot escape, and the State demand limited to a nominal sum per kharwar which lapse of time and ingenious interlarding of words will combine to make permanent.

Para. 72.—Possibility of Leases.

" 73.—Renewed Obstructions.

" 74.—A reasons why we are objectionable.

List of Zillahs and Tehsils in the Kashmir Valley in 1887.

B

HOUSE OF COMMONS, JULY 3

Mr. BRADLAUGH said: I beg to ask leave to move the adjournment of the House for the purpose of discussing "a definite matter of urgent public importance", viz., the taking away by the Government of India from the Maharaja of Kashmir the Government of his state and part of his revenues whilst refusing to allow any judicial or Parliamentary enquiry into the grounds for such action against a great feudatory prince.

The SPEAKER having appealed to the House, and considerably over forty members having risen in their places,

Mr. BRADLAUGH said: I am obliged to move the adjournment of the House, because it is the only possible way in which any appeal for the Maharaja of Kashmir can be submitted to Parliament. The Government of India have deprived this chief of his authority and of his property under cover of allegations which are emphatically denied by the Maharaja himself. The Maharaja, as I shall show, has applied for a trial in India. That has been denied him. The Secretary of State here has been asked to sanction an enquiry, and has refused; the leader of the House has been asked to appoint a Select Committee of enquiry, and has also refused; so that neither judicial nor Parliamentary nor Government enquiry is being allowed, although this gentleman has been subjected to penalties which in the case of the meanest person in this country would entitle him to have the accusations brought before some tribunal and witnesses against him heard. There is no other manner of bringing this matter before the House than by moving the adjournment. Though I can understand the hon. gentlemen opposite may think it unfair that the adjournment should be moved, they must remember than on Indian matters I have always shown the greatest consideration to the Government; so much so that at the beginning of this Session I did not avail myself, as I might have done, of my right to move an amendment to the Address, and I only now make a motion for the adjournment because there are no Estimates in Supply in which, as in any case affecting any other portion of Her Majesty's dominions, a question of grievance may be raised. It is either in the manner I am raising it to-night that this grievance must be submitted, or not at all. Now on May 14th of last year—that is more than twelve months ago—the Maharaja himself asked the Government of India for a fair trial. I will read to the House presently the touching words in which that appeal for a fair trial was met. From then till now, except in a despatch from which it will be my duty to quote, no kind of answer has been made to that appeal, and the Maharaja has been condemned unheard. I should have pressed this claim for inquiry twelve months ago, but there were then no papers before the House. It would have been open for the Government to say in the fashion in which rumours has said that this unfortunate gentleman had been guilty of crime or was suffering the consequences of vice, because these suggestions could be found embodied in official despatches to which I shall refer, and that there was, therefore, a lack of duty in bringing the matter before the House until the Government had put before it the statements on which they rely. Although this unfortunate gentleman was deprived of his authority and his property at the beginning of last year, the presentation of papers has been delayed until last week.

They have been repeatedly pressed for by myself and other members. Until the Government had put their case on the table, any one would have been at a great disadvantage in submitting to this House any matter for its decision. I did not propose to ask the House, in the division I shall challenge, to express any other opinion on the facts I shall submit than that when such a penalty is enforced against a prince with whom we have a treaty—who has recently been regarded as being in the position of a feudatory prince—the man so dealt with is entitled to that which any other subject of Her Majesty, if he be a subject of Her Majesty, is entitled to, viz., a fair trial before condemnation. The Under Secretary must not shelter himself under considerations of State. If considerations of State can justify the Government of India in depriving one man of his authority and property unheard, there is no protection for any one, be he prince or peasant, throughout the whole of our Asiatic dominions. The other day the question was stated as simply as possible in the language of the right hon. gentleman the Under Secretary for India (Sir J. Gorst) in answer to a question put by myself. The right hon. gentleman said, "The action of the Government in Kashmir has been based, not upon grave personal charges made against the Maharaja". I would ask the House to remember that, because this man's character has been rumoured away and lied away with the help of forged letters during the last year and a-half—forged letters used as instruments of political warfare—letters, the authenticity of which has been denied by the Maharaja, letters which have never been produced in his presence and which yet the Government have the face to refer to in their worst fashion in one of the despatches I shall read to the House. I shall be relieved from any question as to the personal conduct of the Maharaja. He may be good or bad. I do not care what he is—he is entitled to justice. If he has been criminal let him be condemned and punished, but do not rob him under cover of a criminality which you dare not bring in evidence against him, and as to which you will allow no inquiry either in India or here. The right hon. gentleman the Under Secretary said the action of the Government was based upon the long-continued misgovernment of Kashmir. Well, this unfortunate gentleman has only been the ruler of Kashmir for about five years, and I will quote, to within a few months of the time he was dispossessed, the testimony of the Government itself that misgovernment did not exist as far as it was in his power to help it. I cannot conceive—I should not be justified in saying before you, Sir, anything more impudent—but I can conceive nothing more cool than the audacity of the confidence that this House would be imposed upon by the statement of the right hon. gentleman the Under Secretary that there had been long-continued misgovernment in Ireland such as justified the dethronement of this man. Vague statements there are here, but not one statement of fact. Misgovernment must be made up of something. You may shadow a man, put him unjustly in prison, or take away his property. None of these things are alleged against this unfortunate gentleman. Well, the right hon. gentleman went on to say that the Government of India have never attached any importance to certain treasonable and criminal correspondence attributed to the Maharaja. It would have been as well not to have so described the character of the correspondence if no importance was attached to it. Why suggest that it was criminal and treasonable if it was not true, as it was not, that he was responsible for it? I do not suggest that the right hon. gentleman has made an inaccurate statement, but I do say he has been ignorant of the facts.

I will read the evidence given by the Viceroy himself with regard to this correspondence which the right hon. gentleman dare not lay before this House, which he dare not put in print, but on which the emissaries of the Government have lied away the Maharaja's character during the last year and a-half. I will dispose of this point at once, because fortunately we have the papers on the Table and are able now to deal with them. So far from its being true that the Government have never attached the smallest importance to the correspondence, the Viceroy himself says the Government were justified "not merely by the disclosure of these letters"—so that they consider themselves in part justified by them (Sir J. Gorst indicated dissent)—The right hon. gentleman shakes his head. It is the Viceroy's head that should be shaken here. I admit that the right hon. gentleman dare not rely on the letters. I admit the right hon. gentleman has too much good sense to use in justification of the position assumed by the Government letters which the man himself declares to be forgeries and which the Government have never dared to produce to his face. But in a long despatch, dated "Simla, June 26th, 1889," I say the Viceroy did say these letters were amongst the things on which the Government acted in condemning this unfortunate gentleman. What did the Maharaja himself say about these letters? In a letter, which unfortunately time will not permit me to read fully to the House, he made a plea for justice first to the Government of India, and then through the Government to the English Parliament. He said, "these letters are nothing but most daring forgeries"; and he suggests that one of the forgers, if not the only forger, is his brother, whom the Government of India has placed in the position of authority of which they have deprived this unfortunate gentleman himself. My allegation will be that it was on those letters—for the papers disclosed nothing else, and further negatives everything else—that this action of the Government was based. (Sir J. Gorst again expressed dissent.) The right hon. gentleman shakes his head, but I have read the papers, which he evidently has not done himself, and I shall read extracts to the House to show that I am within the mark in every statement of this kind I make. Why did the Government of India, twelve months ago, say they did not merely act on these letters? What did that phrase mean if they did not act on them at all? Have the Government since discovered they are forgeries? If so, as they are part of the case on which misgovernment and criminality are alleged against this unfortunate gentleman, the whole story of it does now fall to the ground, at any rate rests on other matters, with reference to which this man demands to be put on his trial, and as to which no evidence has been offered. Lord Cross, speaking last year at Sheffield, used words a little stronger than, and, if I may be allowed to say so, not quite so skillful as the euphemistic language of the First Lord tonight, and of the right hon. gentleman the Under Secretary last week. He said, "we did interfere in the matter of the Kashmir, and why? Because the people of Kashmir were so ground down by the tayranny and misgovernment of the Maharaja that we were bound as the paramount power to interfere for the protection of the interests of the inhabitants." Where in these papers is there one instance of this grinding down? If you want to steal Kashmir, as unfortunately we have stolen State after State in India and other parts of the world, then say so at once, and at least have the merit of honest thieves; don't be hypocritical, by saying you set up self-government where self-government has no real existence. What is the position of Kashmir towards this Country? Fortunately the historry is not long, so far as it affects this unfortunate man, and I will deal with it as briefly as it is possible to do. The history of Kashmir, for the purpose of to- night's discussion, began with the Treaty of 1846, with the grandfather of the gentleman whose cause I am pleading.

Then for a considerable money payment, recorded in the third section of the Treaty, the British Government transferred and made over for ever, in independent possession, to Maharaja Golab Singh and the heirs male of his body, the territory which includes Kashmir and Jummoo. This is not a case of an ordinary feudatory State. So little is it regarded as a feudatory State that in the statistical abstract of this very year you have the evidence of its non-inclusion up to 1881 amongst the feudatory States, and there was never anything to suggest that we had a right to send a Resident there until 1885, on the death of the father of the present Maharaja. I won't trouble the House with what passed until a few days before the commencement of the reign of the present chief. The Maharaja Golab Singh, with whom the Treaty of the 16th of March, 1846, was made, was succeeded by his son about the time of the Indian Mutiny; and Lord Canning, in an official document, gave Maharaja Rumbir Singh, who had succeeded Golab Singh, in 1857, the Sanad of adoption, which provided that in case of failure of issue he and his successors would be competent to adopt an heir and thus perpetuate the line. This was given on the ground of the great service rendered by the Maharaja during the Mutiny. The Maharaja Rumbir Singh was ill in 1884, and I am afraid that some fourteen or fifteen years ago, when Jingoism was specially paramount in the making of great military frontiers and things of that kind, we looked with longing eyes upon the property of others, and were disposed to ignore any sense of justice in our dealings with them. It was then said that Rumbir Singh had misgoverned his country. If he had, it was a matter with which, except as being by treaty the paramount power, in which case we might have made remonstrance, we had nothing whatever to do. But, as a matter of fact, we made no remonstrance to him. The Under Secretary of State dissents. Then why is it not in the papers? The papers began in 1884 with a dispatch relating to the alleged misgovernment during the time of the present Maharaja's father. The words of the despatch preclude the possibility of remonstrance having been made.

But what happens is that while the Maharaja was dying, the Viceroy of India, looking to the matter, as he says, with a view to his troublesome neighbours on the north-west frontier, suggested certain reforms which on the accession of the sòn of the then dying man it would be well should be carried out: and I will read to the House in the words of Lord Dufferin himself the admission that many of these reforms had been carried out during the short period that this gentleman sat on the throne. In 1885 the succession of Prapat Singh was formally recognised by the Government. He came to the throne under the treaty which I have read to the House. One new departure there was against which the Maharaja protested, namely, the establishment of a Residency, instead of Kashmir being an independent possession, which under the treaty it was, subject to the supremacy of the Empress Queen. After the appointment of a Resident it is a monstrously unfair thing to spring a mine four or five years afterwards, and allege as an excuse for confiscating property and power that there had been misgovernment where, if there had been misgovernment, it should have been reported day by day, week by week, month by month, and year by year. There are no such reports. If the Secretary of State has got them he ought to have printed them. I am not asking the House to say that this unfortunate man is guiltless, but I am asking them to say that he is entitled to be tried, and to have an inquiry before he is deprived of his rights. In 1889 the Government deprived this gentleman of his chieftainship. By what right? By no right save the right of force. By what law? By no law save the law of force. Upon what charges? Upon charges of the vaguest description. It is clear these papers are delusive papers. There must have been reports made to the Viceroy, which reports ought to be in the hands of the House. If it is said that they are of a confidential character; if it is said they cannot be produced, at any rate the witnesses who can prove the occasions of misgovernment ought to be produced in some court. Is it because this man is rich; is it because his property is in a place where you want to have possession because of frontier considerations, that he is to be deprived of the right which you admit to the meanest person accused within this country, or within the Asiatic dominions of the Empress Queen? It is a monstrous thing, and I ask the House to look at it without consideration of party; because you must remember it is not a question only of this man, but of every feudatory prince whose property you may want to take and merge in our dominions. The papers have not been put on the table in a hurry. They have been in the skilled hands of the Under Secretary. We all know how frank the Under Secretary can be if he tries, and I ask him to tell the House how many papers relating to these important dispatches between the Government of India and the Secretary of State have been kept back, and why. It is clear some have—the language shows it. Why are any kept back? They have been kept back because the action of the Government cannot be defended. I do not know what the charges are against the Maharaja, and I am only asking that this Parliament shall say that the Government of India, however powerful, and whatever the State considerations are, has no right to rob this man.

On the 14th of September, 1885, the Viceroy sent a dispatch to which I must allude for a moment. It was sent just on the accession of the present Maharaja to the throne, and I allege to the House it makes a clear bill up to the time, so far as any charges of misgovernment entitled our Government to interfere. The Viceroy says: "I trust that your highness's life may be long and prosperous; and that, in all difficulties, of whatsoever kind, you will rely with confidence upon the goodwill of the British Government, which will never fail you so long as you are loyal to the Crown, and earnest in the desire to rule your State with justice and moderation. Your Highness has before you a difficult task. During the illness of your father the administration of the State became seriously disorganised, and it will be necessary for you to introduce many reforms." I will show you that three years after Lord Dufferin's time reforms had been carried out, and that misgovernment is a pretext for stealing the man's property. The Maharaja wrote in reply protesting against the Residency being placed upon him. He said: "I do not hesitate to admit that the existing state of affairs in Kashmir and Jammu urgently requires immediate introduction of substantial reforms into the administration of the country, and now that I have power commensurate with my responsibilities, I beg to answer your Excellency that nothing shall be spared on my part, and no time will be lost to prove beyond any possibility of doubt that it is my ambition to succeed in making my country a model of a well-governed State in alliance with the Government of India." Having got the Resident at the capital, what do we find? We find that the resident wants to get rid of the Maharaja, he submits some report to the Government, the particulars of which we do not know, and a report, the particulars of which we do not know, and a report, the particularrs of which we do know, dated March 5th, 1888. Let me point out in the first place that in the despatch of the 5th of March, 1888, there is nothing to justify any of the words of Lord Cross at Sheffield, or the words of the Under-Secretary of State last week, as to misgovernment, or the words of the First Lord of the Treasury-to-night. Now, what was the decision the Government of India came to in August, 1888? It was that the condition of the State did not seem to demand such action as Mr. Plowden had suggested, and that the Government had therefore determined not to resort to measures which would have the effect directly or indirectly of taking the power out of the Maharaja's hands.

Yet no less than seven months after that dispatch power was taken of his hands, and taken out solely on these letters. Solely, perhaps, is a strong word to use; but it was immediately after coming into possession of these letters, suggesting the worst of crimes—letters which the Maharaja has always denied, and as to which he is certainly entitled to be heard before a Select Committee of this House or before the Viceroy himself. He had confidence in the British Government, but he had no confidence in the officials who he said misrepresented him. The decision that there should be no interference with the Maharaja directly or indirectly disposes of Mr. Plowden's report of the 8th of March, 1888. I come now to April, 1889, when we had some further action. I will first mention that on the 25th of July, 1888, Lord Dufferin wrote: "I do not overlook the fact that since the appointment of the Council of which Diwan Lachman Dass was a member, considerable progress has bee made in the direction of reforms; useful work has been done with regard to the revenue administration, and in the reorganisation of the Public Works and Medical Department. But much remains to be done." This is not the language of condemnation of chronic misgovernment and the grinding down of the people. Misgovernment is only on invention—an excuse for having dipossessed this man, and I think I have a right to quote the evidence given by Lord Dufferin in 1888. This unfortunate prince, hampered by the Resident who dictated the policy he should pursue, did make such reforms as entitled him to the praise of Lord Dufferin—a statesman of the greatest eminence of the keenest judgment, and a man who cannot be charged with being at all partial to the class of man I am defending here this afternoon. Now I come to these forged letters. There is a batch of thirty-four, and the Maharaja says that they are all forgires.

I do not ask you to say whether they are or are not, but I say that if they are used against him he is entitled to go into court and cross-examine the witnesses against him. Other letters on which the Government have relied have been abandoned as forgeries within the memory of many of us in this House. What is the character of these letters as described by the Resident? The character of them is that the Maharaja offered large sums of money to certain individuals on condition that they would murder, or cause to be removed, Mr. Plowden, the late Resident. It is alleged that these letters showed treasonable correspondence with the enemies of England. All these things are denied by the Maharaja. I do not ask you to say whether the Maharaja is right or wrong, but I say that when letters alleging murder are produced against a prince with whom we have a treaty of alliance, immediately after which we take away his property, the commonest and the merest justice demands that he should have an opportunity of being heard before a Select Committee of this House, or some tribunal competent to deal with his offence, if offence he has committed. The Government are not going to stand by these letters to-night, but the Viceroy has stood by them, and I will read you words in which they are so stood by. The Viceroy said "In the spring of this year"—that is last year—"my attention was called to the documents referred to in your Highness's letter. Many of these had every appearance of being genuine, and they have moreover a striking resemblance to those other papers of which I have already spoken, and which came into the possession of the Government of India at a previous time." "Your Highness is correct in expressing your belief that the action subsequently taken by my Government was not justified merely by the disclosures contained in these letters." Where is the report upon which they acted? The man had a right to be tried. The letters are vague statements. The Viceroy goes on: "Notwithstanding the ample resources of your State, your treasury was empty". Well, if you are going to dethrone every Prince whose treasury becomes empty, I do not know how far you are prepared to carry your policy. Does the Government really mean that? If that be so, how is it they took from this man the advance or deposit or loan of a large sum of money, amounting to twenty-five lakhs of rupees? They had this in their hands when the treasury was empty. Why did they take money for Lady Dufferin's admirable fund? Why, if the treasury was empty, did they not reckon the millions of rupees for railway works in the interest of frontier defence? Treasury empty! Why, you and your Resident helped to empty it, and then you tell this unfortunate man it is a reason why he should be dethroned!

Sir J. GORST : Will the hon. gentleman finish the sentence?

Mr. BRADLAUGH : You put on the table what you please, and I have to make the best I can with the House half empty, because every member feels the difficulty when a motion for adjournment is moved. I have, with such knowledge as is supplied, to make what case I can with this far off matter.

Sir J. GORST : I only interrupted the hon. gentleman to point out that he had not read the sentence to the end, and I thought to put the case fairly it should be given to the end.

Mr. BRADLAUGH : I will read it to the end and show that the right hon. Gentleman gains nothing by making me read it. "Notwithstanding the ample resources of your State, your treasury was empty? corruption and disorder prevailed in every department and every office; Your Highness was still surrounded by low and unworthy favorites; and the continued misgovernment of your State was becoming every day a more serious source of anxiety." Well, there is not a word affecting finance there. I was going to deal with each allegation in turn. "Low and unworthy favourites!" Every prince has these even in his own household; every Oriental prince has such. The whole history of our transactions with native princes shows that when we have hankered to take their money, their land, their position, we have used vices which appeared at the time to suit our purposes and help us to gain our ends. I do not know what the right hon. gentleman means by inviting me to read to the end, as if I had ommitted some allusion to the empty treasury. Why, the Indian Government had then twenty-five lakh of rupees of his, and millions of rupees had been laid out in railway works. Who are these low and unworthy people? It is not enough to make a vague statement; where is the evidence? Let the man be tried. A man complains of a burglary in his jeweller's shop, and you say to him, "Oh but you were misusing the jewels". I ask the House to take at least some tone of dignity in this matter. This despotic government of India; as an indian Secretary once said, has no public opinion to influence it, no Parliament to control it, no Press to criticise it. The Government of India is a despotism that has in many degrees been well for India, it is a despotism which has brought in its train advantages which many of these poor people would not otherwise have obtained; but it cannot be denied that in many respects that despotism in the past has been tainted with fraud and crime, and I hope it is not left to the present Government to revive these evil traditions in obtaining possession of Kashmir. The Empress Queen, the paramount Power, acting as Judge, has condemned this man unheard. No man should be under menace of this injustice. The grandfather of the Prince bought these lands, and we by treaty declared they belonged to him for ever. (Sir John Gorst expressed dissent.) The right hon. gentleman does not seem to be acquainted with all these facts in the history of

India. Shall I ask him to read and tell us the exact sum paid for the Maharaja's dominions? How do the Government justify their action? They say the Maharaja resigned. He says he did nothing of the kind. I am more inclined to believe him than even the Under Secretary, for whose statements I have always the profoundest respect. Officially, there could be nothing better than the way he answers questions in this House; but when history some fifty years hence comes to deal with him, the comment of the historian will be how wickedly the Government deceived the Under Secretary, making him say as truth the things that wee not true. It is said the Maharaja voluntarily resigned. It is true that on March 8th, 1889, the Maharaja issued the following document. I will abridge it; if it is said I am incorrect I will read the whole willingly; but I do not think my abridgement will differ from the exact words. The Maharaja appointed a Council who were to govern the country for five years, he reserving to himself all his princely rights and reserving certain powers, but allowing them much the same authority as, allowing for Oriental position, a Cabinet enjoys here. The Government of India do not accept that, yet they say they accepted a voluntary resignation. What he offered they would not have, what they wanted they took from him. The Maharaja says that even in the decree of March 8th he acted under pressure. I do not ask the house to accede to that, but I do say that he is entitled to a Select Committee here—or he would be even content with an inquiry conducted in India, if Lord Lansdowne will give his personal attention to it. The right hon. gentleman is better acquainted with the Government of India than I am. He knows that Residents are not always perfect, that Residents sometimes quarrel with a prince, and that matters are alleged as facts which do not always bear the test and scrutiny of examination. This man through my mouth appeals to this House, not that you, should declare that the Government of India is wrong—he simply asks for an inquiry. He has a right to that inquiry. I regret that the appeal has not been made by an abler tongue, by a better informed man. But I am limited to the information that the Parliamentary papers presented to the House, and such records as the history of India, enables me to present, and I say without fear of contradiction that no case is made out for the action that has been taken. In 1888 the Government of India and the Secretary of State in Council at home came to the conclusion there was nothing for which directly or indirectly the Maharaja ought to be deprived of power; and within seven months they take it all away. If you trample on treaties, if your obligations to the Princess of India are to be broken, and the native rulers are not to rely on your word, and English justice in India is a shadow and a delusion, let that be known; but let those who hold a contrary opinion vote for my motion as the means of protest. The government of India is no party question; alike to Liberal or Conservative, Radical or Whig, it is our duty and our interest that our paramount rule in India should be just.

Motion made that this House do now adjourn.

The UNDER SECRETARY OF STATE FOR INDIA (Sir John Gorst, Chatham): I do not for a moment dispute the right of the hon. member to challenge the action of the Government of India, or to ask the House to order an enquiry, if there is anything to enquire into. If the House will give me its attention for a short time I will tell the House why the Government of India has acted in the manner it has, and why it appears to the Secretary of State this is not a subject which can properly be made matter of inquiry, either by Judicial Commission in India or by Select, Committee of the House of Commons. I need not take the House back to the early history of Kashmir. The hon. member for Northampton has, in the little history he has given, indicated to the House that after the Sikh war we, by force of arms, placed a Hindu ruler over the Muhammadan people of Kashmir; and by doing this, we incurred, as it seems to me, the responsibilitity of seeing that these Muhammadan people, who by the action of the British Government were subjected to an alien dynasty, were at least fairly and properly governed. Now complaints of the misgovernment of Kashmir are not so modern as the hon. member for Northampton seems to suppose. I should like to read to the House the observations which were made by the Government of Lord Ripon in 1884, and Lord Ripon was a Viceroy whose error did not at all events lie in over interference with native chiefs. This was what was said by the Government in 1884. The misgovernment to which the people of this country (Kashmir) have long been subjected.—The hon. member for Northampton asks what the nature of the misgovernment was, and I will try before I sit down to give the House some faint idea of the nature and results of this misgovernment.—Lord Ripon said "The people of that country have long been subjected to misgovernment, and this was some time since brought prominently into notice by Mr. Henvey; we did not take action at once conceiving that a favourable opportunity would offer on the occasion of a fresh successor"—the Maharaja Runbir Singh was then suffering from a mortal illness and his death was expected—"when that event takes place we shall consider that it will be our duty to express on the Kashmir Government its obligations to its own subjects, and to see that reforms so urgently needed are no longer postponed." To those remarks to Lord Ripon's Government an answer was returned by Lord Kimberley, Secretary of State, under the right hon. gentleman the member for Midlothian, and Lord Kimberley stated in his despatch his doubts whether the Government of India was justified in hesitating so long as it had hesitated, to interfere in the affairs of Kashmir. It may indeed be questioned whether, having regard to the circumstances under which a Hindoo family were settled as rulers, the intervention of the British Government on behalf of the Muhammadan people had not already been too long delayed. Well, the Government of India waited eighteen months, and in 1885 the late Maharaja died, and the present Maharaja came to the throne. The hon. member for Northampton has already read some of the warnings which were addressed to the present Maharaja of Kashmir on the occasion of his ascending the throne, but he said—and I really was surprised when he made the statement to the House—that until quite recently no complaint was made of his administration, and in fact he quoted a few expressions from some of Lord Dufferin's despatches, which would have left upon the House the impression that upon the whole the Government had been very successfully administered and many reforms had been carried out. Now, what did Mr. Plowden say in March, 1888. He thought it his duty to call the formal attention of the Government of India to the fearful condition of Kashmir under the Maharaja and his associates, whom he calls a band of corrupt and mischievous men. Mr. Plowden says: "I think, however, that the Government of India should be under no illusion as regards Maharaja Pertab Singh. From first to last I have failed to discover in him any sustained capacity for governing his country or any genuine desire to ameliorate its condition or to introduce those reforms which he has acknowledged to be necessary. More than two years have passed since his accession, but not only has he achieved nothing but he has opposed beneficial measures proposed by others......He will never of his own free will establish a capable and honest administration; nor if any power of interference it left him will he permit any administration approved by the Government of India to carry on the business of the country. He will thwart and oppose it in every way he dares; the only restraint will be the limit of his powers and his fears." Well at the same time that Mr. Plowden made this grave report to the Government of India on the condition of the country and the character of the Maharaja, a proposal was made by the Maharaja himself to appoint a council.

Mr. BRADLAUGH : The right hon. gentleman will pardon me. I stated to the House that on the report of Mr. Plowden the Government came to the decision not to take the power from the Maharaja, and that Lord Dufferin contradicted Mr. Plowden by recognising the fact that since the appointment of the council of which Dinan Lachman Dass was a member considerable progress had been made in the direction of reform.

Sir JOHN GORST: The hon. member is impatient. I am coming to that. I shall have something more to say first. At the time that this report was sent home, application was made by the Maharaja to have a Council appointed, upon which the Government of India decided to give him another trial to see whether by his Council he would govern the country better. I must say, speaking by the light of after events, it was unfortunate that the Government of India accepted the proposal, set aside the report of Mr. Plowden, and gave the Maharaja what in vulgar phrase would be called "another chance". I confess if the hon. member for Northampton instead of attacking the Government of India for having at last relieved the Maharaja of the functions of government had attacked the Government for being so weak in 1888 as to give this second chance, I am sure that I as Under Secretary would have found it difficult to make out a good defensive case. But Lord Dufferin decided on this course. He wrote a complimentary letter to the Maharaja, which the hon. member has read, and no doubt he made use of the expressions the hon. member has quoted as to the success of the Council, since the appointment of Diwan Lachman Dass, under whom considerable progress, he said, had been made in the direction of reform. But will the House believe that the object of that letter, on which the hon. member relies as showing the improvement in the government of the country, was to remonstrate with the Maharaja for dismissing summarily, and without the knowledge of the Government of India, that same Diwan Lachman Dass whose reforms were praised in the passage of Lord Dufferin's letter which the hon. member has quoted as praising the Maharaja for his improvements in the government of his country. The beginning of Lord Dufferin's letter, which the hon. member has not quoted, is as follows: "I cannot avoid informing your Highness that the news of the sudden removal of Diwan Lachman Dass was received by me with some surprise. Your Highness appointed him to your Council after consulting me, and I hoped that your Highness would before making another change of government give me some previous intimation of your views. However this point has already been brought to your notice by Mr. Plowden, and I do not now desire to dwell upon it further." Well, the arrangements for governing the country by means of a Council were made, and in order to give the new scheme the fullest possible chance of success, Mr. Plowden was removed from Kashmir on the occasion of his promotion, and Colonel Nisbet, a personal friend of the Maharaja and in whom the Maharaja placed implicit confidence, was sent to Kashmir. Now I said I would give the House some little idea of the misgovernment which the hon. member for Northampton made so light of, and of which he said no trace was to be found in the papers before the House. Now if hon. members have read the papers, they will see that they close with the report of a certain gentleman of the name of Wingate. Mr. Wingate was a revenue officer of the Bombay Government of nineteen years' experience, and he had also been employed in the revenue settlement of some of the Native States of Rajputana. He was a highly qualified and experienced officer. He was employed by the Maharaja's Government, and his report well deserves the study of anybody who desires to understand the position of Kashmir, although it is full of technicalities and written in a dry business-like technical spirit, but his narrative is enlivened occasionally by the most horrible statements as to the condition of Kashmir. Let me say this gentleman was eighteen months among the people surveying in Kashmir and Jummoo, and he appears to have gone to work in a dry business-like fashion In these Oriental States we know that the foundation of the happiness of the people consists in the correct measurement of their land. The first thing Mr. Wingate discovered was that the measurement of the land upon which the ryots paid their rent was altogether measured against the ryots.

Mr. BRADLAUGH : Does the right hon. gentleman represent that in any way that this was done under the direction of the Maharaja?

Sir JOHN GORST: The evil existed under the Government of the Maharaja and it was approved by the Maharaja's Government there.

Mr. BRADLAUGH: Mr. Wingate's report referred to the existing state of things. Part of the condition of things that existed over Kashmir it was no part of the misgovernment of the Maharaja.

Sir JOHN GORST: It is part of the condition of things in Kashmir under a government of which the Maharaja was the head. I do not know whether the Maharaja shields himself under the allegation that all this had happened in the past and that he was not responsible for the misgovernment which he allowed to exist. I don't think this House will take such a view of the limitations of the Maharaja's duties to his subjects. Besides, we have read Mr. Plowden's report, in which it is stated that the Maharaja opposed those reforms he himself considered necessary. Even the assessment of the ryots is arbitrarily fixed, and a divisional official gets the revenue out of the unhappy cultivators in the best way he can—the result being that from one-half to two- thirds of the gross produce of the land was exacted from these unhappy people, mostly in kind and partly also in cash.

Mr. BRADLAUGH: Does not Mr. Wingate say that began as far back as 1874?

Sir J. GORST: I have been reading the report—

Mr. BRADLAUGH: You have not been reading at all.

Sir J. GORST: The hon. member challenged me to say what the misgovernment was in Kashmir.

Mr. BRADLAUGH: I challenged the right hon. gentleman to prove misgovernment on the part of the Maharaja.

Sir J. GORST: I am in the recollection of the House. I appeal to hon. members whether, if the case rested solely on the speech of the hon. member for Northampton, they would not have gone away in the belief that Kashmir was the best-governed country in the world. I am showing what was the state of affairs which compelled the Government of India to take this action. I am going to show the House why the Government in the interests of humanity were peremptorily called upon to take this step. (A laugh.) The hon member may laugh, but I think it is not a laughing matter. Now let me describe what was done. The assessment was paid at fixed rates in kind: that is to say it was levied on the people in money value and then they were made to give produce at certain fixed and prescribed rates in lieu of paying the assessment in cash. In the case of rice, the main staple which the ryots cultivated, the prescribed rate was extremely unfavourable to the cultivator— All this is in Mr. Wingate's report, and if I am epitomising it unfairly the hon. member can subsequently correct me. I do not see why he should interrupt me now.—But the prescribed rates for cotton, which is grown by the richer ryots, were very favourable therefore it came to this: that the officers of the Revenue allowed the rich ryots to pay on the staple bearing the most favourable rate while the poor ryots had to pay on the staple bearing the most unfavourable rates; and every year, says Mr. Wingate in his report "the bulk of the rice goes into the city", and further, he adds. "these poor ryots often have to buy it back at two or three times the price at which it was credited to them in their assessment", and then this dry technical report contains this statement—"In this fertile valley there are women and children actually starving." Further on it says: "It may be easier now to understand why the Kashmiri cares naught for rights in land, why his fields are fallow or full of weeds, and manure and water neglected; why he has, as I can well believe, even to be forced to cultivate. The revenue system is such, that whether he works much or little he is left with barely enough to get along on till next harvest. He is a machine to produce shall for a very large and most idle city population".

Mr. MACNEILL: Like Ireland!

Sir J. GORST: A city, the population of which consists of officials and of Hindoo pundits who have prepared the brief from which the hon. member for Northampton spoke. These men get their rice cheap, while the ryot who grows it and is forbidden to dispose of it for export, starves. Again, Mr. Wingate says that "the cultivator is compelled to grow rice, and in many years to part with it below the proper market rate in order that the city may be content. If the harvest is too little for both the city must be supplied, and is supplied by any force that may be necessary, and the cultivator and his children must go without. That is the explanation of the angry discontent that filled the valley during the famine.

The cultivator is considered to have rights neither to his land nor to his crops. The city population have a right to be well fed whether there is famine or not", and that is not all; the officials of the revenue contractors are gradually in Kashmir converting themselves into landlords. They get grants of waste land, they foreclose upon ryots who are indebted, and they purchase a considerable part of the land, and as Mr. Wingate says: "Since the death of the Maharaja Golab Singh, from which date central authority appears to have been weaker, there has been a steadily, and latterly, rapidly increasing transference of land from the cultivating to the non-cultivating classes, and a landlord element is intruding itself between the cultivator and the state." I earnestly commend this to the attention of some of the hon. members from Ireland. Then, besides this, there exists among the unhappy ryots a system of begar, or forced labour. This scourge which is peculiar to the Government villages, and from which the villages which happen to be in the hands of these landlords are free is imposed upon the people with the utmost severity.

Mr. BRADLAUGH: I venture to make an appeal to the right hon. gentleman. I fancy that by the rules of the House I have no right of reply. I wish to ask him, in reference to this forced labour, whether it is not a fact that the system prevailed long before the death of the father of this unfortunate gentleman, and whether the Maharaja did not himself issue a decree abolishing it.

Mr. SPEAKER: Order, order! I may explain that the hon. member will be entitled to reply, and it would be more convenient than to interrupt the right hon. gentleman.

Mr. BRADLAUGH: I will, sir, at once take advantage of the right of reply which you have ruled rests with me. The point I wish to state is so important that I think it better to put it before the House at once. I say that the report of Mr. Wingate refers to no specific act of misgovernment by the deposed Maharaja. It relates a state of things which obtained long prior to the Maharaja's birth, and which he has himself partially remedied since his accession to power. In September 1885 he actually issued a decree abolishing forced labour both in Kashmir and in Jammu so far as he could. For three years this unfortunate man step by step took up reforms, and in one of his despatches he speaks of the settlement of the land question as a task which it would take five years to deal with.

I never said that the Government of Kashmir was perfect, on the contrary, I said that, like all Oriental governments, it had many defects, and that the people of Kashmir were in a state of misery and difficulty from which millions of the population of India were not free. I repeat that no specific act of misgovernment has been even pretended to be proved against the Maharaja, and that so far as Mr. Plowden's report is concerned the decision of the Government of India itself was that it did not justify any interference on their part.

Mr. MACNEILL (Donegal Co.); The Under Secretary for India is always interesting and his great abilities add additional charms to what he says. But on this occasion I think it was scarcely fair in accusing me of smiling at the sufferings of these people. I see too much suffering to regard it otherwise than with infinite sorrow and sympathy. What I smiled at was this. Knowing as I do the in famous transactions and secret springs which I intend to expose, I smiled that a gentleman representing a Government guilty of such conduct should claim universal benevolence and pretend to be benefiting the people, whereas they are robbing an ancient prince of his inheritance. The right hon. gentleman was careful to put forward the religious question, and to point out that the Maharaja was an Hindu while his subjects were Muhammadans. But I can tell him that if he would take a plebiscite of the inhabitants of Kashmir he would find that three-fourths of the people favoured the restoration of the prince.

We know that forty millions of our subjects in India are in a constant state of starvation, and that during the famine in 1877 the number of deaths from famine exceeded the population of London. Surely our efforts at administration in India have not been so successful as to justify our bringing more of the natives under our system? I heard the speech of the right hon. gentleman, and I must confess I thought it a most shifting defence. I think I shall be enabled to prove that the Maharaja has been deprived of his inheritance simply by the pursuance of an annexation policy, which was the approximate cause of the Indian Mutiny. What has happened is what is called in Ireland "land grabbing". The Maharaja, who was placed in his position many years ago, has displayed nothing but kindness and loyalty to the British rule. He was placed on that throne, and it was reserved to him and his heirs, and in the meantime he has acted well towards this country. With regard to the letters on which so much stress has been laid, none of them have been read to the House.

Dr. HUNTER: Mr. Speaker, the defence which has been offered on the part of the Government does not explain the degradation from his rank of the Maharaja of Kashmir, an act of unjustifiable spoliation. One remark with which the Under Secretary of State wound up his remarks, intended to be eloquent, was an appeal to this House on behalf of the poor Moslem cultivators. Why the Moslem cultivator? Surely a Hindu, if he happens to be a cultivator, is as much entitled to sympathy as the Moslem. But the right hon. gentleman laid stress on the word Moslem, in order to excite those unhappy religious prejudices which unfortunately prevail in India. We know that in India, unhappily, both Moslems and Hindus are animated by strong fanatical opinions on the subject of religion, leading to collisions and breaches of the peace. And here is the Under Secretary for India in this House pointing his moral by the contrast between the Moslem and the Hindu peasants, and trying thus to fan the members of religious antipathy.

What are the reasons which he adduced why the Maharaja should be deposed. Not one of the reasons had the slightest relation to anything that was done by the Maharaja of Kashmir himself. That I pass by. But what is the state of the country upon which he relies. There were three arguments. The first argument was that in consequence of the mismanagement of the revenue derived from the land, there was a great deal of poverty in the country, and that the population had largely diminished. Well, I was amazed to hear a minister sitting on that side of the House using that as an argument why the Maharaja of Kashmir should be deposed; because the Maharaja has equally good reason for deposing you from the government of Ireland, if that argument has any validity whatever. But that is not the only thing. We are told that the land revenue is extortionate. That is no doubt the reason why you are putting out the Maharaja and putting in yourselves. There is no doubt a margin, a large margin, which excites the cupidity of the British Government, and induces them to take possession of that country. But all this argument simply comes to this point, that according to the view of the Government of India, the ancient, not the recent, mode of collecting the revenue from the land is defective, and that oppressions arise in the exercise of the right; so that, according to the eloquent language of the right hon. gentleman, the people are starving in the midst of plenty. That is precisely the condition of things in Ireland. The case of Ireland is an analogous case. Not a single argument adduced by the right hon. gentleman in reference to Kashmir but is applicable to Ireland, in the eyes of impartial people living outside the latter country. I am afraid the transaction is a very doubtful one, when it has to be supported by such statements as those which have been advanced by the Under Secretary of State.

Sir R. TEMPLE: Mr. Speaker, I feel bound to trouble the House for a very few moments on this subject, because I am one of those members who happen to know this country. I have travelled over every portion of it repeatedly, and for years I was officially connected with it. And though I never had the pleasure of knowing the Maharaja of Kashmir personally, unless I may have seen him as a child, yet I knew his father well, and I knew his grandfather also, and I may say well. Now, sir, much has been said by the hon. member for Northampton and by the hon. member for South Donegal, and again by the hon. member for Abedeen, who has just sat down, regarding the ambitious or greedy eye which England has cast upon Kashmir. Indeed, in effect, the language used by hon. members implied the charge that England is attempting a theft of territory. Indeed the hon. member for Northampton exhausted the resources of phraseology in order to accuse his country of appropriating the lands of others.

But is the House aware that England gains not one rood by the transactions which are now under consideration? All that happens is the transfer of the sovereignty from one brother to another. The power, the wealth, the property, remain in the same family; it is a mere exchange from one person to another.

England remains exactly in the same position as she was before, and is in no wise benefitted. She has acted with entire disinterestedness, and whether she is wrong or whether she is right, her sole object has been to benefit the people of Kashmir. What ground has the hon. member for South Donegal for saying that we want a frontier there.

I am afraid the hon. member does not know what our frontiers are. We have no military frontiers in that direction. It is not from there that we should be invaded. No, sir, the mighty mountains of the Himalaya constitute an impassable barrier to any enemy, either from Asia or from Europe. Then, sir, the hon. member for Aberbeen seemed to find fault with my right hon. friend the Under Secretary for saying that the Moslem of Kashmir must be protected. The hon. member entirely misapprehended my right hon. friend's meaning. What my right hon. friend meant was this, that the Maharaja of Kashmir was a Hindu potentate, and that we interfered by force of arms to place him over a Moslem population—a population which was not Hindu at all by allegiance or by tradition.

They were therefore placed under an alien prince by the action of the British Government. My right hon. friend meant to say that we were bound to see that the Moslem population suffered nothing at the hands of the Hindu masters whom we had put over them. Then the hon. member for Aberdeen spoke of the gratitude which we owe the Maharaja of Kashmir. I am not prepared to deny that sovereigns of this house have behaved well. The grandfather co-operated with us during the darkest days of the mutiny. But after all the gratitude was due from him to us rather than from us to him. He was our ally. We had placed him on the throne for political reasons of our own, and he was bound to act for us when we required his services. Something has been said of the several British residents.

I was grieved to hear the terms of disparagement in which the hon. member for Northampton spoke of those most able servants of the state. At all events, they have no party purpose to serve; they are above partisan considerations. They may, like all men, be liable to error, but they are completely disinterested, and their action is based on perfect impartiality. In this case it was not one or two, but three residents—men of different ideas, but who all come to the same conclusion respecting the Government of Kashmir. Then, sir, regarding the misgovernment, I quite admit that reforms were at one time introduced and carried out to a considerable extent.

I myself in former days have been witness to them. But I am afraid those reforms came to a sudden termination. But, sir, much was said, and with great truth, by my right hon. friend with respect to the mismanagement of the land revenues and the gross oppression which was practised upon the ryots. I quite admit that the abuses are not recent, and the report which has been read to-night is only an enlargement of what I used to hear in former years. But I am afraid that the evils have now reached alarming proportions, perhaps even a monstrous development. The hon. member for Aberdeen speaks of the decreasing population.

Of all countries, Kashmir is the most favoured in climate. It may be severely cold in winter, but in summer it is fertile and bountiful as any place in the world. That its population is decreasing is a sign of misgovernment. I quite admit that there may have been outbreaks of cholera and other epidemics, but as for famine it is the last place in the world where such a calamity could be expected. The question comes what is the nature of the misgovernment? Well now, I submit that that is a question which should be left to the responsible government on the spot. I submit it is our duty to see that a good government is set up in that Empire. But when that has been set up do not harass it, or interfere with it or try to establish committees of inquiry here to investigate the matters, but accept the advice of the responsible authorities. If you are to have a Government at all we must trust to judge of these questions. There is, we are told, a bad system in this State, that the population is decreasing, property is not secure, that communications are not looked after, that the whole land is going rapidly to ruin, and that all departments are falling to a low level. But how are we to examine into these matters by an inquiry such as is asked for? These are the very things which are within the purview of Government and cannot be tested by judicial process. We all know how that would end. It would end in the acquittal of the charged. All these matters should be left to the Governor-General in Council, and to him we should entrust the responsibility. An inquiry such as is now proposed would have a bad effect in India. The hon. member for Northampton speaks as if this political measure of superseding the Maharaja of Kashmir would have a bad effect; but I can assure him that to have an inquiry of this kind, in which the whole government of Kashmir would be overhauled, would be a measure above all others which would be calculated to alarm and would be repugnant to those very persons whom he proposes to serve.

Sir UGHTRED KAY-SHUTTLEWORTH: In this debate we have been placed under this disadvantage, that the papers relating to Kashmir are not yet in the hands of members. But by the courtesy of the right hon. gentleman (Sir John Gorst), I have had the advantage of perusing these papers for a short time and it is only fair that I should rise to say, that so far as I can judge from a hasty persual of the papers and following carefully the speech of the right hon. gentleman, he has stated the case as regards the action of successive Viceroys and successive Secretaries of State in their relation to the late Maharaja of Kashmir and the present Maharaja with perfect fairness. I may venture to say one or two words more as to whether the facts which have been laid before us show a necessity for such an inquiry as is asked for.

I believe if hon. members will examine these papers they will find that there is nothing in them to call for a review by a Parliamentary Committee of the patient and deliberate action of the Government of India, who seem to have hesitated long before taking any strong step, although the misgovernment of the Maharaja has been, I fear, of a very glaring description. I would only venture to make this one remark. It should be a satisfaction to members on this side of the House to find with respect to the Government of India that it has not been drawn into the annexation policy, which my hon. friend (Mr. Bradlaugh) deprecates, but that it leaves the government of Kashmir under a council of natives of India, guided by the Resident of India; and in concluding a despatch addressed by the Viceroy of India to the Maharaja of Kashmir, the Viceroy treats him with the greatest consideration and courtesy, and expresses a hope that it may be possible to give greater power to him in the future. At present the Maharaja is put in an ornamental position. He is not deposed but simply relieved of the powers of ruler of the country and these powers are confided to a council. I hope therefore the House will pause before voting for this motion.

Sir. WM. PLOWDEN: I will not detain the House for more than a few minutes, but I am not at all satisfied with the statement of the Under Secretary of State for India. The course of the debate has rather taken us from the point we ought to have before us, and I am very much surprised to hear the remarks which have fallen from the hon. member who has just spoken, in face of the glaring case which has been made by the member for Northampton. The member for Northampton is condemning the action of the Government of India, and is asking the House to express its sense of the course taken by the Government of India with respect to the Maharaja of Kashmir, and his complaint is that they have not given this man a chance of clearing himself from the charges which have been brought against him. It is not to a Parliamentary inquiry that this man's chance of clearing himself is to be entrusted. Why should we not have a judicial inquiry, and why is it that the Government are refusing to give this man a real investigation into the charges made against him. From what we have had brought before us there is real reason to believe that not only has considerable misgovernment been going on in Kashmir, now and in previous reigns, but that there has been no reproof administered as to this misgovernment. The right hon. gentleman asks us are we going to stand in the way of justice being done in Kashmir, but is he going to stand in the way of justice being done to the Maharaja? If he asserts that he (the Maharaja) is innocent of the charges brought against him.

Sir JOHN GORST: There are no charges.

Sir W. PLOWDEN: Then if there are no charges why is he deposed? Evidently there must be some misconduct attributed to this man, in fact we know there is, because the whole defence put up by the Government is that he has been misconducting the government, and because he has been doing so he has been deposed. He says, "I have not misconducted the government. I am not guilty, and I ask to have my case inquired into." If the hon. member for Northampton pressed his motion to a division I shall be bound to support him unless we get a clear assertion from the right hon. gentleman that he will send out instructions to the Government of India to form some judicial Commission which shall inquire into the charges alleged.

The House divided:

Ayes	.. ..	88
Noes	.. ..	226
Majority		138

The motion for the adjournment of the House was therefore lost.

DIVISION LIST
AYES

W. Abraham (Glamorgan), W. Abraham (Limerick), J. Austin, W.H. W. Ballantine, J. Barran, M.H. Beaufoy, A. Blane, T.D. Bolton (Derbyshire), Henry Campbell (Fermanagh), F.A. Channing, J.J. Clancy, Dr. G.B. Clark (Caithnesshire), H.P. Cobb, W.J. Cobet (Wicklow), D. Crilly, J.J Dallon, J. Dilon, L.L. Dilwyn, S. Evershed, J.C. Flynn, Dr. J.F. Fox, T. Fry (Darlington), E. T. Gourley, E. Harrington (Kerry), H. Harrison, L.P. Hayden, G. Howell, J.A. Jacoby, J.S. Keay, D. Kilbride,, D. Knatchbull-Hugessen (Rochdale), R. Lalor, Sir W. Lawson (Cumberland), J. Leahy (Kildare), R. Leake, T.P. Lewis, (Angelsey), W.A. Macdonald, J.G.S.MacNeill, Dr. R. M'Donald (Ross), J.R. Maguire, W. Mather, S. Montagu, A.C. Morton, J. Nolan (Louth), J.F.X. O'Brien (Mayo), P.J. O'Brien (Tipperary), W.O'Brien (Cork, N.E.), A. O'Connor (Donegal), J. O'Connor (Tipperary), J. O'-Kelly, C.S. Parnell, J.W. Philipps, E.H. Pickersgill, Sir W.C. Plowden, T.P. Price (Monmouthshire), D. Randell, W.H.K. R-Redmond (Fermanagh), Sir E.J. Reed (Cardiff), J. Roberts (Flint Burghs), T. Robinson (Gloucester), T. Roe, J. Rowlands (Finsbury), W.B. Rowlands (Cardiganshire), J. Rowntree, C.E. Schwann, T. Sexton, T. Shaw (Halifax), J.D. Sheehan, F.F.Stevenson (Suffolk), J.C. Stevenson (S. Shields), H. Stewart (Lincolnshire), J. Stuart (Shoreditch), D. Sullivan, (Westmeath), T.D. Sullivan (Dublin), A. Sutherland (Sutherlandshire), A. Thomas (Glamorgan E.), D.A. Thomas (Merthyr), J. Tuite, Captain E.H Verney, S.D. Waddy, H. Wardel, A. Webb, J.S. will, A. Williams (Glamorgan), S. Williamson (Kilmarnock), J. Wilson (Lanark), J. Woodhead, C. Wright (Lanc. S.W.), Tellers for the Ayes, Mr. Bradlaugh and Mr. Hunter.

NOES.

W.G. Ainslie, J. Aird, Hon. P. Allsopp (Taunton), W. Ambrose, W.A.T. Amherst, H.T. Anstruther (St. Andrews), Colonel L. Anstruther (Suffolk), E. Ashmead)Bartlett, H.H.

Asquith, Sir G.S. Baden-Powell, J.G.A. Baird, Rt. Hon. A.J. Balfour (Manchester), T.C. Baring (London), A. Barnes, A.H.S. Barry (Hunts), G.C. T. Bartley, Sir W.B. Barttelot, Sir E. Bates, A.A. Baumann, Rt. Hon. Sir M.H. Beach (Bristol), W.W,B. Beach (Hants.), E.W. Beckett (Yorks., N.R.), W. Beckett (Notts), W.G.C. Bentinck (Penryn), Commander Bethell, J. Bigwood, A. Birrell, Col. H.B.H. Blundell, G.H. Bond, T.W. Boord, Sir A. Borthwick, Col. Hon. F. C. Bridgeman, Hon. St. J. Brodrick, A. M. Brookfield, Sir W.C. Brooks, A.H. Brown (Salop), G. Bruce (Finsbury), Lord H. Bruce (Wiltshire). W. Burdett-Coutts, J. Caldwell, Sir G. Campbell (Kirkcaldy), Marquis of Carmarthen, Rt. Hon. J. Chamberlain (Birmingham), R. Chamberlain (Islington), Rt. Hon. H. Chaplin, Sir E. Clarke (Plymouth), D. H. Coghill, J. Collings, Sir J.C.R. Colomb, C.W.R. Cooke, J. Corbett (Worecestershire), F.S.W. Cornwallis, Sir J.P. Corry Col. E.T.D. Cotton, H.H. Cozens-Hardy, Viscount Cranborne, H.S. Cross (Bolton), Hon. W.H. Cross (Liver- pool), Sir S.B. Crossley (Suffolk), General Sir W. Crossman, Rt. Hon. G. Cubitt, Hon. G.N. Curzon (Lanc.,S.W.), H.J.C. Cust, M.T.S. Darling (Edinburgh), H.T. Davenport (Staffordshire), E.F.D. Dixon-Hartland, R.S. Donkin, Sir J.E. Dorington, R.W. Duff, J.S. Dugdale, Rt. Hon. Sir W.H. Dyke, T.C. Edewards-Moss, Hon. Art. R.D. Elliot (Roxburghs), G.W. Elliot (Yorks.N.R.), P Esslemont, Sir A.O. Ewing, Col. H. Eyre, Lieut.-Gen. Feilden (Lane.N.), A.E. Fellowes R.C.M. Ferguson (Leith), Rt. Hon. Sir J. Fergusson (Manchester), Admiral Field, G.H. Finch, W.H. Fisher, Sir F. Fitz-Wygram, Sir H. Fletcher, C. Flower, A.B. Forwood, Sir R.N. Fowler (London), Gen. C.C. Fraser, L. Fry (Bristol), S. Gedge, J. S. Gilliat, Major-Gen. Goldsworthy, Rt. Hon. Sir J. E. Gorst, Rt. Hon. G.J. Goschen, G.G.L. Gower, Sir E. Green (Wakefield), E. Greene (Suffolk), Viscount Grimston, F.B. Grotrian, R.B. Haldane, Rt. Hon. Lord G. Hamilton (Middlesex), Gen. Sir E.B Hamley, R.W. Hanbury, E. Hardcastle (Salford), Sir E.J. Harland, Marquis of Hartington. A.R. Health, Rt. Hon. E. Heneage, Hon. S. Herbert, Lord F. Hervey, Lord A.W. Hill (Down), Col. E.S. Hill (Bristol), E.B. Hoare (Hampstead), Sir W.H. Houldsworth, J.H.C. Hozier,

F.S. Hunt, Sir G. Hunter (Hackney), Rt. Hon. W.L. Jackson, Sir R. Jardine, A.W. Jarvis, A.F. Jeffreys, L.J. Jennings, W. Johnston, Rt. Hon. Sir U.Kay- Shuttleworth, Sir J.H. Kennaway, W. Kenrick, Hon. G.T. Kenyon, Col. W. Kenyon-Slaney, H Kimber, Sir J.G.S. Kinloch, H. Knatchbull-Hugessen (Kent), L. Knowles, A. Lafone, W.F. Lawrence (Liverpool), E. Lees, T.W. Legh (Lane.), Lord W.C.G. Lennox, Sir R. Lethbridge, Viscont Lewisham, E.H. Llewellyn, G.W.E. Loder, W.H. Long, J.W. Lowther (Cumberland), `Hon. W. Lowther (Westmoreland), L. Lyell, W.G.E. Macartney, C.F. Mackintosh, F.W. Maclean (Oxfordsh.), J.M. Maclean (Oldham), J.W. Maclure, Captain J. M'Calmont, D.H. Madden, W.F. Maithland, Col. J.W. Malcdm, RRt. Hon. E. Marrjoribanks, M.H. Story-Maskelyne, Rt. Hon. H. Matthews, Sir H.E. Maxwell, A.R.C. Mayne, F.B. Mildmay, T. Milvain, R.J. More, Hon. F. Morgan (Monmouthshire, Rt. Hon. G.O. Morgan (Denbighshire), W. Morrison, W.G. Mount, R.G.C. Mowbray (Lane. S.E., P.A. Muhtz, Viscount Newark, Hon. R.T. O'Neill, Sir R.H. Paget, Hon. F. Parker (Oxfords.), Sir L. Pelly, Captain F.T. Penton, Rt. Hon. D.R. Plunket, W.C. Quilter, J. Rankin, Major F.C. Rasch, H.B. Reed (Bradford), T. Richardson, Rt. Hon. C.T. Ritchie, J.B. Roberts (Eifion), Rt. Hon. J.P.B. Robertson (Bute), Baron F.J.de Rothschild, J. Round, T.B. Royden, T. Salt, G.B. Samuelson (Gloucester), Col. E.J. Saunderson, Captain C.W. Selwyn, M.H. Shaw-Stewart (Renfrew), J.W. Side-botham (Cheshire), T.H. Sidebottom (Stalybridge), W. Sidebottom (Derbyshire), W.P. Sinclair, J.P. Smith (lanarksh.), Rt. Hon. W.H. Smith (Strand), J. Somervell, Rt. Hon.E.Stanhope(Lincolnsh.),E.J. Stanley, M. Stewart (Kirkeudbrightsh.), T. Sutheland (Greenock), J.G. Talbot, T.K. Tapling, F. Taylor, Sir R. Temple, J. Theobald, W. Thorburn, W.E.M. Tomlinson, F. Townsend, Sir H.W. Tyler, Hon. A.H.J. Walsh, Sir R.E. Webster (Isle of Wight), W.C. West, Viscount Weymouth, E. Whitley, H. Wiggin, Hon. R. Winn, Viscount Wolmer, N. Wood, H.S. Wright (Nottingham). Tellers for the Noes, Mr. Akers-Douglas and Sir William Walrond.

KASHMIR AND KHIVA

The history of the Russian annexation and absorption of Khiva is one of dissimulation and disgrace, and may be told in few words. On the 8th of January, 1873, Earl Granville, wrote to Lord A. Loftus, the English Ambassador at St. Petersburgh, with reference to the then contemplated Russian expedition against Khiva, that he had a personal interview with Count Schouvalow, by special request of the Czar, who had informed him, that the sole object of the expedition was to punish certain acts of brigandage by the Khan's subjects. 'Not only,' writes Lord Granville, 'was it far from the intention of the Emperor to take possession of Khiva, but positive orders had been prepared to prevent it. He gave me,' he adds, 'the most decided assurance that I might give positive assurances to Parliament on this matter.' The despatch goes on to state, that Lord Northbrook, then Viceroy of India had "given the strongest advice to the Khan to comply with the reasonable demands of the Emperor, and if the expedition were undertaken with the object and within the limits described by Count Schouvalow, it would meet with no remonstrance from Her Majesty's Government.' Unfortunate Khan of Khiva, with Russia lusting for annexation, and Great Britain (of all Powers!) counselling submission! The result is a matter of history. The Russian troops had a 'walk over' into Khiva, and the Treaty which General Kauffman dictated, literally at the point of the sword, to-day gives the lie to Count Schouvalow's pacific assurance.

The Treaty commences in this wise: 'The whole of the right bank of the Amou Darya and the lands adjoining thereunto, which have hitherto been considered as belonging to Khiva, shall pass over from the Khan into the possession of Russia, together with the people dwelling and camping thereon, etc. In the examination of claims between Russians and Khivans, preference shall be given to Russians. Complaints and claims of Khivans against Russian subjects shall be referred to the nearest Russian Authorities. A fine is inflicted on the Khanate of Khiva of two million two hundred thousand roubles (about £ 300,000) in order to cover the expenses incurred by the Russian Exchequer in the prosecution of the late war which was provoked (??) by the Government of the Khan.' Und so weiter. And thus, poor Khiva has been Russianised, at the expense of the blood and wealth of the Children of her soil, while Russia has consequently crept up to within a hundred miles or so nearer of her sole perspective aim and design—the Frontier of British India. All the while, Great Britain, the Power and interested, has according to the despatch of her Foreign Minister, 'offered no opposition' to this wholesale spoliation of one of the outlying bulwarks of defence against Muscovite aggression. On the contrary, she seems rather to admire Russian diplomacy, with its misleading tactics, its false assurances, and its questionable modes of territorial acquisition, and has tried her hand too, a la Russe, that is to say employing the same weapons, in the absorption of Kashmir,—the British Khiva.

Consider we now for a while the modus operandi employed to anglicanise poor Kashmir, and the intelligent reader cannot fail to be struck with the similarity of the means used by the Russians in Khiva and and the English in Kashmir, and can also draw his own conclusions from the political parallel. Imprimus,—of course it was necessary to throw dust in the eyes of our interested neighbours and especially essential was it that England should blind, or try to blind, Russia as to her real intentions regarding Kashmir. Hence, we find both Lord Cross and Sir John Gorst repeatedly and, it appeared to many, unnecessarily, giving the most emphatic explanatory assurances of England's non-intervention,—assurances every whit as unmistakable as those given by the Czar of Russia regarding Khiva. England, we were informed, has not now, nor has she at any time ever had the slightest intention of 'annexing' Kashmir. True, the British Schouvalow did not define his interpretation of the word 'annexing' and herein lies the key of the whole matter.

England might have sought a quarrel with Kashmir, invaded and conquered that country, and then 'squeezed' a war indemnity out of her, thus following the precedent of Russia in Khiva. But, thought John Bull submitted quietly to the Khivan aggression which permitted his foes (to use a Russian expression) 'to sit down' almost at his very door, he knew full well, that Russia would make a very positive and practical 'remonstrance' against the actual annexation of Kashmir by England. Hence, quite a different line of policy had to be observed. After having satisfied the world at large by repeated and plausible assurances that her intentions towards Kashmir were strictly honourable and purely philanthropic, England proceeds, to lay that country at her feet by moral, not military, pressure. First, the Ruler is deposed for no reason except that he was in the way of the Scheme. Then, Rulers, in the shape of a Council, are appointed by England, being controlled and directed by an English Resident. Then, Kashmir is compelled to make a costly military road from the British frontier to her capital. Then, the control of the Kashmir army obtained, and the troops are placed under British officers, while a military colony, under the guise of post of observation, is established at Gilgit. And, lastly, Kashmir is made bankrupt by forced expenditure and a forced loan, and to- day, as we said before, lies as much at the mercy and under the dominion of England as though she had been formerly and officially annexed by that ever-absorbing Power. When comparing the Russian and English methods of extending their frontier by annexation, the balance to the credit of England lies solely in the fact of non-invasion and consequent saving of bloodshed. The violated assurances, the deprivation of power, the transfer to British rule the pecuniary requisitions, all remain the same, and, as surely and certainly as the Agent of the Czar of all the Russians rules and controls the destinies of subjugated Khiva, so surely and certainly does the Agents of the Queen-Empress of India rule and control those of the no less subjugated Kashmir.

D
THE ALLEGED REAL OBJECT OF THE DEPOSITION OF THE MAHARAJA
(Indian Union, Allahabad, June 19.)

THE Foreign Office confidential Memo on Gilgit, published by the Amrita Bazar Patrika, created a sensation that is far from dead yet. In the controversy that caused the Editor by no means came off second best, for the honours of war remained with him decidedly. In fact, the dealings of the Indian Government with Kashmir can only be explained on the basis of the Gilgit memorandum. In the March and April numbers of the Fortnightly Review, an article contributed by Sir Charles Dilke rather tends to establish the Gilgit memorandum on a yet firmer basis. It seems to show that, as early as the autumn of 1888, the practical deposition of the Maharaja and the annexation of Kashmir had been secretly resolved on at Simla. It must be borne in mind that the cock and bull story of the Jammu forgeries did not originate till the spring of 1889. Sir Charles Dilke landed in Kurrachee in November, 1888, as the honoured guest of Sir Frelerick Roberts. January, 1889, saw his return home again. Sir charles Dilke was sorely wanted to popularize among the public of England the Indian Scientific Frontier Defence expenditure. To this end all the secrets of the Military and Foreign Offices were laid bare to him. At page 474 we find Sir Charles Dilke writing:-'The armies of the Native States are being dealt with by the provision of British Inspection, and a beginning has been made in the Punjab, It will be possible to make of the army of Kashmir a very useful force for watching the passes on the Kashmir, side, to the great relief of our field army; but I continue to retain the view with which I went to India, that the armies of the great southern feudatory States should be disbanded as such, that is, reduced merely to police guards.' At page 480 Sir Charles Dilke again writs:-'No large Russian army can venture across the mountains of Chitral or descend upon Kabul from Balkh by the Hindukush. Sir Charles MacGregor, who was there writing of what he knew, has proved this to demonstration, although he did not make the allowance that all would who know Russia, for the use of sledges over the passes in winter time. That the attempt would be made by a small force in case of war is certain. Steps have now been taken to stop any such force descending upon the plains of India without drawing upon our main field army. Colonel Maurice seems to think that a Russian descent from the North might take us in the flank: a small force no doubt might pass by Gilgit towards Kashmir, a small force by Chirtal towards Jellalabad, and a small force by Balkh to Kabul; but until—should this unhappily come about—the Russians have been long at Balkh, no very serious danger is to be apprehended in this direction.' Sir Charles Dike is here slightly disingenuous, to say the least, for Colonel Lockhardt's mission to Chirtal and recent researches have demonstrated that the Hindukush Range is simply honeycombed with easy passes, and the belief now at Simla is that no Russian invasion of India will be attempted by the Candahar route. These extracts show that Sir Charles Dilke was informed in 1988 of what was intended to be done in Kashmir the following year, 1889, when Colonel Nisbet was sent up to force the situation as an agent provocateur.

(1890)

CHAPTER 4

KASHMIRI PANDITS IN BRITISH INDIA

By

Jia Lal Kilam

I

The rise of British power in India, thanks to its superior organization and diplomacy, led gradually to the breakdown of the Mogul and Marhatta Empires. As a result, the country came to be divided into a number of small principalities which sprang up upon the debris of these once magnificent Imperial structures. In the South Haidar Ali founded an independent State in Mysore, and the breakdown of Peshwa's ascendancy led to the formation of a number of Marhatta States. Asaf Jah installed himself as an independent ruler of Haidarabad. Then there were the Rajputana states, and cis-Satluj Sikh States such as Patiala, Jind, Faridkot Nabha etc.,—the other Sikh Misls having been liquidated by Maharaja Ranjit Singh. The chaos was so general and the breakdown so complete that even European adventurers such as Sombre tried to establish small states here or there. And Sombre did establish one near Delhi in Sardhana where his wife Begum Samru a Kashmiri Muslim girl who later became a Christian ruled as a semi-sovereign for long. In Bengal the British installed a person of their choice, Mir Jaffar by name, on the throne left vacant by Sirajuddowlla. In almost all these States there were Kashmiri Pandits though their role may not have been such as may be called historical. But there they were, at such far off places as Bengal in the East and Mysore in the South. Pandit Ganga Ram who later rose very high at the Sikh Durbar was a great dignitary at Gwalior. It was from there that he migrated with a number of Pandits and later settled at Lahore on the invitation of the Sikh Ruler. Some of them were in Tippu Sultan's Mysore; and in the small principalities of Central India the administration was controlled and carried on mostly by the Pandits. And when the British established their direct rule over the country, they found the Kashmiri Pandits almost everywhere in charge of the lower branches of administration. The British left them at their posts and even meted out great encouragement to them. Their attitude towards this community can be summed up in the words of Mr. George Cempbell who says: "The Kashmiri Brahmins are quite high Aryans in the type. Their features are very fair and handsome, with high chiselled features and no trace of intermixture of the blood of any lower race. It may be partly race and partly occupation but they have certainly a great refinement and regularity of feature.... They rule by the brain and the pen and not by the sword It is this character that has gained them the favour of so many rulers of a different faith. Kashmir long belonged to the Kabul Kingdom, but it was never in any degree colonised by the Afghans... The fact seems to be that the valley never belonged to the Afghan nation, but was always retained as a crown appanage of the kings who were very jealous of admitting into it subjects whom they might find it difficult to turn out again and much preferred to govern through the Pandits.....As a body the Pandits excel in acuteness the same number of any other race with whom they come in contact".

With such an opinion formed by the British about the Kashmiri Pandits it was but natural that the former should have extended their unstinted support to them. The Pandits' knowledge of Persian and Urdu was of a very high order and they had taken to the study of English language much earlier than many others. With the reorganization of courts, they came to be appointed in subordinate Judiciary and many amongst them entered the legal profession, from its very start and became the recipients of highest posts in the judiciary and were the first Indians to be appointed to such posts. Mr. Justice Shambu Nath whose father Sada Sheo had migrated from Kashmir in the closing years of the 18th Century was born at Calcutta in the year 1820 A.D. and was appointed as a Judge of the High Court of Calcutta in 1862 A.D. He was the first Indian to be appointed as the Judge of a High Court. So also was another Kashmiri Pandit Mr. Justice Ram Narain Dar who was the first Indian to be appointed as a Judge of the Punjab Chief Court. In United Provinces where the Kashmiri Pandits had settled in large numbers the leadership at the Bar was for years held by them. To name just a few we might refer to the Hon'ble Ajudhya Nath Kunzru, the Hon'ble Pandit Bishamber Nath, Pandit Bishan Narayan Dar, Bar-at-Law Pandit Jagat Narain Malla, Pandit Brij Narayan Chakbast, Rt. Hon'ble Sir Tej Bahadur Sapru, Pandit Kailas Nath Katju, Pandit Janki Nath Chak and lastly the great Pandit Moti Lal Nehru. All these gentlemen were great nation-builders and took a very prominent part in building the National movement. In the Punjab Pandit Sheonarayan Shamim retained the leadership of the Bar for a number of decades. he was a great poet, a great social reformer, a great student of music and a great Budhist scholar to which faith He held allegiance. Even in recent time there has been a galaxy of eminent Kashmiri Pandit Judges such as Mr. Justice wanchoo Mr. Justice S.K. Dar Mr. Justice Kichlu, Mr. Justice Sapru, Mr. Justice T.N. Mulla. Mr. Justice A.N. Malla Mr. Justice P.K. Kaul Mr. Justice R.K. Kaul etc.

It would not serve any useful purpose to multiply names excepting for the purpose of showing the extent of official rise of this community. In the Punjab, Raja Narendra Nath and Raja Hari Kishen Kaul retired as commissioners. Raja Narendra Nath, a great landowner and a grandson of Adjutant General Diwan Ajudhia Prashad took part in politics after his retirement and was elected to the Punjab Legislative Assembly and was appointed as a Minister. Raja Hari Kishen was appointed as

Chief Minister of the Jammu and Kashmir State at a very troublous period of its history. Sir Ganga Ram Kaula, Pandit Brij Lal Nehru, rose very high in the Audit and Accounts Departments. Sir Ganga Ram is a direct descendant of Prabha Kaul who was wrapped in a mat and thrown into Dal Lake to be drowned there along with a number of Pandits under orders of Mir Hazar Khan, the Afghan Subedar in 1792 A.D. But he was saved and fled to India. After having reached the highest rung in the official ladder Sir Ganga retired, and was afterwards appointed as the Chief Minister of Jind State where he served as such for about eleven years. Pandit Manmohan Nath Kaul whose services were lent to Kashmir Durbar was appointed as Governor of Kashmir. Apart from the settlement work which was achieved under his supervision in 1901 A.D. he was a great social reformer. It was he who introduced modern ways of living in the local Pandit population. There is hardly a state in India where at one time or the other a Kashmiri Pandit was not appointed as a Diwan. For instance, Sir Pandit Daya Kishen Kaul was the Chief Minister of Patiala State, Sir Sukhdev Prashad Kak Diwan of Jodhpur, Dharam Narayan Haksar Diwan of Sailana State, Pandit Ram Chandra Kak Chief Minister of Jammu and Kashmir State, Pandit Brij Mohan Nath Zutshi Diwan of Ratlam State, Pandit Maharaja Narain Sheopuri Dewan of Datia State etc. There were other Pandits who were appointed as Ministers in many states, such as, Pandits Col. Sir Kailas Narayan Haksar (Gwalior), P.K. Wattal, (Kashmir,) Radha Krishen Kaul (Kashmir), Diwan Gyan Nath administrator at Nabha, Tribhuwan Nath Sopori (Udaipur), Amar Nath Atal (Jaipur), Narendre Nath Kaul (Kashmir) etc. The last named was a great administrator who solved the problem of the distribution of food grains in Kashmir in a most rational and scientific manner. His name is a byword in Kashmir and the magnificent institution known as Food Control Department built by him and which has stood the test of more than three decades is a living monument to his greatness.

How so ever high positions the Kashmiri Pandits may have achieved in the administration of the country, yet all this pales into insignificance before the magnificent role that they played in building the National Movement. Their urge for freedom their patriotic fervour and singleminded devotion to the cause of their country has carved a place of honour for them in the History of India. It was in the year 1885 A.D. that National Congress was founded. Many Kashmiri Pandits associated themselves with the Congress from its very inception. Even before its birth Pandit Ajudhy-Nath Kunzru started a paper, Indian Herald, in 1879 A.D. which adopted a strong nationalist policy. Ajudhya Nath was a brilliant advocate of his time. He was treated with great consideration and respect by the officials,but he lost caste with them the moment he gave expression to his nationalistic views. Undaunted by official frowns, he went ahead, and joined the National Congress. The fourth session of the Congress was held at Allahabad in 1888 A.D. All sorts of impediments were placed in the path of the organizers of the session by the officials and their non-official supporters. But nevertheless a strong Reception Committee with Pandit Ajudhya Nath as Chairman was formed. Pandit Ajudhya Nath as Chairman was formed. Pandit Ajudhya Nath roused the people with his fiery eloquence. He was ready "to hold the Congress at any cost, wholly at his own expense, if necessary." Pandit Ajudhya Nath had an abundant store of wit and humour which served him well at the most crucial point. He had started a tour of the Provinces for collection of funds for the Allahabad session. The officials and their supporters, side by side with abuse and opposition began to hurl ridicule on the organizers. The Pandit was making an appeal for funds at Agra when oppositionists sent a small boy with a pice to the rostrum, where the boy presented the pice to Ajudhya Nath as a contribution to the Congress. Along with this they shouted and jeered at the Pandit. But Ajudhya Nath at once thundered out that the country was bound to be free where patriotism had found room enough even in the heart of a small boy who having got a pice from his mother offered it to the nation. The pice was put to auction and fetched a few thousands of rupees. He was elected to the U.P. Legislative Council and was a fellow of both the Calcutta and Allahabad universities. He was proposed for the presidentship of Nagpur Congress but before he could preside he was taken seriously ill and breathed his last in the year 1892 A.D. at the age of fifty two years.

There is yet another great Kashmiri Pandit, a close collaborator with Pandit Ajudhya Nath whose contribution to the building up of the Congress movement in its early years has been in no way small or meagre. His name is Pandit Bishambar Nath, a prominent Advocate of Allahabad. He joined the Congress soon after its formation and was elected as the Chairman of the Reception Committee on the occasion of the second Congress session at Allahabad, held in 1892 A.D. On the opening day of the session Pandit Bishambar Nath was taken seriously ill and was advised complete rest by his doctors and friends, but unmindful of his own health and the advice of friends, he attended the session and delivered a very learned address which was greatly appreciated and applauded by the audience. He was elected to the Viceroy's Legislative Council and continued there for a number of years. The depth of his popularity can be gauged from the fact that his return was always uncontested. His Council speeches were brilliant pieces of advocacy characterised by a spirit of fearlessness which should have been unthinkable in eighteen ninety's. After the conviction of Lokmanya Tilak in 1898 A.D. for sedition, the British Government wanted to fight the growing political unrest by further drastic changes in the Penal and Criminal Procedure Codes Pandit Bishambar Nath in his speeches reduced the arguments on the Government side to smithreens and succeeded largely in curbing the mischief that was sought to be done. Pandit Bishamber Nath was proposed for the presidentship, of the Lahore Congress in 1900 A.D., but he refused the honour for reasons of health. He died in the year 1907 A.D. the torch of national service was kept incessantly burning by other men, though small in stature belonging to this community, when we come across with another Kashmiri Pandit by name, Pandit Bishan Narayan Dar, Bar-at-law, who joined the congress with the dawn of the twentieth century. He is the first Kashmiri Pandit to have gone to England for higher studies. Orthodoxy in religion was at its highest then amongst the Kashmiri Pandits and when he came back after having been called to Bar, a howl was raised by a section of Kashmiri Pandits all over India. There were some amongst them who were of the opinion that he could never regain his caste, even after very elaborate Prayachitam, though the Vivasthha of the Pandits from Kashmir was that Pandit Bishan Narayan could be taken back into his caste after due purificatory ceremonies. Pandit Bishan Narayan performed the purificatory rites, and was admitted into their fold by the advanced section of the community, but the more orthodox refused point-blank to have any truck with him. They even nicknamed the advanced Pandits as Bishan Sabhais. For themselves they reserved the pompous title of Dharam Sabhais. There was a huge controversy and apart from any other thing some very good poetry was the result. Pandit Rattan nath Dar Sarshar, a kashmiri poet of Lucknow, has composed some very beautiful verses, called by him as Masnavi in defence of Bishan Narayan. This first public appearance in which Pandit Bishan Narayan made a mark was in the year 1903 at the Madras Congress session, when he moved the resolution on Official Secrets Bill. While moving the resolution, Pandit Bishan Narayan said that "Lord Curzon is astonished that this should be described as Russianizing the administration. I am astonished that any one should be so imperfectly informed regarding the Russian Government as to think that it has got anything in its purely civil Laws so arbitrary and so disastrous to the civil liberties of the people as Lord Curzon's Bill when passed would be in this country". He was elected President of the Congress in 1911 which was held at Calcutta. As President of the Congress he delivered a brilliant address, every word of which breathed a deep sense of patriotism, though as a whole the address was moderate in outlook. No apology is offered to give a rather lengthy excerpt from his address :-

> "The root cause of most of our misfortunes, which if not corrected, forebodes serious disorders in the future, is the growth of an unsympathetic and illiberal spirit in the bureaucracy towards the new born hopes and ideals of the Indian people. While a new India has gradually been rising up, that spirit too has been growing and so a critical situation has arisen. The bureaucracy with its vested interests, its domineering habits, its old traditions of absolute and unquestioned authority, suspicious of knowledge, and averse to innovation like very close corporation, cut off from the people by its racial exclusiveness and wedded to a paternal system of Government under which it has so long enjoyed power and pelf but which is discordant with the more liberal ideas of the day, is antagonistic to the educated classes who are filled with new knowledge and are conscious of their political rights. The Bureaucracy as a body has never been in sympathy with the new aspirations of educated India....
>
> "In the pursuit of a high ideal we must not forget the difficulties that beset our path. Long and weary is the journey that lies before those who undertake to mould a people into the unity of a nation. Our agitation, in order to be effective, must be national, not sectarian, persistent not spasmodic, directed by intelligence and wisdom, and not impulsive and reckless. India needs bold and enthusiastic character, not men of pale hopes, and middling expectations but courageous natives, fanatics in the cause of

their country,

"Whose breath is agitation
And whose life a storm where on they ride".

For such a type of leadership the country had not to wait for long. It was just within less than a decade that there appeared on the political scene some very dynamic personalities "whose breath was indeed agitation and whose life a storm whereon they rode". And it must have been a source of great satisfaction to the departed soul of Pandit Bishan Narayan that this type of leadership was provided by his own community.

Mention may here be made of another Kashmiri Pandit, Mr. Brij Narayan Chakbast, who was a great Urdu poet. Though primarily a poet, he was largely influenced by Pandit Bishan Narayan Dar who infused his own political fervour in him Pandit Bishan Narayan was himself a poet of great merit. Pandit Chakbast resolutionised Urdu poetry in so far as he made a departure from orthodox standards which guided the course of Urdu poetry till then. He is the first Urdu poet who introduced patriotic themes in his poems, and kindled a passion for freedom in the minds of middle class youths in United Provinces. An ardent supporter of Home Rule, a famous line occurring in one of his poems. "We Shall reject even Heaven if offered as an alternative to Home Rule" remained a slogan for long.

Pandit Bishan Narayan Dar died in 1916 A.D. at an early age of fifty two. Soon after did Congress convert itself into a revolutionary body under the unique, unparalleled and unprecedented leadership of Mahatma Gandhi; and with it was a new era introduced in the politics of the country. At the very start of his great movement. Mahatma Gandhi was able to enlist the support of the great Nehrus whose part in building the national movement has been so great that it can be asserted as has been asserted by many without the least fear of contradiction that "the story of the Nehrus is the history of the Indian freedom movement itself". The elder Nehru, Pandit Moti Lal, was in the Congress much earlier than 1907 A.D. Speaking in general terms, he was then quite moderate in politics and was a bitter critic of the advanced section known then as extremists whom he described as mere talkers totally cut off from reality. He was elected as the president of U.P. Congress Provincial Committee and was present at Surat when a schism occurred in the Congress. In short he was not new to the Congress when he later assumed its leadership though his earlier connections with it were that of a "moderate politician".

Mr. C.F. Andrews who has credited Pandit Moti Lal as being "A maker of modern India" has described him in the following words:-

> "Kashmiri Brahmans, to which class Pandit Moti Lal Nehru belonged, are well known all over the north of India both for their intellectual powers and fine appearance. They are by birth, what may truly be called, an aristocratic race, and easily recognized as such. Moti Lal was typical of this distinguished class and in his old age he gained the reputation of being the "aristocrat of the Assembly". His spotless Khaddar dress, with his white Kashmiri shawl, suited him perfectly, and his portrait is rightly given the place of honour in his son's Autobiography. The fine features, which I have mentioned and the fair complexion run through the whole family and have descended from father to son".

Pandit Jawahar Lal has also drawn a portrait of the great Pandit in the following words:-

> "There was in him a strength of personality and a measure of kingliness. In any gathering where he was present he would inevitably be the centre and the hub. Whatever the place he sat at table, it would become, as an English Judge said later, the head of the table. He was neither meek nor mild. Consciously imperious, he created great loyalty as well as bitter opposition. It was difficult to feel neutral about him; one had to like him or dislike him. With a broad forehead, tight lips, and a determined chin he had a marked resemblance to the busts of the Roman Emperors in the museums in Italy. There was a magnificence about him and a grand manner, which is sadly to seek in this world of today".

For his magnificent deeds and achievements, collosal sufferings and sacrifices, Pandit Moti Lal has been quite rightly described as "the father of defiant patriotism" and the "first and foremost pillar of Gandism". Pandit Moti Lal is further described as a great freedom fighter "who transmuted the spineless leadership of the Indian Liberals into a death defying crusade of sterling independence". He was an ardent advocate of Hindu-Muslim unity. The Congress-League Scheme, the first conscious attempt at solving the Hindu-Muslim problem was framed in his house in 1916 A.D. He was apparently very much satisfied with this achievement but his political beliefs were quite in keeping with the Moderate creed though signs were not wanting which pointed that a big change in the mind of Pandit Motilal was in the offing. And the change was soon seen. Afterwards what Pandit Motilal did and what he achieved is a matter of recent history - fresh in men's minds and need not be gone into here with any amount of detail. But it should be noted here that the massacre at Amritsar and the Martial Law atrocities iu the Punjab shook the very foundations of the faith on which his life was hitherto built. And when the call of non-co-operation came, under the leadership of Mahatma Gandhi, he fully responded. No doubt he did it slowly, but did it deliberately realizing all the consequences which it involved. The change-over was not an easy one. Pandit Moti Lal's earnings were very huge and his generosity was equally great. His standard of living was very high. He had many European and Indian friends belonging to high aristocratic circles. To change all this for a life of poverty and privations and give up his huge lucrative practice at the Bar was indeed very difficult. But he did all this. Henceforth his soul did shine in its pristine resplendence and glory. Pandit Moti Lal went to jail many a time. He drafted a constitution for India - now known as Nehru Report, almost single-handed. Twice he presided over the Congress. He organized the first regular opposition in the Assembly and as a leader of opposition and a parliamentary tactician he has not many parallels in the world. His burning patriotism can be gathered from his last political utterance when he said :

> "Decide India's fate in Swaraj Bhawan decide it in my presence and let me be a party to the final honourable settlement of the fate of my motherland. Let me die, if die I must, in the lap of a free India. Let me sleep my last sleep not in a subject country, but in a free country".

Pandit Moti Lal presided over the Calcutta Congress in 1928 A.D. where a sort of ultimatum was given to the British Government that in case Dominion Status was not granted within a year, the country would switch off to independence. The next session of the Congress was held at Lahore under the presidentship of his illustrious son Pandit Jawahar Lal. It was a unique sight to see the father handing over the charge of the Congress to his son. Though Pandit Jawahar Lal was hardly forty, then, yet in the words of Mahatma Gandhi he "possessed dash of the warrior and the prudence of the statesman in whose hands nation was safe". Prophetic words these!— subsequent events have fully shown that the nation has remained indeed safe in hands of Jawahar Lal. As customary with it, the British Government failed to understand the spirit of times and refused to grant even Dominion Status within the year of grace, resulting in the Congress passing a resolution demanding full independence. The honour of raising the banner of independence at midnight of 31st December, 1929 was reserved by an inscrutable Providence for Pandit Jawahar Lal. Thenceforth started Jawahar Lal's Jain going. Nine times was he imprisoned spending the best part of his life in Jails. And when in 1936 there came about a temporary break in his jail-going (after having spent about five years in imprisonment) his friends and foes found him with greater vigour and freshness. Elections were soon in the offing. Pandit Jawahar Lal made an extensive all - India tour in shortest possible time, Wherever he went, he simply conquered. The polls were swept and Congress rule in eight provinces including the Muslim Frontier Province was the result.

II

Pandit Jawahar Lal's solution of the problem that have confronted the country has always been characterised by a very bold and courageous approach. His thought has always been clear and his action therefore always effective. In matters of detail Jawahar Lal may have sometimes compromised here or there but on matters of principle he has never given way. Hard prison life extending over years at a stretch did not diminish his rigid adherence to his principles of life even by an iota even though it meant at times huge suffering and sacrifice. His sixth terms of imprisonment which was quite a long term came to an end on 30th August 1933. Soon after in September of the same year Pandit Jawahar Lal in spite of the fact that his household affairs were none-too-happy—his ailing mother Shm. Swarup Rani, who herself had taken a very prominent part in the freedom movement and had even faced police batons was lying in the hospital, and his brave and noble wife Shrimati Kamla

Nehru on whom had fallen the task of attending on Sh. Swarup Rani was herself unwell he found time to survey the Indian situation in such a bold, cuorageous and detached manner in his three articles entitled "whither India" which baffled both his friends and critics. Unmindful of the troubles which lay ahead, he posed and discussed the question as to what is the aim of our freedom movement in a very very bold and frank manner. Says he :-

"Is our aim human welfare on the preservation of the class privileges and the vested interests of the pampered groups? The question must be answered clearly and unequivocally by each one of us. There is no room for quibbling when the fate of nations and millions of human beings is at stake. The day for palace intrigues and parlour politics and pacts intrigues and parlour politics and pacts and compomises passes when the masses enter politics. Their manners are not of the drawing room; we never took the trouble to teach them any manners. Their school is the school of events and suffering is their teacher. They learn their politics from great movements which bring out the true nature of individuals and classes and the civil disobedience movement has taught the Indian masses many a lesson which they will never forget".

This would show the depth of his convictions before which everything including collosal sufferings and sacrifices paled into insignificance. And in all this he had always the blessings of his noble wife handy who even on death-bed encouraged him to follow the path he had chosen. jawahar Lal was serving his seventh term, when the health of Shrimati Kamala Nehru deteriorated so much that he was temporarily released from Jail to be with her in her last moments. After eleven days Jawahar Lal was again taken back to Jail. Suggestions were made to him on behalf of the Government that if he gave even an informal assurance that he would desist from politics during the rest of his term he would be released to attend on Shrimati Kamala. While he was taking leave of Shrimati Kamala she whispered to him "What is this, about your giving an assurance to Government? Do not give it". This small sentence by itself speaks volumes. The true womanhood of India spoke through her. And what has been the result of all this? A free India and an India which daily goes higher and higher in world's estimation. For all this he has been the recipient of very high tributes from all who count. Some have described him as a great patriot, a fearless freedom fighter. Others have praised his high artistic sense, his great literary attainments and real knowledge of history. There are yet others who admire his high statemanship, his unequivocal support to the principles of international peace and amity. There are many who describe him as a man of great decency with whom the most prized object in this world in full human dignity. And there are not a few who see in him the great upholder of high moral values and ethical standards, which are daily receding to the background in the world of today. Some look upon him as a political prophet who has predicted many world events including the second world war with such precision that it should put to shame all the astrologers, wherever they be.

All this is undeniable. But with regard to Indian freedom movement, his contribution has been in a way unique, It was he who for the first time in India provoked thought on right lines and cleared the minds of the freedom fighters of cobwebs of doubt and confusion which reacted very adversely on their thought and activities. Gandhiji started his great Movement. The whole of India rose like one man. But very few knew as to what was the end to which the movement would lead. Every body had his own notions about the Movement and every body interpreted it according to his own light. Even Gandhiji did not encourage clear thinking on this matter. There is reason for this which may not be gone into here. Sir Valentine Chirol once in 1921 questioned Mahatma Gandhi in Anand Bhawan at Allahabad as to what was his conception of Swaraj; Quick came the answer from Mahatmaji that under Swaraj "the lion shall lie with the lamb". For the time being this might mean a lot, and yet mean very little. When once the things have settled down,—the question as to "for whose freedom did we fight" is sure to crop up then in its grim nakedness. It was after all left for Jawahar Lal to give a definite shape and form to the Indian freedom movement and pull it out of the thraldom of doubt and confusion. In his "Whither India" Pandit Jawahar Lal has posed this question with great clarity and precision. Says he:-

> "Again whose freedom are we particularly striving for, for nationalism covers many sins and included many conflicting elements. There is the feudal India of the princes, the India of the big Zamindars, of small Zamindars, of the professional classes, of the agriculturists, of the industrialists of the bankers, of the lower middle class of the workers. There are the interests of foreign capital and those of home capital, of foreign services and home services. The nationalist answer is to prefer home interests to foreign interests, but beyond that it does not go. It tries to avoid disturbing the class divisions or the social status quo. It imagines that the various interests will somehow be accommodated when the country is free. Being essentially a middle class movement, nationalism works chiefly in the interest of that class. It is obvious that there are serious conflicts between various interests in a country and every law, every policy which is good for one interest may be harmful for another. What is good for the Indian prince may be thoroughly bad for the people of his State, what is profitable for the zamindar may ruin many of his tenants what is demanded by foreign capital may crush the rising industries of the country. Nothing is more absurd that to imagine that all the interests in the nation can be

fitted in without injury to any. At every step some have to be sacrificed for others..." Further on in the same pamphlet He writes :—

"India's struggle today is part of the great struggle which is going on all over the world for the emancipation of the oppressed. Essentially this is an economic struggle, with hunger and want as its driving forces, although it puts on nationalist and other dresses. Indian freedom is necessary because the burden on the Indian masses as well as on the middle classes is too heavy to be borne and must be lightened or done away with. The measure of freedom is the extent to which this burden is removed. This burden is due to the vested interests of a foreign government as well as those of certain groups and classes in Indian and abroad. The achievement of freedom thus becomes a question, as Gandhiji said recently, of divesting vested interests. If an indigeneous Government took the place of the foreign Government and kept all the vested interests intact, this would not even be the shadow of freedom. Swaraj or freedom from exploitation for the masses is not a fine paper constitution or a problem of the hereafter. It is question of here and now of immediate relief. Roast lamb and mint sauce may be a tasty dish for these who eat it but the poor lamb is not likely to appreciate the force of the best or arguments which points out the beauty of sacrifice for the good of the elect and the joys of close communion, even though dead, with mint sauce."

The pamphlet is concluded with the following passage :—

> "Whither India? Surely to the great human goal of social and economic equality, to the ending of all exploitation of nation by nation and class by class, to national freedom within the frame work of an international co-operative socialist world federation. This is not such an empty idealist dream as some people imagine It is within the range of the practical politics of today and the near future. We may not have it within our grasp but those with vision can see it emerging on the horizon. And even if there be delay in the realization of our goal, what does it matter if our eyes look steadily in front. For in the pursuit itself of a mighty purpose there is joy and happiness and a measure of achievement."

Upto the September of 1933, this type of language was certainly unheard of. The articles which constitute the pamphlet created a stir in the whole of Asia and these were translated into many Asiatic languages. In India too it certainly created an unprecedented ideological revolution. But all this was a bitter pill for the British ruler. As hinted earlier by the "Statesman" he was soon arrested and sentenced to a long term of imprisonment.

It is indeed impossible to recount the achievements of Jawahar Lal in the short space available, but yet a brief reference to the solution provided by him of the problems emerging out of the existence of the India states can not be avoided. For this reason or that the Indian States people were a neglected lot, the Congress policy from the very beginning was to leave the Indian States alone. There were some amongst the Congressmen who looked upon the Indian princes" as the visible representation of India's past glory" and there were others who saw in Indian States "self-Government in action.". Least did they know that it was not the love of India's past glory, but their own self-interest, which provided reason to the British Government to continue the princes existence. It was Lord Canning who soon after mutiny said that "It was long ago said by Sir John Malcolm that if we made all-India into districts, it was not in the nature of things that our Empire should last fifty years; but that if we should keep a number of native states without political power, but as loyal instruments, we should exist in India as long as our naval supremacy was maintained." Lord Canning proceeds "of the substantial truth of his opinion I have no doubt, and the recent events have made it more deserving of our attention than ever." Thus did the Indian States spring into existence their justification being consolidation and strengthening of the British rule. The Princes on their part fully justified Malcolm's remarks. Describing the condition of his subjects, the Maharaja of Kotah wrote to the Viceroy on 28th August 1909. "My own subjects are all engaged in their agricultural pursuits, and hardly anybody reads a newspaper and the knowledge of the fact that there are some political activities going on in British India is limited only to some people amongst the upper classes and some state servants."

Kotah's letter was in answer to a circular letter of the Viceroy addressed to the Princes directing them to prevent progressive ideas from percolating into their States. Other Princes also wrote in a similar vein. With the growth of a revolutionary movement in India, the British Government now rivetted its attention more and more on Indian States as its last retreat. The Princes were organized in a "Chamber of Princes." It was proposed that the Indian Federation would constitute of Provinces and the Indian States, and the Princes would act as hereditary Provincial Heads. The States' subjects were nowhere in the picture, and in all matters of interest to them, they were to be represented by the Princes who were described as their "natural leaders." The Princes were encouraged to take their stand on time worn treaties and thus stand as a bulwark against the rising onslaught of democracy. But seeing even all this, the Congress stuck to its policy of non-interference in Indian States. If the things had taken the course visualised by the British Government and the Princes, the problem would no doubt have baffled every attempt at a solution. Pandit Jawahar Lal saw all this. Even at the cost of expressing an open disagreement with some of his colleagues, he raised his voice against all this as early as 1929 when in his Presidential Address he said at Lahore Congress "I must frankly confess that I am a socialist and a republican, and am no believer in kings and princes." Side by side with this bold declaration, Pandit Jawahar Lal organized an All-India organization by name States' Peoples Confeence which provided a platform forr the State's People who were till then a backward and a disorganized lot. Within a few years, this organization became a formidable organization with its branches all over the country though much to the disappointment of Kotah and other princes who had built many a castle on the fact that "their subjects were engaged in agricultural pursuits only and hardly anybody read a newspaper." The result was a general awakening amongst the States' subjects. Many movements were started by them in which many a prince had to eat the humblepie. And when the time of leaving India by British came, the Princes though they had succeeded in securing a verdict of independence from the outgoing British, and were in fact busy building and nourishing dreams of an independent sovereignty, found themselves squeezed out by the pressure exerted by the Indian democracy on one side and on the other by their own subjects, who far from being the docile and backward creatures of Kotah variety, were now fired with a potential revolutionary zeal to secure their own freedom. Had not Pandit Jawahar Lal with the keen political foresight that he has, caught the time by the forelock and organized the States' people in time, it would have really a very tough job for even the tallest amongst the Indian leaders to find a solution of this formidable problem in the manner it has been found. The closest parallel to the situation thus created would have been that of the Portuguese Goa. If Portuguese have their helpers, the Princely Order had no less.

For Kashmir Jawahar Lal brought a new message and a new hope and gave a real shape and form to the movement which was till then not very clear in its aims and objects. He planted the young sapling of nationalism in Kashmir and nourished it under his own tender care and guidance which by the time India came to be partitioned had grown into a mighty tree which provided shelter to many a weary traveller who ran away from the scorching heat of communal fires which were ablaze then in the neighbouring Province of the Punjab. The lesson of nationalism had gone so deep in the minds of the people here that when the time of opting with India or Pakistan came, the leadership of Kashmir which was predominantly Muslim, with one voice declared for India. This was a great victory for the forces of nationalism and an equally great triumph for the ideal of secularism.

Pandit Jawahar Lal is yet in the thick of the battle. It is plainly visible to anybody that destiny has earmarked many achievement yet for him. But it needs being stated here that he has always had the greatest measure of co-operation available to him from everybody including his own house-people. His sister Vijayalakshmi Pandit who has received her political training and inspiration from her great father, Pandit Moti Lal, has always worked in close co-operation with her brother. She came to Kashmir in 1933 and was hardly thirty-three then. Least could it be known then that there was such a spark in her soul, which in 1945 produced a blazing fire which burnt to ashes all the evil effects of a vicious propaganda which was set afloat in America by interested quarters with the active cooperation of some Indians, themselves. She was arrested on 12th August 1942 three days after Gandhiji's arrest. After having remained in jail for nearly a year, she was released. In November 1944 she left India and landed at San Francisco in April 1945. The Conference of the United Nations was held in May 1945. India was represented there by Ramaswami Mudaliar and Feroz Khan Noon who were the nominees of the British Government. At the very outset she challenged the representative character of the so-called Indian representation at the Conference and declared "I desire to make it clear that the so-called Indian representatives have not the slightest representative character. They have no sanction, no mandate from any responsible parties in India. They are merely British Government's nominees. The newspaper comment on this declaration may be given in the words of a prominent journalist Mr. Iftone, who said that "Indian delegates have been chosen without consultation of Indian parties or political leaders, most of whom are in jail, including the far-seeing Nehru who would have shone even in the gathering of gaints." Many Conferences were addressed by her. At one such Conference Mr. Feroz Khan who along with his companion was according to a newspaper report having "Sleepless nights" sent his stenographer Khan to heckle her. The newspaper comments on this episode may be given in the words of Pasbom of the Associated Press of America that :-

> "It must have been most uncomfortable for his boss to learn today that the efforts of, his stooge instead of disrupting Mrs. Pandit's press conference have boomranged and Mrs. Pandit has received much wider publicity both at the radio and the press than she might have otherwise. Yesterday's evening papers and this morning's papers have given her a prominent space with pictures. One paper had a big picture of Mrs. Pandit being garlanded by Amritlal Seth and a small picture of Khan with his name and 'ejected from Conference'."

Though a rebel then with no official recognition, Mrs. Pandit created a great and lasting effect in America. At Baltimore she was given the highest official recognition, the Mayor having received her at the station and presented to her the keys of the city. Besides addressing press conferences and public meetings, she submitted a memorial also to the U.N. Conference and made out a strong plea for an immediate declaration of Indian independence. She was given audience by President and Lady Truman. She entertained the foreign ministers of Egypt, Iran and Saudi Arabia etc, It short even in 1945 she made the voice of India heard in all quarters of the globe.

During freedom movement Mrs. Pandit went to jail a number of times. In 1936 she was elected as a member of the U.P. Legislature and was later appointed as a Minister in the first popular Ministry. She is the first Indian woman Minister. The Ministry was a short-lived affair and had to resign soon after the outbreak of second world war, but yet her achievements in so short a period were in no way meagre or small. For the thoroughness with which she conducted her business as a Minister, she got praises and admiration from all and sundry. What followed next including her election to U.N. Presidentship is a matter of recent history and no detailed reference is called for here.

There is yet another great Kashmiri Pandit, Shri Kailas Nath Katju, whose part in furtherance of the national movement has been indeed great.

A great Advocate and one of the ablest lawyers that Allahabad has ever produced with a very high monthly income, Pandit Kailas Nath enjoyed even before his political career began, a very high reputation for his honesty and integrity. He has ever been known as a person of very deep religious convictions, high moral principles, and ethical standards. Unmindful of the monetary loss and discomforts of a jail life he threw himself whole-heartedly in the national struggle and courted imprisonment more than once. He was appointed as Minister of Justice in U.P. in 1937. After independence he was appointed as Governor of Bengal and later his services were utilized in the Central Cabinet as Home Minister and defence Minister.

There are a good many other Kashmiri Pandits who also have contributed their mite to the national movement. No reference need be made to all of them, but the picture will remain incomplete if specific mention is not made of two Kashmiri ladies Shrimati Rameshwari Nehru and Shrimati Lado Rani Zutshi. Shrimati Rameshwari has always been a true disciple of Mahatma Gandhi. The social uplift work which has been done by her has already created a place of honour for her all over India. Sh. Lado Rani has always been a true Congressite, and she belonged to the first batch of public spirited women who took to Congress work with zeal and seriousness.

There have been other Kashmiri Pandits who though not Congressmen, have also played their part on the Indian political stage. Sir Tej Bahadur Sapru who for decades remained a leading light of the liberal party has by dint of his clarity of thought and cleanliness of action combined with a great intellectual eminent succeeded in carving a place for himself in the country's history. Even his worst critics have never denied what has been described by C.F. Andrews as "his rugged honesty of purpose". Sir Tej was essentially a great constitutional lawyer. Any mention of civil disobedience or non-cooperation greatly annoyed him. His legal training had made him over- conservative in action. He was appointed as a Member of the Viceroy's Executive Council in 1921 when non-cooperation movement was at its highest, but resigned much before this term of office expired. It is said that the Viceroy (Lord Reading) always relied on his counsel, but Sir Tej was also frank enough in giving quite unpalatable evidence. So for as the harsh treatment meted out to Indians outside India was concerned, Sir Tej always raised his voice in the frankest and most indignant manner against it. He attended as a representative at all the three Round Table Conferences held in England to frame a constitution for India.

Pandit Hirday Nath Kunzru has remained a leading light of the Servants of India Society for quite a number of years and has done good service to the country in an un-ostentatious manner.

There have been a number of Kashmiri Pandits who have contributed their mite to the building of modern India as great educationists. Pandit Jagat Narayan Malla, a leading Advocate of his time remained the Vice-Chancellor of Lucknow University for a number of years. His part in organizing the University has been admitted by everybody. He was appointed as a member of the Hunter Committee constituted by the British Government in 1919 to hold an inquiry into the Martial law regime in the Punjab. By his wonderful cross-examination of General Dyer and others, which created a India-wide sensation then, he exposed in its entirety the holloweness of the Government case. He was later elected to the Assembly and became a Minister under the Dyarchy regime. Pandit Iqbal Narayan Gurtu was the Vice-Chancellor of Allahabad University and Diwan Anand Kumar had now been for many years as the Vice-Chalncellor of the Punjab University. After the partition, the University was well-nigh ruined, but by his assiduous work he succeeded in resuscitating it.

Before closing this chapter reference may be made to the contribution made to the Urdu literature and poetry by the Kashmiri Pandits during this period. Pandit Daya Shankar Nasim, who died in 1843 A.D. at an early age of thirty two is even now counted as a great poet. He has composed a poem Guli Bakawli, which has elecited highest praise from all literatery circles. Pandit Rattan Nath Dar besides being a poet of no mean order has made a collosal service to the Urdu prose. His Fasana Azad, in which he has depicted the life of Nawabs of Lucknow is the first Novel in Urdu Language. To Pandits Brij Narayan Chakbast and Bishan Narayan Dar reference has been made earlier, but then as long as Urdu language lives, the names of Pandits Tribhuwan Nath Sapru Hijr Amar Nath Madan, Janki Nath Madan, Brij Mohan Dattatriya Kaifi, Pandit Hargopal Kaul "Khasta", Pandit Nand Lal Talib, Dina Nath

Mast, Master Zind Kaul and about two hundred other Kashmiri Pandit poets will also live as those of great poets.

CHAPTER 5

DOGRAS

By

G.L. Kaul

Gulab Singh, the founder of the Dogra dynasty of Jammu and Kashmir, was born in 1792 (5th Katik 1849 Bikrami Samvat). In his early days he lived under the personal care of his grand-father Zorawar Singh in his Jagir Dyawago. The future ruler of Kashmir received little education but he was trained in all manly arts. He could ride his horse and wield his sword.

After the invasion of Mohamad-ud-Din Ghori the Rajput hegemony in the hilly tract between Punjab and Kashmir was shattered. The Rajput rulers who held sway around the town of Jammu regained their independence when the Moghul kingdom began to show signs of disintegration. They were combined under Raja Dhrou Deo and his son Raja Ranjit Deo. The latter received a jagir from the Durrani king for help rendered against Raja Sukh Jewan of Kashmir in 1730 and ruled for 44 years.

Ranjit Deo had two sons, Brij Lal and Dulel Singh Brij Lal revolted against his father and later succeeded, him in 1780. Mohan Singh who is known to history as the brother of Ranjit Singh was a sworn friend of Brij Lal but he conspired against him and attacked Jammu. Thus the sovereignty of the house of Dhrou Deo over the surrounding country disappeared for the time being.

Gulab Singh was a descendant in direct line from Raja Dhrou through his third son, Mian Soorat Deo. Cunningham doubts the genealogy of Gulab Singh. But Maharaja Ranjit Singh, in his grant of the Raj of Jammu to Gulab Singh, mentioned the fact of Gulab Singh's ancestors having been the rulers of the principality. Raja Dhrou Deo was a Rajput prince of the Surya Vansi (Solar) dynasty who ruled over Jammu in the eighteenth century.

The affairs of Jammu being in confusion Ranjit Singh ordered in 1808 Bhai Hukam Singh to annex Jammu to the Sikh State. It was in this battle that young Gulab Singh fought so well that he won admiration from the enemy even. Gulab Singh intended to go to Kabul to enlist in the army of Shah Shuja but later changed his mind and joinded the army of Ranjit Singh in 1809 as trooper at Rs.3/- p.m. in Mungla, west of Jhelum. Gulab Singh fought many battles and the siege of Multan in 1819 brought him to Ranjit Singh's favourable notice. In the frontier campaigns of Ranjit Singh between 1815 and 1820, Gulab Singh played a prominent role. At this time the hilly area around Jammu was under the influence of Mian Deo. Gulab Singh hit on a stratagem to subdue this bandit chief. His supplies were cut off and his fort attacked. Deo was killed while fighting.

In 1820 Jammu was given to Gulab Singh as a Jagir. Later on he was given the title of Raja and allowed to keep an army. In 1821 Gulab Singh undertook the conquest of Kishtwar and on his way received homage from Dyal Chand, Raja of Chenani. Next Gulab Singh marched on Rajouri whose ruler Ajor Khan had given annoyance to Ranjit Singh in his expedition against Kashmir in 1813. It is in lieu of such services that Ranjit Singh granted to Gulab Singh and his successors the principality of Jammu with the hereditary title of Raja in 1822 A.D.

In 1841 Gulab Singh allowed passage to British army for invasion of Afghanistan which Ranjit Singh had refused at the time of first Afghan War.

Copy of the sanad granted by Ranjit Singh :

"On this auspicious occasion with extreme joy and with heartfelt love, I grant to Raja Gulab Singh in recognition of his conscientious and loyal services, the government of the Chakla of Jammu which from time immemorial has been in the possession of his family. He and his brothers, Dhyan Singh and Suchet Singh appeared in my court at a very early age and loyally and devotedly served me and the State. Their ancestors also served faithfully for a long time under my father Mohan Singh Ji of happy memory. They spared no pains to render their services to me promptly and submissively and to give me satisfaction. They have always been found faithful to me and loyal to the State. They have shed their blood freely in many campaigns, such as the conquest of Kashmir, the seige of Multan, the punishment of the rebels, the suppression of rebellion on the frontier and the fight with the forces of Kabul. In consideration of these and other services I grant the government of the Chakla of Jammu to Raja Gulab Singh and his descendants and I myself mark the forehead of this loyal and devoted servant of mine with the emblem of sovereignty. With great pleasure I also grant Raja Suchet Singh, the Government of Ramnagar to be his own and his descendants, as a reward for the great services he has rendered to me. He and his descendants may dispose of its income on their own account provided that the Rajas be loyal to the State henceforward as they have been till now, that they receive our descendants with no less honour and submission and that their descendants be as loyal to us as our descendants. In witness of this I grant this Purwana of mine with my own hands together with a bunch of saffron."

Dated 4th Ashad 1879 (Vikram).

At the age of thirty, this was indeed a proud achievement for Gulab Singh. Tibet was next to be invaded. But this campaign could not be successful. He and Hari Singh Nalwa repulsed an attack from Kabul in 1823. In 1827 Gulab Singh was the overlord in Jammu having conquered Riasi, Kishtwar, Rajouri and Samarth etc. except Poonch which belonged to Dhyan Singh and Ramnagar which belonged to Suchet Singh. The Illaqa being hilly and the people turbulent, Gulab Singh took great personal interest in the administration. He raised and kept in tact a reserve of money and trained and equipped an army. The death of Maharaja Ranjit Singh on 27th June, 1839 was followed by Court intrigues and internecine strifes. In the Afghan War of 1841 the British enlisted the support of the Sikhs who were not in any way anxious to help them in their Kabul expedition. This provided an opportunity for friendship between the British and Gulab Singh. On 19th January, 1842, the British force was beaten back at the Khyber Pass. In recognition of his services the British Government sent him an appreciative Kharita on 8th April, 1842. Gulab Singh was offered Jalalabad and was asked to give up Ladakh but this he did not accept. The murder of Dhyan Singh, Gulab Singh's brother, by Ajeet Singh in Badami Bagh Fort created further resentment in Gulab Singh against the Sikh Community. The uncle and the nephew, Suchet Singh and Hira Singh, came to gips in 1844 and this resulted in the death of the former. Then followed a dispute between Hira Singh and Gulab Singh. But Hira Singh died on 21st December 1844. The Sikh Sardars combind to smash the "Ulysses of the Hills" but he averted an all round attack. The Sikh army was defeated at Satwari on 3rd April, 1845.

The same year war between the Sikhs and the British became inevitable, for the Sikhs felt convinced that the British Government wanted to annex Punjab. Gulab Singh who had counselled the Sikhs not to go to war with the British, remained neutral for a time. He was, however, persuaded to take charge of the Prime Ministership of the Sikh State on the 27th January 1846. He immediately started negotiations for a settlement. These negotiations failed when the British laid down the condition about the disbandment of the Sikh Army and the battle of Sobraon was fought on February 10, 1846. The British won, though at a huge cost. Gulab Singh again negotiated peace and secured a reasonably fair treaty for his sovereign Duleep Singh who was recognised as ruler on his ceding the territory between Beas and Sutlej and paying £15,00,000 as war indemnity. Gulab Singh's success in negotiating this treaty infuriated his rival Lal Singh who managed to get himself installed in his place. It was now that Gulab Singh realised the precariousness of his position. But Gulab Singh's opportunity was not long in coming. Lal Singh, his successor, in accepting the Treaty negotiated by him, protested his inability to pay the indemnity of £15,00,000. To deprive Gulab Singh of his territory and give the British the option of holding Kashmir—an impossible feat at that time, or accepting a reduced indemnity, he offered to hand over Jammu and Kashmir. This resulted in a revival of the original proposal to make Gulab Singh, the independent ruler of Jammu and Kashmir with this difference only that now he had to pay a sum of Rs. 75 lacs (Nanakshahi). In Gulab Singh's accepting this proposition, the Treaty of Lahore was signed on the 9th March 1846 as originally negotiated by him.

> "In consideration of the services rendered by Raja Gulab Singh of Jammu to the Lahore State towards procuring the restoration of the relation of amity between the Lahore and British Government, the Maharaja (Duleep Singh) hereby agrees to recognise the independent sovereignty of Raja Gulab Singh in such territories and districts in the hills as may be made over to the said Raja Gulab Singh by separate agreement between himself and the British Government with dependencies thereof which may have been in the Raja's possession

> since the time of Maharaja Kharak Singh and the British Government in consideration of the good conduct of Raja Gulab Singh who agrees to recognise independence in such territories and to admit him to the privilege of a separate Treaty with the British Government." This clause of the Treaty of Lahore concluded under force of circumstances cannot exonerate the betrayer.

On the 16th March 1846, seven days after the Treaty of Lahore, Maharaja Gulab Singh signed the Treaty of Amritsar by which he became the Maharaja of Jammu and Kashmir.

The "Sale of Kashmir", which is so much talked about is in reality more a fact than a myth. Kashmir was simply sold to Gulab Singh. The situation is not clarified when it is borne in mind that the areas surrendered by the Lahore Government between Ravi and the Indus were to be transferred to Gulab Singh according to Clause 12 of the Treaty of Lahore with Maharaja Duleep Singh, then an independent ruler, before the Treaty of Lahore was signed because the bargain was struck by the Britishers for their ally. According to Pannikar "The cession of Kashmir was the price paid for Gulab Singh's efforts to bring about a speedy peace which, it he had thrown in his weight with the Lahore Durbar, would not have been an easy matter to achieve. The ease with which the peace was concluded was due to the agreement reached with Gulab Singh by which Kashmir had already been promised to him. It may be that the British could not conquer Kashmir in 1845, much less hold it, with Sutlej as their boundary, Ferozepur as their base, a hostile Punjab on the line of communications and the Sikhs ready to fight. It is true that Kashmir was not a part of India in the eighteenth century, not even till Ranjit Singh occupied it. It was an Afghan Province. And in all schemes for the partition of the Punjab, there may have been many proposals for allotment of areas, not necessarily Kashmir, as that would also lead to consolidation of

Afghan empire and thus be a perpetual danger to the British. The British wanted to divide up the Sikh empire which would be a great menace if it extended from Multan to Gilgit. By snatching Kashmir out of it and passing it on to an ally the object was achieved, thus killing two bi ds with one stroke. Sir George Clark, Agent to the Governor-General at Lahore, wrote in March 1849 :-

"I have been under the necessity on more than one occasion of testing, rather severely, Gulab Singh's loyalty to us. My belief is that he is a man eminently qualified by character and surrounding territorial possessions for the position of ruler there, that all his interests lie on the side of friendship with us, that he will always desire and some time or another may need our countenance of his authority against enemies. Their aggressions, whether Chinese or Goorkhas on one side of him of Afghans on the other, will be retarted rather than precipitated by his proximity to them in that form instead of our being in more direct contact with them." Why did Ranjit Singh himself create a Dogra kingdom it may be argued? He put off the Afghans. Lord Hardinge did the same for more cogent reasons.

Some do accuse Gulab Singh of treason against the Lahore Durbar and the death of Nao Nihal Singh, caused by the fall of the archway, was designed by him. Though incidentally he lost his eldest son, Udham Singh (Randhir Singh), Lord Hardinge says, "Was he (gulab Singh) not the Minister and were not four other Commissioners associated with him for setting the terms of peace?" Sir W.R. Lawrence says that when the second Sikh War coloured the map of Punjab red, some regretted the transfer of Kashmir to the Dogra Chief. But in his opinion based on some knowledge of the possibilities of Kashmir it was fortunate that the English did not annex Kashmir because they had not annexed the Punjab yet.

Cunningham is of opinion that the English bargained with Gulab Singh. Mr. Sapru in his monograph No.14 (Punjab

Government Record Office Publication) pleads that the circumstances of the transaction fully justified it. "No one then imagined that the Punjab would become a British province in less than three years and it was deemed a good stroke of policy to weaken the Sikh Durbar by rewarding one who had been favourable to their own cause. Lal Singh wanting to get a dreaded rival out of the way, enabled the Governor-General to appease Gulab Singh in a manner sufficiently agreeable to the Raja himself, thus further reducing the importance of the successor of Ranjit Singh." Sir Richard Temple also says that Lord Hardinge aimed to divide the Sikh power between the Lahore Court and Gulab Singh, and thus effectively weaken it. The Maharaja remained faithful to the British to the last.

A.P. Nicholson in his famous book "Scraps of Paper" referring to this question says :

"We sold the right to keep it, if he could conquer it, to Gulab Singh."

In the "Life of Hardinge" appears the following account, "It was necessary to....to weaken the Sikhs by depriving them of Kashmir. The distance from Kashmir to the Sutlej is 300 miles of very difficult mountainous country, quite impracticable for six months. To keep a British force 300 miles from any possibility of support would be an undertaking that merited a strait-waist coat and not a peerage. The arrangement was the only alternative. The Government took away with one hand and gave with the other as the exigencies of the case required." To Lord Ellenborough, Lord Hardinge wrote : "It was always intended that Gulab Singh whose troops had not fired a shot should have his case and position fully considered ... After the war commenced were we to abandon our policy and to treat the only man who had not lifted up his arms against us with difference because he came to headquarters especially deputed by the Lahore Durbar to confer with us as one who had joined in their unprovoked invasion? His forbearance was rewarded because his forbearance was in accordance with an intended policy...." Again in a letter to the Secret Committee, the Governor-General wrote on March 14, 1846.

> "On the other hand, the tract now ceded included the whole hill possessions of Raja Gulab Singh and the Jammu family. Its possession by us enables us at once to mark our sense of Raja Gulab Singh's conduct during the late operations, by rewarding him in the mode in accordance with his desires."

The treaty only transferred to him the legal title, as no actual possession over Kashmir was handed over to him. He acquired the territory for himself though he did so with the help of the British. "sold even a thousand times, Joseph is no slave."

> "Their fields, their crops, their streams,
> Even the peasants in the vale,
> They sold, they sold all Alas!
> How cheap was the sale.
>
> —Iqbal.

Maharaja Gulab Singh despatched Dewan Lakhpat Rai to take possession of Kashmir but Imam-ud-Din, the then Governor, did not surrender and offered resistance. The Hari Parbat Fort was siezed by him but subsequently the General was killed and his army was in imminent danger. Maharaja Gulab Singh then applied to Sir Heney Lawrence for assistance in taking possession and when the combind forces of the Maharaja, the British Durbar and the Sikhs marched against the Governor, Imam-ud-Din he surrendered declaring that he had acted according to the written instructions of Lal Singh. When Maharaja Gulab Singh came to Kashmir he found the land divided into three categories—one part under mountains, one part under water and the rest under Jagirdars.

Gulab Singh belonged to the school of Nepoleon, burning with a desire to conquer. But his contemporaries were too formidable to allow him to extend his conquests. He sought his game elsewhere and made war with the hill tribes on the frontiers. Wazir Zorawar Kalhoria who is believed to have led these campaigns has carved a name in the annals of Kashmir. He (Gulab Singh) conquered Ladakh and Tibet in 1842, annexed Chilas in 1850 A.D. and subdued Gilgit in 1852 A.D. To conquer these hill Rajas was no easy task. They had forts built everywhere. Their army consisted of people who were proof against any kind of hardships. To-day they were routed and tomorrow they would again make war and re-capture the lost places. They never appeared on the battlefield to kill or to die but like guerillas played "hide the seek" game. To fight such people was to do battle with the air or to give blows upon water. Gulab Singh who was a great soldier showed sound knowledge and practical experience during his campaigns against the Frontier tribes. He was a great unifier and he welded together various patches of his kingdom. His encouragment of art and patronage of learning besides his grand personality and noble character raised the town of Jammu from a mere barrack to the first rank among the many stately cities of the Indian Empire. "Once Gulab Singh watched with interest the construction of a bridge constructed by convict labour. One convict solicited the Maharaja for pardon. The offence was the murder of a girl for her jewels. the Maharaja was infuriated at this and he enhanced the sentence. While sitting in judgment the hire-apparent was ordered to be nearby. Once a complaint came that a hen was stolen. The offender was summoned and the barber was commanded to shave half of his moustache and he was paraded in the open bazar." This provided instruction for the Yuvraj in the administration of justice.

He died of dropsy on 25th Sawan 1914 (August 1858 A.D.), the year which witnessed the horrors of the Indian Mutiny and his death was marked by an earthquake. He was only 66 years old.

The tribes of Hazara rose in rebellion in 1847. At first it had not become possible to cope with it but subsequently it was suppressed. Gulab singh thereupon asked th British Government to exchange Hazara with Mandi and Garhi. Hazara was assigned to Lahore and Gulab Singh got Kathua and Suchetgarh with part of Manawar. The boundary was further altered in 1847 under the supervision of the British officers, Cunningham, Strachey and Thomson. Poonch which had passed on to Gulab Singh was given to Jawahar Singh, the eldest surviving son of Dhyan Singh. But soon after, he claimed a share in Gulab Singh's property on the ground that they were the joint family property of all the brothers. The claim was settled on 12th May 1948 by Frederick Currie and Gulab Singh was declared as the rightful master. The claim of Chamba was further adjusted by the transfer of Bhaderwah to Gulab Singh and taking away Chamba from his territories.

In 1848, when the second Sikh War broke out, Maharaja Gulab Singh stood by the side of the British although he was approached by both Dost Mohammad Khan of Kabul and Sardar Chattar Singh to help them. The Sikh were defeated again.

It was no easy job for Gulab Singh to look after an administration which had gone from bad to worse in the time of the Sikhs. The shawl industry which was the main source of livelihood for the people was taxed very heavily. Reckless governors had given away much of the land in the valley as rent- free concessions, forced labour told upon the peasantry, sati and infanticide were common, robbers infested the hills. Nicholson records in his diary on 19th November 1847:—

"Had some conversation with a party of Kabul merchants taking tabacco and snuff to Kashmir whence they intend returning with pattoo and tosh, which at last fetches a very high price in Kabul. They complained of the oppressive duties in their own and Maharaja Gulab Singh's territories but remarked that in the latter their goods were protected whereas they frequently ran great risks from the plundering tribes between Kabul and Peshawar." A number of men were determined in each village for begar and every man on begar duty was paid a khirwar of rice per month and given food. Another step which he took was to ration rice in the vallye. This system of grain control was revived immediately after the first Great War. The re- organisation of the shawl department or the Dagshawl received his attention next. The shawl tax was reduced, the Moulut (carrying accounts to the 14th month) was abolished and Chuttiana cancelled. The efficiency of his forces was always a matter of deep concern to him.

In 1851, trouble arose on the Tibetan frontier over the refusal of the Zamindars of Ladakh to allow full transport to Western trade mission from Tibet. The dispute was settled by representatives of the Maharaja and the Dalai Lama.

There is no doubt that it was an uphill task for Gulab Singh to consolidate his dominion. A characteristic of his personality was that he was ready to listen to complaints. Even in a crowd one could catch his eye by holding up a rupee (as Nazar) and crying out, "Maharaja Arz Hai." He would jump down like a hawk upon the money and listen to the petition. Once a man shouted in the customary manner and then closed his hand and said, "No first hear what I have to say". Gulab Singh did not lose patience, he heard the petition, and when the hand was opened he gave orders about the case.

Gulab Singh was a remarkable man of the nineteenth century. He began as a petty official and founded a kingdom. "He was after Ranjit Singh, the greatest lord in the Punjab." He knew tricks and stratagems. Opportunism was so near him that he always availed of it. Cunningham writes : "He must be judged with reference to the morality of his age and race and to the necessities of his own position. If these allowances be made Gulab Singh would be found an able and moderate man who does little in idle or wanton spirit, and who is not without some traits both of good humour and of generosity of temper." Major Smyth states, "With all this he was courteous and polite in demeanour and exhibited a suavity of manner and language that contrasted fearfully with his real disposition." The present Jammu and Kashmir is his monument. "It is at once a memorial of that foul act when, like the arch traitor of old, we bartered innocent lives, which fate placed in our hands, for a few pieces of silver."

"Gulab Singh had agreed to pay 68 lakhs to his Paramount before the war broke out. He should have paid the deficient million of money as a Lahore subject, instead of being put in possession of Lahore subject, instead of being put in possession of Lahore Provinces as an independent prince."

"For purposes entirely selfish we deliberatelly sold millions of human beings, into the absolute power of one of the meanest, most avaricious, cruel and unprincipled of men that ever sat upon a throne."

Mr. Lepel Griffins (Punjab Chiefs) says :—

"There are perhaps no characters in history more repulsive than Raja Gulab Singh and Dhyan Singh."

Immediately after the sale of Kashmir, the British imperialists realised their mistake as the following quotation from Canon Tyndale Biscoe's Autobiography makes it clear :—

"Wazir to Lt. Urmston—but that order was for India, not for Kashmir. Urmston—now watch my hand. He drew a red line right round the boundaries of Kashmir joining it to British India. This happened in 1857." It is since then that the British had an eye on Kashmir, particularly Gilgit.

It is clear beyond any doubt that 1846 created an independent state of Kashmir recognising Gulab Singh as an ally of the British, not a vassal. But the latter did not mean it. They started penetrating through needlewhole under one pretext or another until they succeeded in installing a British Resident in Kashmir whose policy of interference went so far in Pratap Singh's reign that the Maharaja could not appoint any one even to a post carrying a monthly salary of Rs.100/- Missionaries were deputed, men at large were sent from time to time to undo what had been done unconsciously in 1846. Troubles were fomented in Twenties and Thirties only to annex the State with British India. Man proposes, God disposes. The British themselves were destined to march out in 1947 but the wrong done could not be rectified.

TREATY OF 1846 A.D.

Treaty between the British Government and Maharaja Gulab, concluded at Amritsar, on 16th March 1846.

Treaty between the British Government on the one part and Maharja Gulab Singh of Jammu on the other, concluded on the part of the British Government by Frederick Currie Esquire and Brevet Major Henry Motogomery Lawrence acting under the orders of the Right Honble Sir Henry Hardinge, G.C.B., one of Her Britannic Majesty's Most Honourable Privy Council, Governor-General, appointed by the Honourable Company to direct and control all their affairs in the East India and by Maharaja Gulab Singh in person.

Article 1 "The British Government transfers and makes over, for ever, in independent possession to Maharaja Gulab Singh and the heirs male of his body, all the hilly or mountainous country, with its dependencies situated to the Eastward of the river Indus and Westward of the river Ravi, including Chamba and excluding Lahol, being part of the territory ceded to the British Government by the Lahore State according to the provisions of Article 4 of the Treaty of Lahore dated 9th March 1846 A.D.

Article 2—The Eastern boundary of the tract transferred by the foregoing article of Maharaja Gulab Singh shall be laid down by Commissioners appointed by the British Government and Maharaja Gulab Singh respectively for that purpose and shall be defined in a separate engagement after survey.

Article 3—In consideration of the transfer made to him and his heir by the provision of the foregoing Articles, Maharaja Gulab Singh will pay to the British Government the sum of 75 lakhs of rupees (Nanakshahi), fifty lakhs to be paid on ratification of this Treaty and twenty-five lakhs on or before the 1st October of the current year 1846 A.D.

Article 4—The limits of the territories of Maharaja Gulab Singh shall not be at any time changed without the concurrence of the British Government.

Article 5—Maharaja Gulab Singh will refer to the Arbitration of the British Government any disputes or questions that may arise between himself and the Government of Lahore or any other neighbouring States and will abide by the decision of the British government.

Article 6—Maharaja Gulab Singh engages for himself and heirs to join with the whole of his military forces the British troops when employed within the hills or in the territories adjoining his possessions.

Article 7—Maharaja Gulab singh engages never to take or retain in his service any British subject nor the subject of any European or American State without the consent of the British government.

Article 8—Maharaja Gulab Singh engages to respect in regard to the territory transferred to him under the provision of Article 5, 6 and 7 of the separate engagement between the

British Government and the Lahore Durbar, dated 11th March 1846.

Article 9—The British Government will give its aid to Maharaja Gulab Singh in protecting his territories from external enemies.

Article 10—Maharaja Gulab Singh acknowledges the supremacy of the British Government and will in token of such supremacy present annually to the British Government one horse, 12 goats (6 male and 6 female) and three pairs of Kashmir shawls.

This Treaty consisting of the above Articles has been this day settled by Frederic Currie Esquire and Brevet Major Henry Montgomery Lawrence, acting under the directions of the Right Honourable Sir Henry Hardinge, G.C.B., Governor-General, on the part of the British government and by Maharaja Gulab Singh in person and the said Treaty has been this day ratified by the seal of the Right Honourable Sir Henry Hardinge, G.C.B., Governor- General.

Done at Amritsar this sixteenth day of March in the year of our Lord, 1846 corresponding with the seventeenth day Rabi-ul-Awwal 1264 Hijri.

True to the very words of the Treaty of Amritsar, Jammu and Kashmir State has always stood by the Paramount Power in their hour of need.

"At the outbreak of the Mutiny", says the author of "Letters from India and Kashmir," "the late Maharaja Gulab Singh enjoined, nay, ordered his son "Ranbir Singh) to proceed with all his troops to the aid of the British, an injuction promptly obeyed and the soldiers of Kashmir fought by our side at the seige of Delhi."

The Jammu contingent consisting of 2,000 Infantry 200 Cavalry and six guns, under the political charge of Lt. Col. R. Lawrence, reached Delhi at a critical moment in the history of the Mutiny. The troops were commanded by Dewan Hari Chand. His Highness the Maharaja also sent valuable cash contributions to the Government of India.

After this the Kashmir State troops fought side by side with the British troops in the various campaigns on the frontiers of India including the Tirah and the Chitral campaigns.

Maharaja Gulab Singh despatched Zorawar Singh with a force for conquest of Ladakh in 1834 A.D. In the first skirmish the Ladakhis were defeated at Pashkyum but they again attacked the Dogras with an army of 15,000 near Langkartsa between Kargil and Suru. But this time they were completely routed losing 400 of their number and 200 who were taken as prisoners. The king of Ladakh submitted, agreeing to pay a war indemnity of Rs.50,000 and an annual tribute of Rs.20,000. While the Dogra troops were engaged in these operations, the Chief of Sod attacked Dogra fort at Suru but Zorawar Singh retook the fort and beheaded 200 insurgents.

Gulab Singh again despatched Zorawar Singh from Jammu with 12,000 troops in 1841 A.D. to take possession of Lhasa. The Dogra reached Guhrak and defeated the Lhasa troops. On return to Mantalan they seized the fort of Gurbang and Parang by storm. But the Lhasa troops came back under Chhgjut, retook Gurbang and defeated the Dogra under Zorawar Singh. Twentyfive soldiers only survived to tell the dismal tale, On hearing this Gulab Singh sent another force of 6,000 under Dewan Hari Chand and Wazir Ratnu. They defeated the enemy at Kargil who lost 3,300 soldiers. They then besieged Chamarh Gunpha where Bakhshi Achhinjut and Karam Shah had concentrated themselves. The Generals surrendered and were brought as prisoners to Leh from where they escaped after nine days. But the Dogra force again pursued them till they were humiliated and brought as prisoners to Gulab Singh who had encamped at Nasim Bagh. The Maharaja pardoned them after concluding a peace treaty with Lhasa in September, 1842 according to which Ladakh came permanently under Jammu and traders of Ladakh and Lhasa got the reciprocal concession of conducting trade freely in both the countries.

Baltistan,—The Rajas of this place are said to be the descendants of Sikandar of Kashgar. They were under the kings of Kashmir but in the time of Chaks they were independent. When the Moghuls came they again lost independence which, however, they regained under the Afghans. In 1837 A.D. Raja Ahmad Shah was at war with his son Mohammad Shah who got Tilel as Jagir from Col. Mian Singh, the Sikh Governor. During Zorawar Singh's expedition Mohammad Shah was caught and taken as a prisoner to Skardu by his father. Thereupon Zorawar Singh marched but restored it to Ahmad Shah on his paying a heavy war indemnity. When Zorawar Singh was killed at Mantalan, Ahmad Shah rebelled again but was over- powered a second time by Dewan Hari Chand who brought him as a prisoner to Jammu where he afterwards died. Mohammad Shah received an allowance from the Maharaja at Skardu. It may be noted here that Baltistan consists of the following subdivisions : Kharmang, Khaply, Skardu and Rondu.

Dardistan.—The district of Dardistan consists of the following sub-divisions : Astore, Bunji, Chilas, Gilgit, Hunza, Nagar, Punial, Yasin and Chitral.

During the time of the Moghuls, Gilgit was under Kashmir but when the Afghans appeared it broke away. In the time of the Sikhs, its ruler Mohammad Khan was over-powered by Suleman Shah of Yasin. The latter himself was murdered by Azad Khan of Punian who declared himself the master of the country. Azad Khan was in turn killed by Tihar Shah of Nagar. Tihar Shah ruled for some time and after his death was succeeded by Gauhar Aman son of Suleman Shah who then usurped the throne.

In 1842 A.D. Ghulam Mohiuddin, the Sikh Governor of Kashmir, sent troops to Gilgit under Nathu Shah and Mathra Das to help Karim Khan, brother of Sikandar Khan against Gauhar Aman who sustained a defeat and fled to Punial—Karim Khan then assumed the sovereignty of Gilgit. Nathu Shah who remained there and married the daughter of Gauhar Aman to himself and the daughters of the chiefs of Hunza and Nagar to his sons.

Maharaja Gulab Singh appointed the same Nathu Shah as Governor of Gilgit in 1845, but the Chief of Hunza killed him together with Karim Khan for bringing two European Officers with him. Gauhar Aman, the Chief of Punial and Yasin, with the help of the people of Delel, invaded Gilgit. Bhup Singh and Sant Singh, in command of Gulab singh's garrison, gave a crushing defeat to Gauhar Aman. Soon after the sons of Gauhar Aman namely Mulk Aman, Mirwali, Mirghazi and Pahalwan Bahadur, assisted by Dards and Hunza people, held Bhup Singh into an ambuscade at the Niladar Hill and massacred 100 of his troops and took 200 soldiers as prisoners who were sold as slaves after forcibly converting them to Islam. Only one woman escaped who crossed the Indus by holding the tail of a cow to tell this horrible tale at Bhunji. This made Gauhar Aman again the sole master of Gilgit. In 1856 after his death, Maharaja Ranbir Singh despatched General Devi Singh with a large force to re-conquer Gilgit. The enemy fled away before this force and the whole district as far as Yasin was occupied again. The victorious General installed Uzmat Shah and Isa Bahadur as Governors of Yasin and Punial respectively.

In 1859 A.D. Gilgit was permanently annexed to Kashmir when Mulk Aman who had revolted again was given a severe defeat by the Dogra force under the command of General Hushiara.

Chilas and Delel were annexed in 1851 and 1866 respectively. Yasin was taken in 1859 and was subsequently. Yasin was taken in 1859 and was subsequently ceded to the sons of Gauhar Aman with whom a Treaty of Peace was concluded.

The Chiefs of Hunza and Nagar, though tributary to Kashmir often gave trouble to Maharaja's garrison at Gilgit, but in December 1891, these two principalities were subjugated by British Indian and Kashmir Imperial Service Troops under the command of Col. A Durand, the then British Political Agent at Gilgit. When the Chinese were thrown to Rudok, a peace treaty was signed between the Lhasa Government and Maharaja Gulab Singh in 1842, which reads : "We shall neither at present nor in future have anything to do or interfere at all with the boundaries of Ladakh and its surroundings as fixed from ancient times and will allow the annual export of wool, shawls and tea by way of Ladakh according to the old established custom."

RANBIR SINGH

Maharaja Ranbir Singh, the third son of Gulab Singh, was born in the fort of Ramgarh in Samvat 1887-1889 some say at Ramnagar. His eldest brother Udham Singh was born on 27th Assuj 1874 and died on 22nd Kartik 1897. His elder brother Randhir Singh alieas Sohan Singh was killed in action in Samvat 1901. Maharaja Gulab Singh who was not keeping good health for some years before his death asked Ranbir Singh to look after the administration of the State and this enabled the Prince to equip himself for the duties which he had to fulfil as the ruler of Jammu and Kashmir State. About two years before his death Maharaja Gulab Singh himself gave Rajtilak to Ranbir Singh on the 18th Phagan 1912. According to Thakur Kahan Singh Billawaria, soon after his accession, three unsuccessful attempts were made on the life of the Maharaja in close succession by a band of intriguers. They were all punished in 1915 Samvat when the intrigue was traced. Sir Richard Temple who had known Maharaja Ranbir Singh since 1853 A.D. when he paid a private visit to Jammu, writes : "He was at that time 30 to 32 years of age. Handsome in face, with a very long moustache and a mien indicating high birth. His figure was small and his legs inclined to bend outwards but he rode and shot well". The author of the "Letter from India and Kashmir" wrote in 1870 AD. : "His Highness is in person handsome and of a complexion—I know not how to express it with a more expressive epitheton than olive—an olive colour his face presenteth, fair for the people of his country with features of the Grecian type, nose and forehead a straight line with a short black curly beard. His puggery of lawn with a lawn of gold tissue was relieved in colour by one scarlet gold. On his forehead was painted a yellow symbol with green centre that indicated the followers of Shiva and he wore the Brahmanical cord, also a necklace of barries inlaid with gold resembling the rosary of Romanists and used for the same purpose. The rest of his dress was of white cambric and a ribbon of scarlet and gold lace across his badge of authority."

"Government and other agencies would get 20 traks (trak is 5 seers 3 chataks) and 6-1/4 seers plus 22-1/2 chilkis (chilki anna is half Company anna) upon 192 traks in Rabi crop and 21 traks and 13-1/4 seers, plus 17-3/4 chilkis upon 142 traks in Kharif corp. The revenue in kind was collected through Tehsildar, Thanedar, Kardar, Mokhdam, Patwari, Shukdar, Sazawal, Taruchdar, Harkar and Doom who all fleeced the Zamindar (food grower)." The following taxes were in force :-

House tax 4 to 20 annas.
Fruit tax 3/4 of the price.

Animal tax 2 to 3 animals a year from each village yielding 500 khirwars of grain (khirwar is 16 traks = 83 seers), I pony, loi (blanket), 1/2 seer ghee for each milch cow, 1-10 fowls from each house, 2/3 of honey whereever produced.

Shawl tax Rs. 47/8/- in 1867 or Rs. 18/12/- per cent for stamp at Dagshawl.

Marriage license fee Rs. 3/- (license fee to purchase a girl for prostitution was 100 chilkis). Every nautch-girl paid 80-100 chilkis a year and was not permitted to marry.

Begar or forced labour was paid at the rate of 4 to 7 chilkis for double journey from Srinagar to Gilgit or Astor which involved a period of 24 days.

According to Robert Thorp (Kashmir Misgovernment 1870) Kashmiri character is exhibited in a marked degree in honesty and loving kindness.

"Shali sold at Rs. 2/- (chilki) a khirwar (chilki rupee is ten annas). It was sold at half this price when Gulab Singh came."

Gulab Singh created a kingdom which the new ruler consolidated. He spent a considerable sum of money upon education and roads. In his time crime and drunkenness became almost unknown. The economic conditions were such that a rupee would buy 80 lbs. of rice, 12 lbs. of meat and 60 lbs. of milk. Fruits grew in abundance and had little value. But as Mrs. Bruce says, the year 1877 was a cruel time on account of a very bad season. Maharaja Ranbir Singh's anxiety for improvement of the administration and the lot of his subjects is reflected in the talk recorded by Sir Richard Temple in his Journals. Sir Richard says : "I tried to hint delicately that, like all other places, Kashmir would benefit by increased care. The Maharja said that he was conscious of many defects and that as soon as he had leisure from affairs at Jammu, he would go to Kashmir and introduce several reforms, adding that he felt himself responsible to God for the care of his peoples. He then went on to say that Kashmir's population did not increase as much as he hoped, that many of his people had emigrated and that much land was lying waste...... In the afternoon I went again to bid the Maharaja farewell. He told me that he was endeavouring to improve the judicial system and that he had Doctors of Hindu and Mohammedan law in the work." Rev. Robert Clark founded Church Missionary Society in Kashmir in 1864 A.D.

During the reign of Maharaja Gulab Singh there was practically no change in the then existing judicial administration which was conducted by the Governors and other officials. The Maharaja himself could be easily approached by any of his subjects who sought justice at his hands. It must be remembered that Maharaja Gulab singh had to devote much time in the consolidation and building of Jammu and Kashmir State and it fell to the lot of his son, Maharaja Ranbir Singh, to set up an administration. He divided the administration of the State into three main heads : Daftar Nizamat, Daftar Diwani and Daftar Jangi.

For the first time a Penal Code, containing 100 Sections only, was published in Dogri characters. At every Police Station the Maharaja appointed an officer known as "Chakladar". This officer used to settle all petty civil and criminal suits.

An Adalat Sadar was created at Jammu and another at Srinagar. All cases of importance used to be decided by this Court. The Maharaja himself used to take keen interest n the administration of justice which was very cheap. It only required a stamp worth annas eight for getting a case decided by his Highness. The Maharaja used to hold his Durbar daily. Describing the Maharja's Durbar, Frederick Drew who saw one himself says :

"It is when the Maharaja is sitting in public Durbar, holding open Court for the hearing of petitions that the Mandi has its liveliest apppearance. For the morning Durbar he will take his seat at nine or ten o' clock beneath one of the arches of the arcade on the cushion which here answers for the throne, accompanied by his eldest son and surrounded by his minister, and with, may be, from fifty to hundred other courtiers and attendants seated round against the wall at distances according to the degree."

"Thus seated, and supported, the Maharaja looks down on the petitioners who stand in the Square which is some feet lower than the room. Each coming succession according to their petitions, previously written on stamped paper and given in, are called on, stands in front with hands closed, in the attitude of supplication, which the prayer is read out. The subject of the petitions are wonderfully varied ; perhaps an employee will ask leave to return to his home, or to take his mother's ashes to the Ganges ; next, may be a criminal is brought to receive final sentence ; then a poor women, with face veiled, will come to complain of some grievance or other or a dispute about a broken of marriage will have to be decided. These are all listened to patiently enough and on the simpler cases the decision is given at once and written on the petitions. The civil and criminal cases have usually been previously inquired into by judicial officers, in the courts of first instances, and perhaps have been adjudicated on by the Appeal Courts of Jammu or of Srinagar, but it is open to the suitors and complainants to try their fortune with the Maharaja himself. The Maharja does his best to find the truth, will examine and sharply cross-examine the witnesses. It frequently ends in his referring the matter to the magistrate for investigation in which case it will be again brought before him for final decision."

In Samvat 1848 (1891-92), a new State Penal Code called 'Sri Ranbir Dandh Bidhi' was compiled and issued.

The Jammu and Kashmir State Civil Courts Regulation of 1877 defines the powers of HIgh Court which was created the same year, as follows:

> "The High Court (Adalat-i-Alia) shall be deemed for the purposes of all enactments for

> the time being in force to be the highest court of appeal or revision, subject to the control and the judicial powers exercised by His Highness the Maharja Sahib Bahadur. The general superintendence and control over all other Civil courts shall be vested in, and all such courts shall be subordinate to the High Court."

There were in all 25 courts of which 14 were Wazarat courts. Besides there was a court in Srinagar called Adalat Dag-i-Shawl and a Panchayat Court consisting of eight nominated members (four Hindus and four Muslims) to look after general welfare. There were also three courts at Ladakh, Gilgit and Skardu. Two Sadar courts at Srinagar and Jammu heard appeals against Wazarat Courts. A Law Department under a Secretary was also established.

In the very beginning of his reign the Maharaja had a devote much attention towards military activities. He supervised drilling of soldiers. In 1857, when Mutiny broke out, he led a contingent consisting of 2,000 infantry, 200 cavalry and six guns to the aid of the British. It was due to these services, says Young-husband, that his right to adopt from collateral branches an heir to the succession on the failure of heirs (male) of Gulab Singh on whom alone the country had been conferred by the British was recognised. The Sanad was conferred in March, 1862.

After the termination of the Mutiny, the Maharaja turned his attention towards strengthening his position in Gilgit. In 1860, he sent a force under Colonel Devi Singh, which reduced the fort built by Gauhar Rahman who had just passed away. The forces then advanced towards Yasin and took it. After the reconquest of Gilgit, Raja Isa Bahadur of Punial, who had incurred the wrath of Gauhar Rahman, sought refuge principality. At the time of his reinstallment he acquired the territory of Ishkoman. In 1865, the disturbances which originated from Hunza, made the retention of Gilgit difficult again. The ruler of Chitral assisted the insurgents. Reinforcements were sent by the Maharaja and Darel Valley was occupied. The garrison was re-established at Gilgit. In 1867, Punial was invaded by its enemies from Yasin. But relief was sent from Gilgit and order restored. About this time the valley of Chaprot was occupied by the Hunza ruler. In 1877 the then ruler of Nagar occupied Chaprot and Chalt, and from that day these areas were held by the Nagar and Kashmir troops. In 1876 Yasin, Kuh-Ghazr and Ishkoman were under the rule of Mehtar Pahlwan Bahadur who belonged to the ruling dynasty of Chitral and professed allegiance to the Maharja of Kashmir. But he proved teacherous and Aman-ul-Mulk was permitted by the Maharaja's Government to incorporate the whole country. He partitioned the districts among paid Governors under the Maharaja after their severance from Chitral in 1895.

The Maharaja introduced many reforms in the administration of the State. As already referred to above he divided the administration into three main heads, Daftar Nizamat, Daftar Diwani and Daftar Jangi. The Jammu Province was divided into seven Wazarats—Jammu Khas, Jasrota, Ramnagar, Udhampur, Reasi, Nowshera and Manawar. The land revenue assessment was considerably improved. The Jammu Wazarat had four Tehsils and 30 Parganas.

Out of the total area of 686,450 ghumauns, 33,344 ghumauns were under cultivation and the land revenue was assessed at an average rate of Rs.1/9/3. The Kashmir Province was divided into six Wazarats—Shahar-i-Khas, Anantnag, Shopian, Pattan, Kamraj and Muzaffarabad. Taxes had increased in Kashmir from reign to reign. Ranbir Singh remitted many of them such as Tarki which was imposed on Zamindars from old times (it yielded an income of 209,000 chilkis though hardly one-fourth of the total produce was left with the tiller of the soil and sometimes even less). The imposition of the tax is explained thus : "Out of every two Khirwars of the produce one Khirwar was taken away as land revenue. Out of the balance of one Khirwar, eight traks were taken away as the so-called rasumi Tarki, rasumi Manwati and Qanungoi and Girdawari and the part of Shakdars and Sazawals.

Moorecroft who visited Kashmir in 1824 A.D. describes how heavily the Shawl trade and other trades were taxed in Kashmir. He says "Every Shawl was taxed 24 per cent upon the estimated value, besides which there was an import duty on the wool with which they were manufactured and a charge was made upon every shop or workman connected with the manufacture. Every other trade was also taxed." The trade of Kashmir received a great set-back partly on account of heavy taxation and partly on account of the heavy fall in the export trade brought about by the Franco-German war of 1870. Prior to this the Kashmir Shawl known as Cashmere was the fashion in aristocratic societies in Europe and was exported to the continent in large quantities. The tax on Shawls which was called "Dag-i-Shawl" is dated as far back as 1197 Hijri and was a great source of revenue. In the time of Ranbir Singh the tax at the old rate yielded a revenue of 12 lakhs. The Maharaja remitted this huge tax altogether just to help the industry. The other taxes on different arts, crafts and trades were as under : Taxes realised from Srinagar (trades) Rs.45,687/11/- ; taxes realised from Srinagar (arts and crafts) Rs.16,621/8/- ; taxes realised from Anantnag Rs.4,280/6/- ; taxes realised from Shopian s. 1,079/4/-, taxes realised from Pattan Rs.304/5/- ; taxes realised from Wazarat Kamraj Rs.9,151/8/- (Total Rs.77,125/4/-). These taxes were all remitted: Besides many petition boxes were set up, import duty abolished, marriage tax withdrawn and kidnapping put down.

The following extract from the administration report of the Punjab for 1864-65 will be read with interest :-

"The reduction of customs affected by His Highness last year had let to a considerable increase in the trade with the adjacent districts in the British territory. The trade with Sialkot is reported to have increased in value from Rs.1,35,000 to Rs. 1,71,000 per annum, that with Jullundur and Hoshiarpur to have more than doubled.

Chiefly in regard to the items of saccharine produce and native cloth, in Gujrat there is said to have been a general increase in the trade with Kashmir. The export of silk from Jhelum is stated to exhibit a similar increase and the value of shawl, wools and saffron imported to the Kangra district, showed an increase of Rs.9,000." In 1867 His Highness decided to apply the rate of five per cent, charged for goods in transit from the Punjab to Yarkand from all imports from Central Asia or India of which the bond was not broken in the State territories. In 1870 a trade treaty was concluded with the British Indian Government. Under its terms, His Highness the Maharaja undertook to forego all duty on the trade between Central Asia and British India, in return for the same concession made by the Indian Government for goods imported into the State through British India.

There occurred a severe clash between the Shias and the Sunnis in 1872. The disturbance was brought under control and the Maharaja gave Rs. 3 lakhs to the Shias by way of relief because they had suffered much. The famine of 1877 was of a severe type. Foodstuffs could not be easily imported from the Punjab because no motorable road existed then between Rawalpindi and Srinagar though the construction of a cart-road had just begun. The Maharaja, however, ordered grains to be purchased worth about a lakh of rupees from the Punjab. Besides, an Irshad was issued saying that "Anyone who imported foodgrains to the value of Rs.20,000/- will be awarded Rs. 1,000/- as Khilat and will receive the pleasure of His Highness." In the meantime some grain purchased at Sialkot arrived. The grain had cost the State Rs. 15/14/6 per khirwar but it was sold at the rate of Rs. 4/4/- only. Free langars were started to feed the poor. About 195,714 maunds of grain were imported.

The State met a loss of about Rs. 33,64,195/3/3. Those who emigrated during this famine were later on induced to return.

Under such circumstances the question of transport would draw any ruler's attention. The construction of the Jhelum Valley Road already started. The cart road between Jammu and Srinagar was also started with a bridge over the Chenab at Ramban. This bridge was built at a time when over 2-ton motor lorries were unknown but it has existed up to this day in spite of heavy vehicular traffic that runs over it. The bridge was built by the local people and the steel used in its construction was brought from the rich mineral areas in Reasi district. A telegraph and a postal system was introduced to link up various parts of the State.

To increase th speed of mails 129 stages were set up between Jammu and Srinagar and it took only 25 to 30 hours for the mail bags to reach Srinagar from Jammu and vice versa. Settled condition in Kashmir valley attracted many visitors to Kashmir and in order to afford facilities to European visitors a direct mail line from Jammu to Lahore was established in Samvat 1921.

Anxious to further develop the postal system the Maharaja invited Mr. Hogg, the then Postmaster-General of Punjab to Jammu and discussed with him all possibilities of improvement. In 1934 (Bikrami) the Maharaja thought of connecting Gilgit with Srinagar by a telegraph. And he did it with the help of an officer from the Punjab Government. Later, Jammu was also connected with Srinagar. Telegrams addressed from Srinagar to British India were sent from Jammu to Sialkot thrrough horse service but in Samvat 1935 the State telegraph line was extended to Suchetgraph which brought the State nearer to British India telegraphically.

While earlier the visitors were looked after through the Punjab Government, in 1877 an officer on special duty was placed directly under the Government of India who replaced the mixed court of 1872 consisting of British and State officials, for deciding civil suits between local people and the European visitors. In the Afghan war of 1878-80 the Maharaja sent a contingent of troops and artillery to assist the British. He introduced vine cultivation at various places and brought productions of the country on a firm footing. Silk industry received a great impetus during this time. He imported seedlings of mulberry trees from China. Tea gardens were laid in the Tehsils of Reasi and Basohli.

In Samvat 1931, production of hand-made paper was started for Government use. Shawl manufacture, paper-making and sericulture were already introduced into Kashmir by Sultan Zain-ul-Abdin. Paper-making spread as a cottage industry round Vicharnag and survived till the earlier days of Maharaja Partap Singh, when mill-made paper pushed it out of existence. Opium cultivation which was restricted to Bhaderwah and Kishtwar only was extended to other parts of the State as well. A brewery was established at Gupkar and the Kashmir wine won a gold medal at the Calcutta Exhibition. Sir Oliver St. John, officer on special duty in Kashmir, conveyed Viceroy's appreciation to the Maharaja on this successful manufacture.

Ranbir Singh was a great patron of art and letters. As early as 1867, when the idea of founding a University at Lahore was first mooted by Sir. E. Mcleod, the then Lt. Governor of the Punjab, the Maharaja gave a donation of Rs.6,25,000. When the University was founded in 1882, Maharaja Ranbir Singh's name was incorporated as the First Fellow in the Charter. A Translation Department was created to translate books on various subjects for use in the schools of the State. Subjects like Geology and Physics were also dealt with. The chief books published then are Sri Ranbir Parkash (diseases and their treatment), Ranbir Vrat Ratnakar (Dharm Shastra), Ranbir Bhakti Ratnakar (Purans), and Gulabnama (history of Gulab Singh in Persian). Scholars were sent to Tibet to learn the Tibetan language and many Tibetan books were translated into Hindi. Vidya Bilas Press was the first printing press introduced in his time in the State. Writing about the languages in vogue then Frederick Drew writes : "Besides the Persian character which is these territories in hardly ever applied to any but persian language there are three written characters used for the spoken languages.

These are Dogri, Kashmiri and Tibetan. The Dogri alphabet in its old form was imperfect and not easy to read either accurately or quickly. For this reason a few years ago the Maharaja recommended its modification. It was brought nearer to Devnagri, so near that the system is quite one with that, though the forms are somewhat different. New Dogri is used for the petitions that are read before the Maharaja, for this purpose it has replaced Persian in which petitions were written when I first visited Jammu but it has not generally displaced either Persian in which petitions were written when I first visited Jammu but it has not generally displaced either Persian or old Dogri." In every Wazarat and Tehsil a school was opened and provision was made for higher studies in oriental languages. A big Pathshala was opened at Raghunath Temple, Jammu and another at Utterbhani where instructions were imparted in the Vedas, Grammar, Kavya Shastra and Niyay. Books were supplied free and scholarships granted. Frederick Drew was incharge of mineral survey and under his direction iron and coal were worked to certain extent.

Considerable attention was given to irrigation and one of the most important canals in the State is known after him, though it was completed in the time of his successor. Earthquakes occurred in 1883, 1978 and 1884 A.D. Famine visited in 1864 and 1877 A.D. Cholera broke out in 1557-58, 1867, 1872, 1875-76 and 1879 A.D. and fires caused a devastation in 1875 and 1878 A.D.

These are Dogri, Kashmiri and Tibetan. The Dogri alphabet in its old form was imperfect and not easy to read either accurately or quickly. For this reason a few years ago the Maharaja recommended its modification. It was brought nearer to Devnagri, so near that the system is quite one with that, though the forms are somewhat different. New Dogri is used for the petitions that are read before the Maharaja, for this purpose it has replaced Persian in which petitions were written when I first visited Jammu but it has not generally displaced either Persian or old Dogri." In every Wazarat and Tehsil a school was opened and provision was made for higher studies in oriental languages. A big Pathshala was opened at Raghunath Temple, Jammu and another at Utterbhani where instructions were imparted in the Vedas, Grammar, Kavya Shastra and Niyay. Books were supplied free and scholarships granted. Frederick Drew was incharge of mineral survey and under his direction iron and coal were worked to certain extent.

Considerable attention was given to irrigation and one of the most important canals in the State is known after him, though it was completed in the time of his successor. Earthquakes occurred in 1883, 1878 and 1884 A.D. Famine visited in 1864 and 1877 A.D. Cholera broke out in 1557-58, 1867, 1872, 1875-76 and 1879 A.D. and fires caused a devastation in 1875 and 1878 A.D.

Maharaja Ranbir Singh introduced his own currency. The State Mint was closed twelve years after his death in 1897 A.D. when the British currency was introduced. Similarly the State Postal system was amalgamated with the Indian Postal system in 1894 A.D.

Sir Richard Temple bears testimony to the high character of the Maharaja. He says : "His private domestic life seemed to be good. He came out daily and was certainly free from many frivolities and vices which but too often disfigure the private conduct of Oriental Princes." Maharaja Ranbir Singh was granted G.S.C.I., and a royal salute of 21 guns in lieu of his services to the British Empire. Earlier he had been offered a jagir in Oudh in return for the State force's assistance in putting down the Mutiny. He declined the offer because the help rendered was given as an ally.

Maharaja Gulab Singh had established the treasury of Shri Raghunathji with a fund of rupees five lakhs, the interest to be spent of Sadavarts. Ranbir Singh was appointed Trustee to look after the Devasthans. Ranbir Singh enjoined upon his sons, heirs, descendants etc. to lend their help to his Trust and to see that the Trust-deed was respected in letter and spirits. This was issued on 20th Katik, 1950.

Rajas Pratap Singh, Ram Singh and Amar Singh accepted the injunction of their father with heart and soul by a declaration dated 25th Baisakh 1941. The oath administered in the name of hundred thousand sacred cows is incorporated in the Ain-i- Dharmarth which governs the administration of the ecclesiastical department.

Ranbir Singh breathed his last on 14th September, 1885 A.D. Conveying his condolence to his successor, Pratap Singh, H.E. the Viceroy and Governor-General in a letter dated Simla, the 14th September, 1885, wrote : "Maharaja Ranbir Singh rendered valuable service to the British Government. I feel that his loss is the loss of a friend."

Maharaja Pratap Singh G.C.S.I., G.C.I.E., LL.D., etc., was born in 1850 A.D. and succeeded to the throne in 1885 A.D. Ranbir Singh had four sons, namely, Raja Pratap Singh,. Raja Ram Singh, Raja Amar Singh and Raja Lachman Singh. Pratap Singh was the eldest. Raja Lachman Singh died in 1848 A.D. Raja Ram Singh was a soldier who would admit no defeat in battle. He passed away in 1897 A.D. Raja Amar Singh was one of the richest princes of India and served as Prime Minister and

Commander-in-Chief in the State for some time and died in 1907 A.D.

Maharaja Pratap Singh's forty years' reign was epoch-making. The greatest contribution of the Dogra Rule in Kashmir are the two trunk roads which were completed in his time. The first drawback of Kashmir was its lack of the means of communication with British India. In 1889 there was no continuous road to drive through in Kashmir, althogh there existed every kind of roads between different towns. In addition to numerous short roads constructed throughout the country plans of two main roads, one joining Srinagar with Kohala and the other with Jammu, were designed for motor traffic. The Jhelum Valley Road covers a length of 132 miles from Srinagar to the Kohala Bridge and the Banihal Cart Road covering a length of 203 miles was completed in 1922 at a cost of rupees forty-three lakhs. Bridges were constructed at Domel, Kohala and other places.

The Sialkot-Jammu Railway which linked up Jammu with British India was thrown open to traffic in 1890. Many projects have been prepared from time to time to bring Srinagar on the Railway map of India but the idea so far remains unrealised. The Sangam bridge was built in 1910.

Crops in Kashmir usually depend upon snows and not upon monsoons as in the plains. Naturally the greater the number of irrigation canals, the less apprehension of a famine. Pratap Singh constructed a number of these—Martand Canal, Lal Khul, Pratap Canal, Ranbir Canal (this being the largest, serving an area of about 1,26,000 acres) Basantpur Canal, Ujh Canal and Upper Jhelum Canal. The Zainagir Canal was completed in the year 1931 at a cost of Rs.11 lakhs. A flood spill channel for diverting the waters of the Jhelum was constructed between Ram Munshi Bagh and Pandrethan. Dredging operations were conducted below the town of Baramulla for removal of silt etc. A weir was constructed across the Jhelum at

Chatabal to maintain enough water in the river during winter and draughts. Arrangements were made for supply of pure water on sanitation lines to the cities of Srinagar and Jammu.

Pratap Singh was an orthodox Hindu. Though deeply devoted to the Royal House of Windsor, neither he nor his brothers ever crossed the "black water". Even moving about India meant a cumbersome, elaborate business. "It pleased him that his Imperial Service troops—no Kashmiri among them—had the honour of guarding the Northern passes into India". He avoided alcohol but an "opium peg" brightended his wits and his outlook.

Though himself not a very great soldier, the army was his great concern. He reorganised the military force, supplied it with modern equipment and brought it on modern footing. Kashmir being so rich in forest wealth its conservancy was needed. (India probably gets her best timber supplies from Kashmir). The First Great War caused great unrest in the grain market by high fluctuation. Pratap Singh took cue from Gulab Singh's food policy and introduced rationing which led to grain control that exists to this day A step was taken in the direction of local Self- Government by establishing two Municipalities—One at Jammu and one at Srinagar. Two first grade colleges were founded at Jammu and Srinagar with a net-work of schools spread all over the country to fight ignorance and illiteracy. Two up-to-date hospitals were also opened at the capital cities. Numerous dispensaries were set up in towns and villages to combat sickness and disease and to promote public health. A well-equipped technical institute was established at Srinagar to train artisans in various crafts. Few of its kind existed in the whole of India then.

Since Gulab Singh's time revenue was obtained in kind. Probably salaries also were given in kind. One of the greatest measures of Pratap Singh's reign is the land revenue settlement of the country under the able supervision of Walter Lawrence.

The revenue in kind was replaced by revenue in cash. The old Kardars who fleeced the peasantry no more exist now. Soon after followed the co-operative movement which saved zamindars from the clutches of Sahukars. In his time one State monopoly Dagshawl (shawl industry) was abolished and another, Sericulture, was set up. Silk Industry in Kashmir provided work to thousands of people in the State. "He accomplished all this in spite of the fact that he had succeeded to a bankrupt kingdom," says Lawrence.

In 1889 A.D., only after few years of his reign, the relations between Pratap Singh and the Paramount Power became somewhat strained. By now—1885 the British had succeeded in installing a Resident in Kashmir. The mixed court appointed in 1872 was abolished and the Resident and his assistants were invested with powers to dispose of certain kinds of suits. Col. Nisbat the then Resident, brought a charge that Pratap Singh was intriguing with Russia and Dalip Singh against the British which resulted in virtual abdication of the Maharaja in 1889. The charge of plotting murder of Plowdon, the British Resident, was also brought against him. "Condemned Unheard" gives the full background. A council was constituted for the administration of the State with Raja Amar Singh and two officers from Delhi ; just before his death after the conclusion of the first Great War in which the Maharaja had given great assistance and displayed deep loyalty he was once again in enjoyment of full powers.

Pratap Singh had some trouble on his frontiers also. In his time, conquest of Hunza was effected and Chitral War was fought. The Dogra soldiers resisted attacks, offered counter attacks and finally won wherever they went.

As in the previous reign, Kashmir saw a number of natural calamities. The earthquake shock of 1885 A.D. destroyed much life and property. Cholera epidemics of 1888, 1892, 1900, 1902, 1906-7 and 1910 wrought untold havoc. Plague that broke out in 1903-4 in Jammu, created panic in the whole State. People fled into interior to save their lives. There were big fires in 1892 and 1899 which entailed much loss of property—as if these had not been enough, there were heavy floods in 1893 and 1903. The former alone swept away about six thousand souls. The first Census operations were conducted in Kashmir in 1891 and this was followed by three other decennial Census operations in 1901, 1911 and 1921. The population of Kashmir in 1891 was only 949,041 ; in 1941 it was 1,728,705.

The visit of a Prince of Wales to a State was a rare occasion. During Pratap Singh's reign, two Princes of Wales visited Jammu. Their visits further strengthened the bond of friendship between Kashmir, Delhi and London. Pratap Singh spared no pains to help winning the first World War. His contributions in men, material and money were huge.

In 1914 A.D. Kashmir sent Second Kashmir Rifles to the front, the main strength of which was reinforced throughout the war. Another despatch consisting of two battalions and 2/2nd Kashmir Rifles was sent in 1917 A.D. The total number of these despatches amounted to 1,200 and 1,070 strong.

Two Kashmir Imperial Lancers (1915 A.D.) and Kashmir Mountain Battery furnished with six guns (1916 A.D.) largely added to the numerical strength of the war contribution. The total monetary contribution amounted to about Rs.1,11,00,000/- in all. In addition to this, the State supplied 31,000 recruits to the British India Army. This was the largest number of recruits supplied by any Indian State during the war.

"In recognition of the signal services rendered by these Units at the various theatres of the war, many battle honours were conferred on them".

Yuvraj Hari Singh, who was then the Commander-in-Chief, made the following contribution from his Privy Purse.

Investment in War Loans and Bonds	Rs. 13,00,000
Donations etc. ---- ----	Rs. 2,91,000

The war began in 1914 and ended in 1918 A.D. with victory for the Allies.

During this war prices of commodities soared very high. Death by starvation was averted by the timely intervention of the Government. Narindra Nath Kaul, Revenue Minister, assisted by Salam Shah, Tehsildar, brought into being Shali Stores (now known as Food Control Department) of which every consumer was made a share-holder on payment of Rs.11/- as share money. After a few months share money was returned and the concern was taken over by the Government. Shali was priced at Rupees five per khirwar, hatab (firewood) at annas eight per maund, bread five tolas one pice, milk annas two a seer, meat annas eight a seer and so on. Grain dealers, stockists, gujjars, and butchers were rounded up and their stocks seized if they refused to sell at fixed prices. Novel punishments were given out of court such as cutting the beard on one side, dragging through the streets bare-headed and bare-footed. "Salam Shahun Suchh" became a house-hold term. When Narindra Nath Kaul died even stones and bricks of Srinagar wept. Never was an administrator given such a funeral as he. He was the brain behind the economic revolution while Salam Shah was the executor of the policy. This revolution catered to the urban consumer at the cost of rural producer and voiceless labourer. Kashmir was deaf to what was happening beyond her North across the Himalayas.

During the summer of 1924, there was an uprising by the labourers of Srinagar Silk Factory and this incident was immediately followed by possession of a plot of land belonging to the State by the Muslims at Anantnag. For the first time a people politically oppressed appeared in revolt and the seed took roots. Young husband writes in "The Light of Experience" that Pratap Singh was a great gentleman and remained staunch in his loyalty to the British Crown and sedition had never the slightest chance in Kashmir. That is a reason why this movement did not receive external support then. The movement was suppressed and obviously it disappeared.

Maharaja Pratap Singh was a pious ruler. Though a Rajput, he did not take meat nor did he shoot any game. Every day from morn up to noon he would be busy with his "Puja". In the afternoon he would come in the open Durbar. Right up to the evening the Vitasta put up an appearance of lotus crop which he had offered to the Deity earlier. The Maharaja himself watched it from his window as did his "humblest subjects". These lotus flowers came from his "place of worship". The Khir Bhawani Mela on 8th day in the solar half of Jeth attracts large crowds at Tulamula. Maharaja Pratap Singh was a frequent visitor to the shrine on this day. He would go there in all pomp and distribute alms to the poor and the needy.

Arya Samaj preachers and Qadiani Muslims, also Biscoe Schools, gave a shaking to orthodox thinking.

His simplicity and unostentatiousness are proverbial. He was extravagantly liberal in Dan (charity). The current history has not come across a single anecdote that Pratap Singh had ever refused a gift or a charity. Some times he would relieve a widow. Some times he would come to the rescue of an orphan. May be that some times his charity was misplaced or his generosity abused. His Privy Purse which was one lakh per month minimum hardly made way outside the State, and there were few charges of luxury and extravagance. He would puff native tobacco all day long and he was accessible to the humblest of his subjects.

In his time law courts had begun to function. Ranbir Dand Bidhi was in force, and he would him self take up investigation if a complaint came to his notice. This he had inherited from his father and grand-father. But the punishments he awarded were not severe.

As there was unrest in the country, Gulab Singh had ordered to fire gun three times in a day—twelve noon, ten P.M. and four A.M. (winter) or three A.M. (summer). Twelve noon indicated time. Ten P.M. a signal to remain indoors and 4 A.M./3 A.M. indicated time limit within which the people were required to remain indoors. This practice continued up to Maharaja Hari Singh's reign, though in theory only because time had changed and "law and order" had come to stay. His successor discontinued this practice because it was needed no more.

Maharaja Pratap Singh was very fond of cricket. He maintained a cricket team and was himself one of the eleven. Thousands of spectators were attracted to see the Maharaja hitting the ball on the playground. He was exceptionally short-statured.

Maharaja Pratap Singh's State entry into Srinagar every year between May and June was a picturesque scene. At Shalteng he would take his seat in a specially decorated chakwari with Wazirs round him and as the chakwari moved up towards Shergarhi, thousands of people were attracted and watched the procession from roofs, windows and river ghats. The river Jhelum was literally littered with Shikaras moving to and fro.

Organised public opinion was suppressed as before though a solitary organisation or a solitary newspaper did make its appearance to mould the policy of administration as inspired officially. It was Dogra Sabha and Ranbir started from Jammu under special permission. When the author sought permission to start a paper from Srinagar he was told in writing by the then District Magistrate that it was not desirable to grant permission to a newspaper being started from Srinagar.

Mirwaiz and Hargopal Kaul lead Muslims and Pandits of Kashmir but inspiration and patronage from Government guided their activities which were restricted to social land religious spheres only in fitness of the times.

Kar-i-Sarkar or forced labour survived to his day but it was paid for. It may be that it was some times abused but it was not so rigorous as previously.

As education spread, a wave of resentment arose among the local intelligentsia against the outsiders who had almost all the services in their hands. The administration was mostly manned by them. The slogan of "State for States' People" came to be heard everywhere, but the Maharaja paid little heed to this growing movement. Least did his councillors imagine that this pukar would become a public slogan one day and lead to a political movement that would be faced by his successor and one day culminate in "Quit Kashmir" slogan.

Pratap Singh was not blessed with a son. Once or twice a child was born to him but none survived. He adopted Jagat Dev Singh of Poonch Ruling family but Raja Amar Singh taking exception to his (former's) claim of succession frustrated the intrigue at the very initial stage. Jagat Dev became waterson to perform obsequies only and Hari Singh, the only son of Raja Amar Singh and nephew of Maharaja Pratap Singh, became thus the heir-apparent. And when he grew up, he became the Commander-in-Chief and later Senior and Foreign Member of Council.

Pratap Singh died on 23rd September 1925 A.D. at Srinagar. Jagat Dev Singh later succeeded to the gaddi of Poonch, a Jagir under the sovereignty of Kashmir Durbar.

Since his virtual deposition earlier, Pratap Singh was over loyal to the British Government. In his time a Britisher (Bara Sahib) moved about as God's anointed. The revenue of the

State had risen to about rupees two crores. Rajputs were recruited in the army. Brahmins of Jammu and Kashmir lived upon his orthodoxy. Muslims were backward. In Kashmir it is labour and trade that kept them just going 85 per cent of the civil administration was usurped by the people of the neighbouring province of Punjab. A few low jobs such as a Patwari, schoolmaster, forest guard and clerk went to Kashmiri Pandits who flocked to schools and were utilised by the British Departmental heads. Punjab, 15 per cent to Jammu and 10 per cent to Kashmir out of which Muslims got a negligible share. Civil liberties there were none. If there was any association its motto was 'God bless the king'. Pratap Singh would say "Don't give too much to Rajputs, use Kashmiri Pandits as much as you can and see that Muslims do not starve". He started a move to attract people from outside to settle in the State. Lands were doled out to them. The economic and political condition of the people was very backward so much so that joint family system had come to stay by dire need as hardly one in a family was an earner. It is only after the Great War I that people started converting earthen utensils into brass or copper ones. People were so poor that even Hindus could not change earthen utensils on such days as Shivratri or Shrada day. The custom prevails even now in some houses inspite of changed economic position. Pratap Singh was accessible to people and he was in touch with what happened around him. Some times he would baffle official informers. A kind word pays in the long run. When he died Kashmiris did say that he was a pious ruler.

Maharaja Hari Singh, the ex-ruler of Jammu and Kashmir, was born in September 1895. He was the son of Raja Amar Singh and a great grandson of Maharaja Gulab Singh. He joined the Mayo College, Ajmer in 1908 at the age of 13. Later on he was sent to Dehra Dun for military training. On his return he was appointed the Commander-in-Chief of State forces in 1915 when he was only 20 years of age. He took up the post of Senior Member of the then State Council in 1922.

Maharaja Hari Singh ascended the Gaddi in September 1925 but Rajtilak ceremony was performed in February 1926 at Jammu. The new Maharaja announced agricultural reformes and further extension of educational and other facilities.

As mentioned before both Dogras and kashmiris were demanding representation in services At last, due to the support of the ruler himself, came the State Subject's Definition in 1927 which protects the children of the soil in recruitment to services and other privileges against outsiders. According to the Definition only those persons who settled in the State before Samvat 1942 came to be recognised as hereditary State Subjects of class I. This measure was implemented by training local talent for different offices. Its rigidity is over now. Writes Alberuni—"People of Kashmir are particularly anxious about the actual strength of their country and therefore take always great care to keep a strong hold upon the entrance and roads leading into it. In consequence it is very difficult to have any commerce with them ....At present they do not allow any Hindu whom they do not know personally to enter, much less other people". This has got to be reckoned as a historical background for this move.

Writes (Justice) Jai Lal Kilam in his book 'A History of Kashmiri Pandits' :—

"Those were the days when the whole of India was pregnant with many great revolutionary potentialities. Though there was no freedom of press or platform in the State, yet a stir was clearly visible in the whole State excepting in the powers that were. The movement went under-ground. The present writer and a number of educated Pandit youngmen alongwith a Kashmiri Pandit journalist—Pandit Gwasha Lal Kaul—wrote extensively to outside papers and issued hand written and some times cyclostyled posters in which the short comings of the ruling Junta were discussed thread bare. This went on for some time till contacts were established with writers in other states".

Following the movement launched by the Muslims in 1931 for political reforms and civic rights the Maharaja appointed a Commission (Grievances Enquiry) of representatives of communities which was presided over by a British Officer, Mr. (later Sir) B.G. Glancy. As a result of this enquiry religious places that had passed into the hands of the Government were restored back to the Muslims and other communities, adequate representation to different communities in services was guaranteed and proprietary rights to zamindars on their lands were granted. The freedom of the press and the platform also came in its wake. The movement of 1931 created a mass leader in the person of Sheikh Mohammad Abdullah who in the initial stages placed a communal view-point before the people. Later on, say in 1939, he became wedded to the nationalist school of thought asking for responsible Government. The ideology attracted to him non-Muslims as well. There were stirs in other communities also and the most important of these were the 'Bread Movement' of Kashmir and the 'Cow Agitation' of Jammu. The former followed the publication of the Grievances Enquiry Commission Report and was led by Kashmiri Pandits who interpreted the report as an anti-Hindu document which would bang all doors of services against them and even impede the course of their development. Prem Nath Bazaz, Kashmiri Pandits' representative on the Commission, who had pleaded for recreation facilities in I' dgah was publicly hooted. The High Court had reduced punishment prescribed by law for cow killing in a single case. The Dogras protested against this.

Praja Sabha (People's Assembly) was established in 1934 and about 6 per cent of the population only was given the right of vote. The Praja Sabha consisted of 75 members, 33 of them being elected. In 1939, the elected element was raised from 33 to 40 and the constitution was further liberalised but increased representation was given to vested interests to hoodwink democracy.

Judicial reform was not lost sight of. In March 1928, a High Court comprising a Chief Justice and two Puisne Judges was established. In 1930, the jurisdiction exercised by Residency courts was transferred to the State courts. This decreased the influence of the Political Department on local administration. A Judicial Advisory Board akin to the Privy Council in the case of British India, was also established to advice, His Highness in regard to the disposal of Judicial cases going up to him in appeal. On 10th September, 1943, Letters Patent, was granted to the High Court thus bringing it in line with modern canons of law. The judiciary in the State was thus made completely independent of the Executive.

Before the introduction of Settlement of Land under Mr. W. Lawrence the status of cultivators was awfully bad. The State's share of revenue revised to 30 per cent of the gross produce contributed some relief. The total area under cultivation was 2,256,000 acres. The Settlement itself is repeated after 40 years. The Agriculturist's Relief Act specially relieved the cultivator from the clutches of the money-lender. The Village Panchayats gained impetus from 1937. They attend to medical relief, education, sanitation, rural uplift etc., and dispose of petty cases. Out of 300 and odd Acts passed during the last 20 years, Alienation of Land Act of 1928 and Consolidation of Holdings Act 1940 did much to ameliorate the lot of Zamindars. Free and compulsory primary education for boys was introduced to fight mass illiteracy. Trade, commerce and industry received impetus through the Exhibition which was founded in 1929.

On March 9, 1931, Her Highness the Junior Maharani who had accompanied the Maharaja to London in 1930 gave birth to a prince—Maharaj Kumar Karan Singh Ji,(heir-apparent) at Cannes in the South of France. Since Pratap Singh's times the Dogra House had not been favoured with a male issue.

Social Reform :— Marriage of boys under 18 and of girls under 14 was prohibited, even before the Sharda Act had been passed in British India. Rajputs who killed their daughters after birth were forbidden to do so. During the previous reigns, Rajputs and Brahmins were immune from capital punishment. This disparity was ended. The Juvenile Smoking Act was passed to save the rising generation from a bad habit. Harijans against whom the doors of temples had been banned were allowed freedom of worship on 2nd November 1932. Traffic in women was put an end to. Restriction against Hindu widows that they could not re-marry was removed.

The seed for local self-government was sown in earlier days. The Municipal Committees at Srinagar and Jammu were official bodies in the initial stages. As education advanced and civic sense developed, municipal reforms also came. The first step was taken in 1913, then next in 1921, again in 1927-28 and finally in 1936. Just as measures were adopted to discourage emigration of labour, so was overcrowding in the cities guarded against under Town Planning which recommended extension. Old maps were redrawn.

The introduction of the basic system and recognition of the Double Script (persian and Devnagri) for education were experiments which did not make much headway. The construction of three new hospitals at Mirpur, Jammu and Srinagar on modern scientific lines at an immense cost was designed to provide improved medical aid. For the last so many years plague has not been heard of in Jammu.

In 1935, Gilgit was leased out to the Paramount Power on certain conditions under an agreement reached between the two Governments.

The flood of 1929 was one of the severest ever witnessed by Kashmir. It caused immense loss of property. This was followed by another in 1931.

In the domain of industries besides the Silk Factory which is the largest of its kind in the world there came into being Match Factory, Santonine Factory, Tannery, Pottery Factory, Woollen Mill, Silk Weaving Factory, Sheep Breeding Farm, Pyrethrum Cultivation, Resin and Turpentine Factory, Half Wrought Factory, Drug Research Laboratory, Kashmir willows, Sugar Mill, Indianite Factory. The Jammu and kashmir Bank reflects prospects of these and other industries.

The World War II broke out in 1939. Like his predecessors the ruler left no stone unturned to help the war effort. He offered services of one Infantry Brigade Signal Section and four Battalions of Infantry (1st and 2nd Mountain Battery), 3rd Rifles, 4th, 7th and 9th Infantry, Artillery Training Centre), 18 completely equipped motor ambulances, Kashmir House at Delhi without rent, Lock-heed plane besides contributions in money and men. The total number of recruits supplied was nearly 65,000 and the total aid amounted to Rs.9,87,315/8/- (war aid), Rs. 2,79,247/1/6 (Privy Purse), £40,000 and £1,000. The State troops won distinction at Keren (Eritrea) and Damascus (Syria). The ruler personally visited the Middle East in October 1941 and Italy in 1944.

At the first Round Table Conference held in London, Maharaja Hari Singh boldly advocated India's freedom. And at the time Sir Stafford Cripps came to India with an offer, he issued a historical statement advocating the same ideal. In 1944 he himself appointed two Popular Ministers and in 1945 he gave the Premiership to a mulki just giving an opportunity to State Subjects for manning the highest posts in the administration but times had gone much ahead to hypnotise people with such eye-wash reforms.

Maharaja Hari Singh was fond of polo and shikar very much as his predecessor was of cricket and puja. The two palaces of Gupkar and Ramnagar, the Hari Singh High Street and the Boulevard round the Dal Lake reveal taste of a builder.

The revenue which the State yielded in 1945-46 was Rs.4,24,54,000.

But in spite of this, differences continued to exist between various communities. Muslims, HIndus and Sikhs presented a separate stand-point each. The politics of Kashmir was greatly influenced by the politics of British India. "Akhand Hind" and "Pakistan" slogans assured to sweet promise. In spite of obvious clash of interests both province- wise and community-wise there was a common ideal before all—responsible government under the aegis of the ruler which later on culminated in the "Quite kashmir" movement.

Writes Maud Diver in Royal India, "The position of Kashmir is that of Hyderabad reversed and given the moral support of the British Government, there is every possibility of a peaceful solution that may be reasonably expected to endure". The British mind though like this.

The Civil Disobedience Movement started in 1931 rooted itself deeply into the soil as champion of the rights of the peasant, the artisan and the worker. The sponsors of the movement were Muslims. That was only natural. It is they who had been reduced mostly to a position of servitude since the coming of the Sikhs. The non-Muslims opposed the rising tide with the result that communal clashes could not be averted. Both as petty officer or as landlord and shahokar (money-lender), the HIndu had played no small part in shaking the confidence of his countrymen. But communal discord subsided soon. In 1933 support of the Sikhs and the Hindus was enlisted to work jointly for the welfare of the masses. In his presidential address at the J & K Muslim Conference in 1932 Sheikh Mohammad Abdullah said : "We stand for the rights of all communities. Our country's progress in impossible so long as we do not establish amicable relations between the different communities. This is possible only when each community learns to appreciate the view point of other communities". The Muslim Conference became extinct in 1939, its place was taken by the National Conference. The same year gave birth to the famous National Demand which was signed by representatives of all communities. The "Quit India" movement started by the Indian National Congress in 1942 was followed by "Quit Kashmir" movement led by the National Conference in 1946 preceded by adoption of "New Kashmir" as the goal in 1944 which promised freedom from all form of political and economic exploitation. The National Conference in its historical memorandum to the Cabinet Mission declared "Today the national demand of the people of Kashmir is not merely the demand of a responsible Government but their right to absolute freedom from the autocratic rule of the Dogra House". This was followed by the arrest of Sheikh Mohammad Abdullah on May 20, 1946. And from that moment onwards there was "blood, sweat and tears". Pandit Jawahar Lal Nehru was taken into custody in June 1946 near about Kohala, while on his way to Srinagar which further changed the course of history in the country. On July 22, 1946 Sheikh Mohammad Abdullah was sentenced to nine years imprisonment and Rs.500/- fine.

Mr. M.A. Jinnah, the founder of Pakistan, spared no labours to convert Sheikh Mohammad Abdullah to his way of thinking but he met with no success. Mr. R.C. Kak dreamed of isolation for Kashmir but he was asked to quit from his office six days before India and Pakistan were declared independent. Mahatma Gandhi who visited Kashmir in his time was also not heard. He stated, "The Kashmiris had one language, one culture and so far as I could see, they are one people. The Treaty of Amritsar was in reality a deed of sale". The question of the State's accession remained undecided. Too late was Abdullah released.

Kashmir was passing through a crisis. Kak was followed by Janak Singh, Batra and Mahajan. None of them could cope with the situation. Batra even inspired R.S.S. training and set up one medium wave transmitter at Jammu feeling that if Kashmir could not be retained a front would be created whether independently or within the Indian Union to ward off the enemy from Jammu. The transmitter was secured through Sardar Patel and the Radio Station came to be known later as Radio Kashmir. One unforgettable incident in mentioned here.

The day Baramulla was making last resistence a deputation waited upon Mahajan. He plainly told the deputation that since further resistence was impossible he would advise the people to cross Banihal on foot, by tonga, by bus, by boat and in this task Police boss and District Magistrate would render all possible help. He also said that he was making arrangements for the Maharaja to reach Jammu. District Magistrate was available no where. Inspector-General of Police was helpless as transport was scanty. And whatever he could lay his hands on he managed to supply to Dogras who took to heels during the whole night and day that followed. This was an hour of great trial for non-Muslims who could not imagine what was coming ahead and for Muslims who were making every effort to promise protection. The deputation consisted of Bhagat Karam Chand, Bala Kak Dhar, Thakur Kartar Singh, B.N. Nehru, Satyapal Vohra and the author. Planes that brought in troops carried back refugees mostly Punjabis. The whole sight was dreadful.

Extract from "Mission with Mountbatten" :—

"One Sikh Battalion consisting of 330 men was flown on Tuesday, October 28, 1947 to block a major invasion by North-West Frontier tribesmen—the Kashmir Government accused Pakistan of failure to provide supplies of several essential commodities and protested about a number of small border raids."

"Three days before the transfer of power and the accession time limit the Kashmir Government announced its intention of signing Standstill Agreement with both India and Pakistan. Subsequently the India Government's policy has been to retrain from inducing Kashmir to accede. The Maharaja's choice in decision must be accounted a big factor in the present crisis. Almost any course of action taken quickly would have saved his State from this turmoil. Procrastination alone was fatal but in combating major crisis it would seem that, as with the Nizam, this is the only weapon in-his diplomatic armoury."

"5,000 tribesmen had attacked and captured Muzaffarabad and Domel on 25th October and were already little more than 35 miles from Srinagar. The rush of events had unnerved the Maharaja who felt lone and helpless. He left Srinagar with his wife and son on 26th October on strong advice of India's representative who was on the spot. The same day the Maharaja signed the Letter of Accession. There was only one squadron of cavalry left to hold the invaders. "While urging th Maharaja to make up his mind about accession before the transfer to power Mountbatten had all along, from his visit in June onwards, exerted his whole influence to prevent him from acceding to one Dominion or the other without first taking steps to ascertain the will, of his people by referendum, Plebiscite, election or even if these methods were impracticable, by representative public meetings". Jinnah, on the other hand, was hoist with his own petard, as it was he who chose over Junagadh, to take his stand on the ever-riding validity of the ruler's personal decision."

"You can't build a nation on tricks. Jinnah at Abbotabad had been expecting to ride in triumph into Kashmir. First there was Junagadh. Then Hyderabad. India's readiness to accept a plebiscite had been declared from the outset. A large scale massacre, including a couple of hundred British residents in Srinagar, by Tribesmen would have been inevitable if no military move had been made. The Maharaja's accession gave complete legality to the action so far taken"

—Mountbatten.

"Jinnah had given orders for Pakistan troops to be moved into Kashmir but these were called off subsequently when

Auchinleck explained to Jinnah that in so far as Kashmir had acceded to India the Government of India had a perfect right to send troops in response to the Maharaja's request."

"The result was in the hands of God, men could but do or die. He would not shed a tear if the little Union force was wiped out like the Spartans barvely defending Thermopylae nor would he mind Sheikh Mohammad Abdullah and his Muslim, Hindu and Sikh comrades, dying at their posts in the defence of Kashmir. That would be a glorious example to the rest of India."

—M.K. Gandhi.

"Pakistan did not recognise the accession describing it as based on fraud and violence. At the Jinnah-Mountbatten meeting at Lahore the latter maintained that accession had indeed been brought about by violence but the violence came from the tribes for whom Pakistan was responsible. Jinnah's attitude to a plebiscite was conditioned by his belief that the combination of Indian troops in occupation and Sh. Mohammad Abdullah in power meant that the average Muslim would be far too frightened to vote for Pakistan. Mountbatten proposed a plebiscite under U.N.O. auspices whereupon Jinnah asserted that only the two Governors- General could organise it."

"On November 3, Nehru made a broadcast offering a United Nations controlled plebiscite for Kashmir which did not react so well in Jinnah who objected to the presence of Indian troops in Kashmir before any plebiscite could be held. Had Maharaja joined Pakistan before the transfer of Power, India would not have regarded the act unfriendly, says Alan Campbell Johnson."

"With Pakistan's knowledge India lodged an appeal with the United Nations on January 9, 1948. No attack was developed on Uri and the Indian troops there made no contact with hostile forces as that would be an event which could well touch off the wider conflict. This was meant to be avoided, the issue being subjudice before the Security Council according to Mountbatten."

—Alan Campbell Johnson.

Pakistan had meanwhile an "economic crisis" for Kashmir, in spite of Standstill Agreement with her Sheikh Abdullah who had been released by this time stressed that it was the people's right to decide their own future. While negotiations were going on both at Lahore and Delhi about the future settlement, Muzaffarabad was raided on October 22, 1947. Trouble in Poonch had started earlier. With Brigadier Rajendra Singh making desperate stand against the raiders near Buniyar, the civil administration collapsed at the head-quarters, the Peace Brigade and the National Militia of the National Conference took up the defence crying "Raiders beware; we Kashmiris are ready" Baramulla fell into the enemy hands on October 26. And what happened. The Maharaja left for Jammu, leaving poor Kashmir to her own fate. At the joint request of Hari Singh and Sheikh Abdullah India at last accepted accession on Oct. 24 and "decided to intervene with the armed forces of the Union" who landed in Srinagar on October 27 when raiders were sacking, burning and looting round the northern walls of the city. Wave of joy again spread in the country. The raiders were driven off and Baramulla was recaptured on November 7. Sh. Mohammad Abdullah was sworn in as Head of Emergency Administration on October 30. The necessities of life having been stranded at Rawalpindi the price of salt at once rose to Rs.16/- per seer.

One thing important to mention here is the Lal Chowk pledge which history cannot overlook. While raiders were being driven out Jawaharlal Nehru and Sheikh Mohammad Abdullah gave pledges to each other on behalf of their respective countries in presence of a huge gathering. Since 1953 there has been parting of the ways. What those pledges were and who violated them are mystery to the common man?

The year 1948 was a period of great pressure on home front as well as war front. The cease-fire line was ultimately drawn by which Muzaffarabad, Gilgit, Mirpur and a part of Poonch now known as "Azad Kashmir" (occupied Kashmir) were allowed to remain with the insurgents under an over-all control of Pakistan. Mohammad Ibrahim, Ch. Ghulam Abbas and M. Yusuf Shah held command there. While Ibrahim organised revolt from Poonch the latter two joined him after partition.

On the home front, the duly constituted Government headed by eight popular Ministers looked after refugee problem and introduced many a reform mostly agrarian. Canals were dug and roads constructed to increase production and promote communication. Food and other essential supplies were imported. Land was particularly passed on to the tiller. Jammu, where communal madness had shown its head, was cooled down. Jagirdari and Zamindari were liquidated. Transport Service was built up. Ejectment of tenants was stayed and moratorium was laid on non- commercial debts. The common man was in the picture and relieved. Chenani which was a jurisdictional Jagir having an area of 95 square miles and a population of 12,000 was taken over on April 5. Muqarraries amounting about Rs.1,77,925 reverted to the State Exchequer. Co-operative movement received a further fillip and the institution of Zaildars and Nambardars was re-organised on elective basis. Emporia were established in important towns of India.

Maharaja Hari Singh went into voluntary exilement and his place as constitutional head of the State was taken by his only son Yuvraj Karan Singh. This took place in 1949 when the question of Kashmir was already pending before the Security Council of the United Nations where India and Pakistan figures as complainants and defendants respectively. The five man Commission which reported failure was followed by 1. Sir Owen

Dixon and 2. Dr. Frank Graham, United Nations' representatives who also reported failure.

Hari Singh followed a policy which was opposed to that of his uncle. It was for show that he fixed his uncle's photo on his crown. He went out of his way to help the Rajputs. He became conscious of the inherent strength of the Muslim and the more he tried to raise their standard the more they became critical of him. The "Mr. A. Case" had already demoralised him. As ruler he offended the Britishers. As Head of the Ruling family he did not behave well with his aunt and the Poonch branch. His own three wives died in grief. He inspired 'State Subjects Definition' which was a challenge to the people of the Punjab and all aliens. British Departmental Heads were gradually replaced by Rajput upstarts. The revenue of the State had risen to over Rs. 4 crores out of which he took away more then 12-3/4 per cent in cash and kind. 40 per cent still went out. Out of the balance 30 per cent went to Jammu and hardly 17-1/4 per cent to Kashmir. This could not feed the growing population.

He was not accessible to his own people. He would love a polo pony more then his ryot. He would not trust his advisors whoever they were. Around him the times were changing at atomic speed. His gifted intelligence and acquired education did not guide him well. He never paid a visit to the far flung areas of his kingdom. Thus unrest at home and transfer of power beyond his boundary brought to end 100 years of Dogra rule. Overcome by provincial bias he once ordered fixation of headquarters at Jammu in place of Srinagar. The resentment of Kashmiris at this ludicrous move was natural. The move was dropped after a few years' sad experiment.

Sheikh Mohammad Abdullah, Lenin of Kashmir, was born in December 1905 in the family of shawl makers at Soura, 6 miles away from Srinagar. Poverty greeted him on his birth. The seeds of a revolution were sown in a simple reading room at Fateh Kadal where he and his friends met and discussed the future of Kashmir. The first storm blew across Jammu. The long waiting was exhausted and the stage set. Mr. Abdullah defied tyranny when he delivered his first speech at Jama Masjid. Since that moment he courted arrests until one day the tale echoed in the plains of the Punjab attracting persons like Iqbal at the earlier stages. First a communalist (1931), then a nationalist (1939) and later a socialist (1944) Sheikh Mohammad Abdullah rode a high horse. To such a man, Jinnah and his hymn of hate could have no attraction. His instinct took him towards Nehru and his hymn of love. But he was not prepared to go whole hog.

On coming to power what did he do? He installed an University and a Radio Station to spread education and to promote culture. The ancient Kashmir was once again put on the cultural map of world. In the eyes of some he was a Muslim as Gadhiji was a Hindu.

The greatest achievement of Sh. Mohammad Abdullah was the convening of the sovereign constituent Assembly for the State which met in october 1951, seventy-five members of which were were returned on basis of adult suffrage and joint electorates. But only one political party fought elections. The Assembly took bold decisions, refused compensation to landlords, abolished hereditary rule and designed a new State flag and emblem.

About 150,000 absentee landlords were made to surrender 4,500,000 kanals of land. The Text Book Advisory Board evolved a common script (Persian Arabic-Nasakh Style) which has not become popular though.

Girls' Colleges were established. The Transport Service commands a fleet of 400 vehicles. Debts amounting to about six crores of rupees were liquidated. Hundreds of Multi-Purpose Co-operative Societies for distribution of necessaties of life were established throughout the State.

Zainpur canal (50,000 acres), Sumbal canal (5,000 acres), Mawar canal (4,000 acres), Kishtwar canal (5,000 acres) and Udhampur canal (24,000 acres) are under construction. The Sindh Valley Hydro-Electric Project to irrigate 2,000 acres and to produce 13,000 kwts of electricity is now complete. This Project was conceived in 1942, a taken beginning was made in 1946 and actual work was redoubled after 1955. Two generators have already been installed and two more are to be installed. The project has cost Rs.2.75 lakhs. The present yield is 6,000 kwts. President of India congratulated Kashmir while performing its ceremony.

B.C.G. team of the World Health Organization vaccinated more than a lakh of people against chest diseases. Five years were ear- marked for vaccination of entire population. Flood control bunds have been erected by Co-operative effort. Before the Second World War the revenue of the State never exceeded Rs.2,50,00,000. It rose to Rs.5,75,00,000 by 1945. It dropped to Rs. 2,74,00,000 in 1947. In 1951 it as estimated to be Rs.4,57,00,000. About 4 lakh kanals of cultivable land were made available to speed up production.

While all this is said the impartial historian cannot suppress the other side of the picture. As popular administration continued on mass discontent also stepped up. This is not so much due to Indo-Pakistan controversy as it is due to taxation, corruption, unemployment, high prices and security measures. While prices have shot up four to eight times incomes have not correspondingly increased. The Government itself raised the price of Shalia from Rs. 8.25 to Rs. 10.50 per Kirwar. It is on the price this staple food that prices of other commodities revolve. Taxation at the base hardly goes long way to balance a budget.

Extracts from Mehar Chand Maharajan's (Prime Minister of Jammu and Kashmir during the fateful period of 1947) diary :—

"Jinnah's British Military Secretary came thrice to Srinagar with letters from Jinnah to persuade Maharaja Hari Singh to accede to Pakistan. Jinnah's Private Secretary was in Srinagar for a number of weeks creating hatred against India. Maharaja Hari Singh had already declined Jinnah's desire to spend summer in Kashmir as Governor-General of Pakistan. Standstill Agreement was signed with Pakistan before 15th August. (According to R.C. Kak no such agreement was signed upto 11th August). Mountbatten in his three days visit to Kashmir hinted at Kashmir's accession with Pakistan both to Maharaja Hari Singh and Mehar Chand Mahajan. (This is confirmed by R.C. Kak to whom Mountbatten had said—you must consider your geographical position, your political situation and the composition of your population and then decide). (Mehar Chand Mahajan had taken over on 15th October). Chitral and Hunza had wired their loyalty to the Maharaja but at the same time pleaded State's accession with Pakistan. Major Shah compelled me to see him. He had accession draft in one hand and sword in another. This was Pakistan speaking. Then came trade blockade, communal frenzy in Jammu, border raids. Jammu mosque was fortified and a plan was hatched to kidnap the Maharaja and abduct M.C. Mahajan at Bhimber Dak bungalow but it was frustrated as the Maharaja changed has programme on the way. The raid was initially organised by Ex-Army Officers. The British Commander- in-Chief had maldistributed the State forces which weakened defence against the raid that came on 23rd October. There was no reply available to the request for help and the accession Deed on 24th the 25th October. Sheikh Mohammad Abdullah himself took a plane flight to Delhi on 25th October. Jinnah made a programme to celebrate I'd at Srinagar. His Commander-in-Chief pushed two brigades on 27th October via Sialkot and Rawalpindi. Indian troops were also flown on 27th morning. This halted Pakistani brigades. Delhi took this decision on 26th. M.C. Mahajan and Sheikh Mohammad Abdullah who were on the spot agreed for such a decision. If this decision had not been taken M.C. Mahajan was instructed to surrender to Pakistan on 25th October when suddenly Menon came who advised the Maharaja to leave for Jammu and M.C. Mahajan for Delhi. Thus was the State saved and the war between the two dominions averted".

According to R.C. Kak the policy of his government was that Kashmir should accede neither to India nor to Pakistan but should execute Standstill Agreement with both to meet the needs of the immediate future.

"I would crave the indulgence of the House if I delve into the history of Jammu and kashmir before 1947 and soon after that. We find that from times immemorial Kashmir has been a part of India excepting for a short period when it came under the Afghan sway in the early part of the nineteenth century. It was the brave Sikh ruler of Punjab, Maharaja Ranjit Singh, who reconquered Kashmir for India, and later on the Dogras took over in 1846.

"The Dogra rulers were always patriotic and they conquered Ladakh in 1824 and Gilgit soon after that, and brought them into the map of India. They gave good and stable government to the people of Jammu and Kashmir. I might recollect with great pleasure on this occasion that it was Maharaja Hari Singh who kept up the family tradition and the flag of Jammu and Kashmir flying high up when he spoke at the First Round Table Conference in 1930. When Sir Samuel Hoare, the then Secretary of State for India, opposed the move of independence for India on the plea that His Majesty's Government had given solemn assurances to the Indian Princes to keep their integrity in tact. It was Maharaja Hari Singh, who at that time as Pro-Vice-Chancellor of the Chamber of Princes, spoke in London some time between the 12th November 1930 and 19th January 1931.

"As allies of British, we stand solidly, behind the British connection. As Indians and loyal to the land whence we derive our birth and infant nurture, we stand as solidly as the rest of our countrymen for our land's enjoyment of a position of honour and equality in the British Commonwealth of Nations".

"It was a period when very few of the Princes could ever dare to use such words in favour of the independence of India. It was later on really a bad turn of destiny that this patriotic son of Jammu and Kashmir made a mistake by not joining India before 15th August 1947, in spite of the advice of Mahatmaji and Acharya Kripalani, the then President of All India National Congress. But it should not be forgotten that it was never the intention of the ruler of Jammu and Kashmir to join Pakistan, in spite of the machinations of Mr. Jinnah through Colonel Webb, the then British Resident who was hand to glove with the creator of Pakistan. It was the then Prime Minister of Jammu and Kashmir, Rao Bahadur Ram Chandra Kak and his Scotch wife that were the instruments of Colonel Webb to influence the Maharaja.

"It is known that the later events made the Maharaja give up his dream of being an independent ruler like the Nizam of Hyderabad due to the invasion by Pakistan on the Kashmir territory—and made him request for help from India to stem the invasion, that was a threat to the four million people of Jammu and Kashmir. His accession to India at that time was an event which was hailed as an act of patriotism by all sections of the people of Jammu and Kashmir, and it was also considered a step in the right direction. Thus, a new chapter opened in the history of Jammu and Kashmir.

"It is pertinent for me to point out here that the leader of the National Conference, Sheikh Mohammad Abdullah himself, supported the Maharaja in his move to accede to India with a view to achieve the ideal for which the National Conference struggled for many years, namely, responsible Government of a secular nature as an integral part of India. The National Conference confirmed this action of the Maharaja and the decision of Sheikh Mohammad Abdullah in their election manifesto. The official seal of this decision was given by the President of India on May 14, 1954".

Lakshman Singh Charak
(Lok Sabha Debate 27-9-1954)

(That Ram Chandra Kak influenced Hari Singh in favour of independence is against facts. It was Swami Sant Dev the Raj Guru, who inspired Hari singh. Swami Sant Dev and Ram Chandra Kak did not see eye to eye with each other.)

Though fanaticism has still survived in the land there are also possibilities of Kashmir turning red in the near future. It is becoming explosive day by day.

The U.N.O. has made Kashmir into gun-powder magazine which may burst any moment. The longer a fair solution is delayed the worse it is, not only, for Kashmir but for the whole world. The findings of the Security Council during the last twelve years have repeatedly reported a failure.

Prime Minister during Hari Singh's reign :—

1. Sir Albion Bannerjee —he sent mulkis for foreign trainings. "Kashmiris are hewers of wood, drawers of water and tillers of land."
2. Mr. G.E.C. Wake-field —he instigated Hindu-Muslim tension.
3. Raja Hari Krishen Kaul —he saved Hari Singh.
4. Col. E.J.D. Colvin —Gilgit was his problem.
5. Sir N. Gopalaswami Ayyangar —he was an iron man.
6. Sir B.N. Rao —he dreamed of Kashmir turning into Paradise.

7. Sir K.N. Haksar —he was old 'wine put in new bottle'.
8. Sir Maharaj Singh —he was a sportsman but non-serious.
9. R.C. Kak —he was more loyal than the king.
10. Janak Singh —the state was over run.
11. R.L. Batra —he organised R.S.S.
12. Mehra Chand Mahajan —he marched to put down revolt in Poonch with wooden sticks.
13. S.M. Abdullah —he bargained.
14. Bakshi Ghulam Mohammad —opportunist and realist in action.

Shree Maharaja Karan Singh Ji was born in the city of Cannes (South of France) on 9th March 1931. The Maharaja received most of his primary education at home, although he attended the Presentation Convent College in Srinagar for two seasons. In 1942, at the age of 11, he was sent to the Doon School, Dehra Dun. He was perhaps the first heir-apparent to go to a public school in India. He studied there for three years and in 1945, at the age of only 14, he appeared for the Senior Cambridge Examination which he passed in the first grade and in 1947 passed the Intermediate Examination of the Allahabad University as a private candidate. He graduated from J & k University in 1951, again as a private candidate passed M.A. from Delhi University in 1957. He was sent to New York for medical treatment at the beginning of 1948 and he returned to India after a year. On June 20, 1949 he took over as Regent of the State. He was married in Bombay to Princess Yasho Rajya Lakshmi, grand-daughter of His Highness Maharaja Mohan Shamsher Jung Bahadur, Rana of Nepal. He has a daughter from her.

The State Assembly unanimously elected him as the first Sadar-i- Riyasat on 14th November, 1952. He assumed office on

17th when a salute of 21 guns was given to him. The rejoicings broke all previous records, the occasion being 'Magna Carta' for the people of Kashmir. The new flag and the new emblem were also publicly adoped on this day under Indo-Kashmir agreement of 1952. He was re-elected Sadar-i-Riyasat on November 6, 1957 and functioned also as Chancellor of J. & K. University.

Karan Singh Ji is fond of Indian Classical music, tennis and chess. He is a prolific reader and his favourite subjects are political science and philosophy.

The people of Jammu led by Praja Parished launched a satyagraha movementimmediately after the above decisions were implemented which spread throughout the Province. There was a mob violence also on various occasions and at various places which resulted in firing. The agitation demonstrated that the people of Jammu were not with the people of Kashmir, in spite of India's common link. The movement received momentum when later on Hindu Mahasabha, Jan Sangh and Ram Rajya Parishad supported it. Dr. Shyama Prasad Mukerjee, President Jan Sangh entered the State without obtaining a permit. He was taken into custody on the border and removed to a villa in Nishat Bagh (Kashmir) where he died as a detenu. Shri Jawahar Lal Nehru at last made an appeal for the withdrawal of the agitation but the wrong was already done. The movement was however, formally withdrawn in July 1953.

It is many a local grievance which led to the agitation. The Dogra pride had been stirred up. Sheikh Mohammad Abdullah had repeatedly referred to Jammu massacre of 1947 in his public speeches. Durga Dass mounted to the same fame as underground leader as Mohi-ud-Din (Kara) had mounted during the "Quit Kashmir" movement in 1946. Praja Parishad agitation did not go unnoticed in Kashmir where for the first time since 1947 pro- Pakistan slogans were publicly raised. A fresh chapter was opened in the history of Kashmir when on August 8,

Sadar-i-Riyasat dismissed Sh. Mohammad Abdullah and appointed Bakshi Ghulam Mohammad as Prime Minister who took over on August 9. Of late Sh. Mohammad Abdullah who was mentally confused all along was planning to drift away from India subtly to carve out an Independent State of Kashmir with or without Jammu. While arguing the case privately or publicly Sh. Mohammad Abdullah desired complete internal autonomy for the State which others interpreted as independence. This created a rift in the Cabinet as well as in the National conference High Command. There was a stir in the Valley but it was soon overcome. Bakshi Government at once announced many salutary reforms such as abolition of 40-year-old mujwaza (compulsory levy) reduction in the price of shali, free education upto post-graduate standard, reduction in Abiana,reorganisation of Government services, abolition of customs duty from 1954, extension of co-operative credits, appointment of Public Services Commission etc. The new Government also ratified Indo-Kashmir Agreement of 1951 after it was unanimously voted by the Constituent Assembly on February 6, 1954 as part step since the Kashmir problem had not yet been solved through the good offices of United Nations Organisation. What followed from this was (a) financial integration with India ; (b) internal autonomy ; (c) amendment of State Subjects' Definition of 1927 entitling every one to become a State subject after ten years of continuous residence in the State ; (d) formal transfer of ceded and centrally administered subjects to India.

Bakshi Ghulam Mohammad was born in a poor family at Nawa Kadal. His father was a petty tailor and his mother an 'aya'. Bakshi went to School but could not cross Matriculation bar. In his early age he accepted a teachers job in the frontier illaqa and became a Christian also for some time. He struggled hard with many jobs and finally plunged into politics in 1931 under the leadership of Sheikh Mohammad Abdullah whom he accepted as Sixth eeman. Luck favoured him through and through.

Bakhshi diagnosed the disease which was eating into the vitals of the society like a cancer. The disease was scarcity and high price of food stuffs, small pays, growing taxes, costly education, debts, mujwaza and what not. Sheikh Mohammad Abdullah probably wanted to use mass discontent as a trump card in favour of independence. To say he was blind to this is to do him injustice. Bakhshi turned the corner. But armies of India and Pakistan are still facing each other across the Cease fire Line as they have been since 1948. Kashmir is the apple of discord. What is coming ahead baffles even surmise. And yet it is no bed of roses for Bakhshi so long as Abdullah is under detention.

In spite of huge economic and educational projects undertaken by Bakhshi Government the revenue of the State mounted to Rs. 5.5 crores for 1954-55 turning the deficit of 34 lakhs into surplus by fiscal integration with the Government of India which extended a grant of Rs. 250/- lakhs to the State. Since 1947 when the State acceded to India the total loan obtained from India amounted to 8 crores and 63 lakhs. This was necessary to adjust the reduced revenue of the State to increased demands. Over and above this there came a huge aid also and yet the economic distress mounted up. The leadership was tried and it was found wanting. A University Degree is not necessarily the key to success. Bakhshi apparently proved a greater success than Abdullah. Even a backward district like Ladakh received a fair deal and her representative was taken into the cabinet.

A high altitude cosmic rays research observatory was formally inaugurated on April 4, 1954 at Gulmarg (9,000 ft. hight) under the joint auspices of the Universities of Kashmir and Aligarh thus reviving the ancient intellectual integration between India and Kashmir.

A wire ropeway upto Khilanmarg has been suggested which, apart from serving the research station, will also open up the entire area and make it an attractive centre for tourists and for winter sports and training for the defence forces.

The advantage of a high altitude station was that the number of cosmic ray events of different types increased rapidly as we rose higher in the atmosphere and it, therefore, became possible to study the newer events in a reasonable length of time. Some phenomena were only found in the uppermost layers of the atmosphere, and those could only be studied with the use of balloon-borne equipment.

Other phenomena could only be studied by the use of heavier and more elaborate precision apparatus and a high altitude station was essential for such work so that rare events could be recorded for sufficiently long periods to enable quantitative conclusions to be drawn.

After discussing the merits and demerits of the various sites, the Tangmarg-Gulmarg-Khilanmarg-Apharwat group was found quite suitable from the point of view of location. Two proposals are in hand:

(1) A high altitude cosmic ray research station should be established at Khilanmarg, provided it can be connected by ropeway with Gulmarg. The station would provide basic facilities for cosmic ray workers from all parts of India to carry out their experiments. It would also provide limited facilities to worker in other branches of science, such as Physiology and astrophysics;

(2) A firm of experts should be asked to make a preliminary survey and cost estimates of connecting Gulmarg with Khilanmarg; Gulmarg with Tangmarg and Khilanmarg with Apharwat by wire ropeway, so designed as to form a continuous connection when all links were completed.

Jammu turned en fete during the four days visit of President of India in April 1954 who was greeted with nation building projects such as Arts and Crafts Exhibition, Boulevard round the Tawi, widened old old Bhabra bazar, Gandhi Bhawan etc. His first official visit to Srinagar in 1950 had provided a similar fillip to Kashmir. These visits are unlike the visits of former British Viceroys. Previously the host used to be the Maharaja. Now the hosts are people. The previous hospitality laid greater stress on catering, shikar and presents. Jammu had never known such an exhibition before. Replying to an address of welcome presented by the Jammu Municipality the President of India. Dr. Rajendra Prasad, said that the history and mutual understanding had cemented the ancient ties between Kashmir and India to such an extent that any break in the relationship was inconceivable.

India all along made it clear that she would abide by plebiscite she had voluntarily offered, provided:—(a) The lawful administration of the State was recognized. (b) Pakistan withdrew her forces from occupied part of the State. (c) Refugees returned to homes and were rehabilitated. (d) Normal conditions prevailed. (e) Plebiscite administrator nominated by U.N.O. was appointed by the legal government of the State. (f) Aggression by Pakistan was admitted. Since no final agreement was reached between India and Pakistan on these issues and since American Military Aid to Pakistan changed the entire context India backed out of her pledge under force of circumstances that the need for a plebiscite did no longer exist. Development projects in the meanwhile had already carried the State forward. There are other factors also which lowered Abdullah's prestige in the public eye—hot temper, lust for power and wrong company. A few Kashmiri Pandit adventurers in politics who exploited the situation in 1946 for their own ends were pushed into power by him. Abdullah of 1953 was a changed man from Abdullah of 1946, politically as well as mentally. And when he was arrested, sinners at once changed sides and he was left in wilderness. Muslims for whom he essentially toiled had turned backs against him.

The customs barrier between India and the State was removed from April 13 giving way to octroi duty chargeable on weight. Goods coming from abroad entered in the State under bond. It yielded a revenue of over one crore of rupees. This included the amount payable from various departments in State account. The Government of India made this loss good having already included it in the 250 lakhs grant. This gave a great relief to the people after a period of about 18 years.

Karan Singh's birth abroad was simultaneously followed by popular uproar at home. As he grew up he saw the throne shaking. But he is unlike his father. He has no vice. He has adjusted himself to the changed environment. Though he has lost all claim to hereditary rule he has not lost all chances of a bright career.

The revenues of the State have exceeded five crores. India to which Kashmir has acceded is giving enormous aid in cash and kind which has brought about a great change in the economic condition of the people.

Both Abdullah and Bakhshi received aid. During Abdullah's time much of it did not reach masses. But during Bakhshi's time the quantity of aid was greater and a larger percentage did reach the masses through labour etc. If the total aid in the shape of loan or free gift had been well utilized it would have brought about a great change in the country. The expenditure was not scrutinized. The plan was not whetted. As in India the first Five-Year Plan was completed with the close of 1955. About Rs. 1274.15 lakhs mostly contributed by India were spent which did some spade work in the development of the country. While money was freely circulating there grew up an organisation known as Plebiscite Front which demanded plebiscite in the State. It did not attract much notice, the ruling party being opposed to it. Only pro- Abdullah elements sponsored and fanned it. The greatest event of the year was the visit of Russian leader—Bulganin and Khrushchev. When they stated that Kashmir was a part of India and "the present boundary need not be altered" the so-called Plebiscite Front received a great set-back and the people continued hoping against hope.

Like India Kashmir also stepped into the new year heralding the Second Five-Year Plan with an ambitious project of Rs. 51 crores and 27 lakhs mainly contributed by India. The emphasis was laid mostly on education, agriculture and industry. Two bridges—one at Sonwar and the other at Maisuma, raised the figure of already seven bridges to nine in the city.

Municipal elections under the new Constitution were conducted both at Srinagar and at Jammu after a period of about 17 years. A keen contest was noticed but the ruling party finally won. These elections were earlier preceded by Town Area elections in rural areas where also keen contest was noticed.

Again, all speculations were laid at rest when Jawahar Lal Nehru, Prime Minister of India, declared that no useful purpose would be served by holding a plebiscite in Kashmir, since Pakistan had accepted military aid from America and become a party to SEATO and Baghdad Pacts and that she was not prepared to accept any plea advanced by India whether within United Nations Organisation or without it. Not only this Nehru also stated subsequently that Chitral, Hunza, Nagar, Punial and Yasin were still part of the State. This silenced the people inside though it caused some flutter outside. The issue is still hanging until the other party also closes the chapter.

With the growing of Schools and Colleges in the State and subsequently spread of education under an indigenous University the State became rejuvenated culturally. Poetry, drama, music, research, literature, dance and what not received a great impetus. Old order changed. Broadcasting continued to attract classes as well as masses from both sexes. With the introduction of broadcasting in 1947-1948 illiterate girls were prevailed upon to come and sign and now educated girls come forward to offer their co-operation. Similar is the case with sport. Olympic games became popular day by day.

The city today is immensely changed—many roads widened, new houses erected and congestion mostly removed. Money being abundant compensation is paid several times the actual cost. People are heard whispering B.B.C. meaning Bakhshi Brothers Corporation whose slogan is—make hay while the sun shines. People are also heard talking against imported rice which sells at 25 nP. per seer and salt because they come from India. The old economics of Kashmir devolved on 'Shali, Shawl, Shalgam' and cheap rice should have revolutionised the entire market but no, the shoe is on the other leg. It is also a trait of Kashmiri character to find fault with those who are in power. Foreign yoke for over 600 years has developed many vices in the whole race. It is Abdullah who projected Kashmir to India. Bakhshi only cemented integration in the interest of both Kashmir and India. And Bakhshi did no wrong to Muslims in any walk of life—services trade, labour, art and what not. If some people call him a traitor who pushed out his leader they are unfair. Sometimes the leader and the follower can also differ on a vital issue.

India did not give only aid and loan to Kashmir but did all that was possible to promote the economic condition of the people. Indians were pushed to Kashmir as visitors, official conferences were scheduled in Kashmir—even a special sitting of the Supreme Court was held at Srinagar and surveys were conducted. All this helped to build up the economy of the country. Some offices like the Information Centre and Mineral Survey were opened in the State to further cement the accession. The policy of India was to feed the people, educate them rightly, raise their moral and material standard and possibly not to colonise them. Contrary to the expectation this policy did not produce the desired effect. Love for India is wanting in many a heart. The non-Muslims submitted to the inevitable all along since the raid. The secular policy of India was on trial in Kashmir. Viewed from all aspects Kashmir stands as a unique instance which has baffled statesmen and politicians and defies all approaches to a fair solution. It should be no job of a historian to predict coming events. An armed conflict between India and Pakistan to decide the Kashmir Issue cannot be ruled out unless a miracle happens which may bring about the settlement.

August 9 was being observed as a jubilation day since 1953 by pro-Abdullah element. But this year the National Conference itself observed it as the deliverance day. There was illumination throughout.

September 9, 1956, will go down in history as a landmark day. On this morning the first vehicle passed through the new tunnel near about lower Munda thus linking Kashmir with India. The work on this tunnel was started in 1953 by German Engineers. The tunnel is one of the six longest tunnels of the world. It has cost over Rupees three crores. The tube about 1½ mile long (8,120 ft.), 18 ft. high and 14 feet wide has been bored at a height of 7,000 feet. It has shortened distance between Srinagar and Pathankot by about 20 miles and saved time by about two hours. Before this Banihal used to remain closed to traffic from December to April. Now it remains open throughout the year. The second tube which is also under construction is expected to be completed by now. Such a tunnel was considered an impossibility before—credit for this achievement goes to India which sponsored the scheme and German Engineers who accomplished the fact at minimum cost and in shortest possible time. The winter immediately following witnessed through traffic for the first time in history.

The month of September 1956 was celebrated as 'Festival of Kashmir' throughout the province. It was indeed a cultural, lingual and social gala month. Kashmiri, Dogri, Ladakhi and Bhadarwahi life was illustrated through drama, dance, poetry, sport and music. Politically it diverted the attention of the people from growing prices. Every item of programme was over shadowed by fun and frivolity where sobriety had no entrance. At any rate the idea was to attract visitors and provide recreation on a larger scale. Government spent Rs. 2,40,000/- on this.

For the first time since the raids, a draft constitution for the State was placed before the Constituent Assembly on September 10th at Srinagar providing (a) elective office of Sadar-i-Riyasat subject to approval by the President of India (b) two houses—one consisting of 100 members (25 reserved for occupied area) and the other of 36 members, 1/3 to return after three years—11 each for Jammu and Kashmir, 8 returned by teachers and Town Area Constituencies and 6 nominated by Sadar-i- Riyasat (c) adult franchise minimum age 21 years (d) Auditor- General, Public Services Commission, Advocate-General, Independent High Court of Judicature, (e) Financial Integration (f) Urdu as State language while Kashmiri, Dogri, Ladakhi and Bhadehwahi as regional languages. During the same session Bakhshi Gulam Mohammad announced a dearness allowance for State employees whose pay ranged from Rs. 30/ to Rs. 300/- p.m. with retrospective effect from April involving an annual expenditure of about sixty lakhs of rupees. This provided relief to over 40,000 people.

A jeepable road to Leh via Kargil and electrification of the town by utilizing the waters of the Indus are under way. The monasteries are likely to receive cash grants equal to rent to enable land reforms to be extended to Ladakh as well. The prohibition of polyandry there is in itself a great social reform. Air service was established on September 28, 1955.

1,63,300 maunds of wheat, 4,91,522 maunds of rice and 3,58,884 maunds of paddy were imported during one year.

8,000 acres of dry land were brought under paddy cultivation through lift irrigation near Sangam. 15,000 maunds of sulphate ammonia were distributed among the farmers. Educational institutions rose to 1,820 and expenditure thereon to 70.31 lakhs. Mobile schools function for Gujjars and Bakarwals. Expenditure on health has gone up by 75 per cent. Carpet, namda, tweed, khadi received great fillip. Paper and cardboard, paints and chemicals, bamboo furniture and tanning industries etc. are being organised on a large scale.

About 19 lakh kanals stand transferred among two lakh tillers. Besides 13 lakhs kanals belonging to Government are being distributed among refugees and landless tillers. Co-operative debts amounting to over 35 lakhs were remitted. The rural debt has come down from about two crores to less than a crore. In the Second Five-Year Plan Rs. 12 crores were earmarked for the Kandi Canal Scheme in Jammu which remained neglected so far.

Maisuma Bridge was named Badshah Bridge and its opening ceremony was performed on 24th October 1956, by Sadar-i-Riyasat Shri Karan Singh. The bridge is 285 feet long and 40 feet wide and has cost Rs. 15,66,000.

Mirza Mohammad Afzal Beg and his eight colleagues who were released last week walked out of the Constituent Assembly where draft constitution bill was under discussion on the directive of the Plebiscite Front which is still breathing. The Constitution was lunanimously passed on 17th November. Out of 10 members of the Plebiscite Front one joined the National Conference (Mr. Abdul Gani Goni form Doda district). The members (66 out of 75) put their seal on the Constitution on 19th November. There was State-wide jubilation and prayers were offered at the 1931 Martyrs Grave-Yard. Never was such an illumination seen before. If R.C. Kak could earlier snatch away Mian Ahmed Yar Khan from the National Conference, Bakhshi Ghulam Mohammad also could snatch away Mr.

Abdul Gani Goni from the Plebiscite Front as he did Mr. Durga Das from the Praja Parishad a short while before. People have a price which power and money can bid for.

22nd December (1956) was a jubilation day for the State. Dr. Radhakrishnan, Vice-President of India, opened the Jawahar Tunnel in Banihal for Public traffic. Thousands had flocked to the place to witness the great engineering feat of the modern age. Kashmir's physical accession with India was cemented this day.

25th January (1957) took the State nine years back when the fresh resolution of the Security Council passed on 24th was announced reiterating that the final disposition of the State would be made through free and impartial plebiscite under United Nations auspices in continuation of its previous resolution dated April 21, 1948; June 3, 1948; March 14, 1950 and March 30, 1951. Wide- spread protests followed throughout India. According to Government of India the accession was completed in 1947 and Pakistan had committed aggression in Kashmir and unless these two basic facts were accepted there could be no further discussion. The Security Council passed another resolution on February 21, sponsored by four nations, requesting Mr. Gunnar Jarring of Sweden to examine any proposals which would contribute towards settlement of dispute having regard to all its previous resolutions and report back not later than April 15. The proposal for the use of U.N. force and demilitarisation prior to plebiscite was turned down by Russia.

While people watched the movement of Mr. Gunnar Jarring across the border during the month of March (1957) they had a busy time on this side of the border where second general election since 1947 was due. National Conference, Praja Parishad, Praja Socialist Party and independent were in the field. Out of 75 seats election for 5 and 2 was held in the last week of May due to snows in Doda and Ladakh districts. Kashmir Province mostly featured with unopposed returns and Jammu with keen contest. While about 75 per cent votes were polled in Jammu hardly about 50 per cent were polled in Kashmir. The results were National Conference 61+7, Praja Parishad 5, Independents 1, Harijan Mandal 1. The leader of Praja Parishad lost in south Jammu and Speaker of the Assembly, a candidate of National Conference, in Khanayar Nawa kadal Constituency.

Jarring report was out before the end of April. Two main points featured in the Report. He stated that if plebiscite were at all held grave problems might arise. "I could not fail to take notice of the concern expressed in connection with changing political, economic and strategic factors surrounding the whole Kashmir question together with the changing pattern of power relations in West and South Asia". This came under Security Council resolution on January 5, 1949. To resolve differences between India and Pakistan under Security Council resolution of August 13, 1948, arbitration was suggested which was accepted by the later and rejected by the former. The report was again a failure.

Rains which usually end in March continued upto end of May which hit hard local economy. Fruit, oil-seeds, rice, maize, wheat crops were adversely affected. The rains had forty times greater radio active count than that due to cosmic ray action. Introduction of decimal coinage into the country with effect from April in the same year and the reception given to new coins brought Kashmir still nearer to India fiscally also.

Results of election to the Legislative Council consisting of 36 members held on 26th June and subsequently were as under:—

(a) Eight by—election; one each by the constituencies of local authorities and teachers in Jammu and Kashmir.

(b) Two by each two member constituencies of Panchayats of Jammu and Kashmir.

(c) Twenty-two seats—eleven for Jammu and eleven for Kashmir elected by J&K Assembly.

(d) Six nominated by Sadar-i-Riyasat.

Kashmir was not only seat of learning but Centre of Philosophy in times of yore. Shaiva philosophy has had its birth here. It was in fitness of things that the All-India Philosophical Congress chose to hold its 32nd Session in Srinagar on June 16. Shri Karan Singh told the Congress to interpret fundamental truths taught by religions as the world was faced with danger that progress of science created. Dr. G.P. Malalassakera of Ceylon, President World Buddhist Federation who presided over the session, stated that Panch Sheela constituted a challenge from Asia to the world. Already 25 countries constituting 3/5ths of the world's population had accepted these five principles of co-existence, enunciated by the Buddha, 2,500 years ago and which Kashmir Bhikhshus propounded elsewhere.

The elections to both houses were complete by the middle of July. Some contests such as teachers' constituencies revealed a trend towards Leftism. Out of the total strength of 111 members at least 12 could be safely counted as Leftists. Then came the election of the leader and the formation of the cabinet. Bakhshi Ghulam Mohammad was unanimously elected leader. All National Conference nominees to the Legislative Council were elected. Among the six nominations by Sadar-i-Riyasat, while backward classes received representation and defeated ex-Speaker found accommodation, art and literature were neglected. The two houses met on July 26 when the cabinet was also announced. From the cabinet formed after the raids only two ministers survived. Bakhshi Ghulam Mohammad himself and Shyam Lal Saraf. Many old comrades were dropped and new blood introduced. The Assembly had for the first time two opposition groups—one led by Praja Parished and the other by the Communists Block who formed progressive wing within the National Conference. G.M. Sadiq was associated with the freedom struggle from the beginning and the cabinet from 1947.

Bakhshi Ghulam Mohammad's 1957 Cabinet consisted of:—

1. Bakhshi Ghulam Mohammad.
2. Shyam Lal Saraf.
3. Dina Nath Mahajan.
4. Ghulam Mohammad Rajpuri.
5. Shams-ud-Din.
6. Kotwal Chuni Lal.
7. Vacant.

Plus six ministers of State—a team unparalleled in local annals.

The two Houses were addressed by Sadar-i-Riyasat on 27th July. The address outlined the new Cabinet's policy which assured still greater integration with India. But it did not augur all well because of internal faction, between Leftists and Rightists so much so that six of the former tendered resignation from the governing body of the National Conference. This organisation was adulterated by mixing up elements that opposed it before 1947 such as a former Minister, a former I.G., Police, a former communal leader, an agent of former administration and so on. Two more resignations from the governing body and country-wide resignations from the organization followed which created widespread flutter and headed for a trouble. Growing high prices, corruption and personality cult gave support to the Leftist' bid for an overhaul.

1957 Budget of the State rose to Rs. 765.70 lakhs with the imposition of a few taxes. The claim of the budget being surplus was rejected by critics who discovered a deficit of Rs. 2 crores.

The flood in August crossed the highest recorded level of 1950. While it caused immense loss to the rural area, the city was saved by raised bunds and digging and widening of canals. Loss of property was much, particularly in Southern Kashmir and loss of life also no small. 3,16,000 kanals of land were flooded. About 68 persons were killed in the whole State mostly in Jammu. The total loss could be roughly estimated at Rs. 250 lakhs. Rivers Chenab and Tawi alone swept aways about 600 heads of cattle and devastated about a 100 villages, while river Jhelum not less than 500. 19 small bridges or culverts and 20 canals were affected involving a loss of about sixty and twenty-five lakhs respectively. 41,000 acres of land were submerged. In absence of exact records of previous floods this year's flood would be considered as unprecedented.

All Leftists who either resigned from office or governing body of the National Conference brought into existence a new political party called "Democratic National Conference". The parent body thus broke into three parts—Abdullah group, Bakhshi group and Sadiq group since 1947 which was not a happy sign for future. As assessed on September 9 the Leftists commanded 14 members in the Assembly and 2 in the Council.

Bomb explosions created a grave situation in the State since June. The one which exploded in Maisuma on September 8 killed two persons. It was put in a mosque to give it a communal colour. It is possible that Pakistan may be behind this. It is also possible that local workers may be behind this just to blackmail India. The guess cannot be ruled out that explosions may have been organized both to defer as well as to precipitate the impending release of S.M. Abdullah. Some parties wanted it and some did not. There were 38 explosions killing six persons in all (13 in Kashmir and 25 in Jammu).

September 11 was a day of joy. Jawahar Lal Nehru visited Srinagar after about 4½ years. The peoples' welcome was unprecedented. He reiterated India's latest stand on Kashmir and assured of his full moral support to Bakhshi which put Abdulla's release again in cold storage and discouraged dissident group from the National Conference.

The months of October, November and December broke the lull by India sponsored food discussions, trial of enemy agents (16 in number) in connection with bomb explosion, re-election of Shri Yuvraj Karan Singh as Sadar-i-Riyasat for the second term and fillip to Second Five-Year Plan. Shortage of food due to floods told on the economics of the State. Community Development Projects were put to severe test and strain to tide over the gap.

The final blasting of the second tube of Jawahar tunnel at Banihal was completed on 19th October. The same day the first two day convention organized by National Conference Democratic Front was held at Srinagar. The Front reiterated Kashmir's accession with India and placed its own programme before the country.

For the first time during the last 50 years or so Kashmir Valley witnessed its first snowfall on 20th October. The year 1957 was omnious—there were unprecendented rains in spring, there was unprecedented flood in summer and there was early snowfall in autumn. Chinar leaves had not yet turned red. They were still green. Famine stared in the face. Late sowing of seed, flood when crops were in bloom and early snow when harvesting was on crippled all grain crops. If India were not at the back as she has been hitherto there would have been disease, death and devastation unknown in past history. About 5 ft. snowfall over the Banihal pass suspended life-line for a few days. Local food stocks being near exhaustion did present a grave situation so much so that the price of a khirwar of rice rose to about Rs. 150/-. But no death by starvation came to notice. This year's responsibility of feeding the entire population roughly estimated at about 18 lakhs in Kashmir Province devolved on India which rushed supplies in season and out of season. The State received a food subsidy amounting to Rs. 4,55,70,862 between 1948 to 1956.

In Chrar-i-Sharif bye-election contest and Town Area elections both National Conference and Democratic National Conference set up its own candidates. Severe skirmishes were reported from Badgam, Sopore and Srinagar in November. Beating at Lal chowk was personally witnessed. Leaders of the Democratic National Conference demanded President's rule in the State. Lawlessness and resentment against the ruling party was manifest.

Budget increased by five times from the initial outlay of Rs. 38.49 lakhs and it now equals pre-partition budget. Food deficit grew from more to more inspite of 25 per cent increase in food production. Smuggling across the border was also a reason.

Ten years ago the State had only 2.5 miles of roads per 100 sq. miles. During the period over 500 miles of new roads were constructed, 482 bridges built and about 1,500 miles of roads are in hand to bring towns and villages closer to one another.

For Community Development Projects this year the villagers contributed Rs. 50 lakhs against the Government subsidy of Rs. 87 lakhs. There are 1,000 Panchayats and the figure is rising to 5,000.

Community Centres in the Second Five-Year Plan—The Sindh Project has attained a generating capacity of 10,000 k.w. and the country is still grievously short of electric power which has hampered industrialisation. During the last ten years the State has received a total assistance of Rs. 18 crores most of which was consumed by food and transport.

The year 1958 opened with a sensation. Sh. Mohammad Abdullah was released from detention in Kud Sub-jail four days earlier to Dr. Frank Graham's visit to the Indian sub-continent as representative of the Security Council. S.M. Abdullah remained in detention for fifty-three months less by one day. After his release he stated that the real solution of the Kashmir question lay with the people who were the final arbiters. He was given a hero's welcome enroute to Srinagar on 12th January. In his address at Hazaratbal on the following day he stated that accession was never finalized and ratification by the people was still due. Kashmir had temporarily acceded to India in defence, foreign affairs and communications. He maintained that one of the solutions was Independence for the valley guaranteed by United Nations and he would not mind Ladakh and Jammu going to India. Procession taken out on 26th January under Bakhshi's leadership was a reply to 12th January ovation given to Abdullah. If bodies were on one side, hearts were on the other. Friday following Miraj-ul-Alam (2-12-1958) turned prayer day at Hazratbal into a miniature Kurballa when followers of Abdullah collided with the workers of the National Conference killing one and injuring dozens of people, even officials on duty for first aid were not spared. This resulted in police action who rounded up many a noted person. A case was started against 86 persons and the trial was conducted in Central Jail.

For the first time since 1947 the annual session of the National Conference was held in Jammu from 14th to 16th March under the Presidentship of Bakhshi Ghulam Mohammad. Among other resolutions one endorsed Kashmir's accession with India as convened under the leadership of Sheikh Mohammad Abdullah and demanded vacation of aggression by Pakistan.

The period 1957 to 1958 following unprecendented flood gave big economic surprises. Not only food grains were imported in abundance, but even things like fodder for animals, milk and its derivatives, straw made articles and what not for which Kashmir had never felt want found their way in. Had grass also disappeared from the grounds and leaves from the trees poses a question for the historian? September flood and early October snow wrought untold havoc. People from the rural area were seen begging in the streets of Srinagar in spite of First Five-Year Plan that was over and Second Five-Year Plan that was on.

While Dr. Frank Graham's report created a political flutter in the sub-continent of India and Pakistan Kashmir went ahead with spring festival. Dr. Graham had proposed among other things that the Prime Ministers of India and Pakistan should meet under auspices of U.N. Representative and that after withdrawal of Pakistan forces from 'Azad Kashmir' area U.N. forces be stationed on Pakistan border and India to withdraw her military forces from Kashmir which was not acceptable to India at all. The absence of Bakhshi Ghulam Mohammad from Hazratbal on 21 February (Miraj-ul-Alam) and I'd Gah on the same day two months later gave wind to the impression that Abdullah was the defacto leader.

Prices of commodities in the second decade and fifth decade:—

Article	II Decade	V Decade
Meat	-/4/- seer	3/- seer
Milk	-/1/- "	-/12/- seer
Oil	-/4/- "	2/8- "
Ghee	-/12/- "	5/8- "
Eggs	-/-/3 "	-/2/6 each
Fuel (willow)	7 mds. per rupee	1/12/- per md.

Vegetables six times, suger five times, timber 12 times, rice twenty times and so on. There was increase in income also but not to the same extent and it varied from one social group to another. The middle class split into two flanks—extreme riches and extreme poverty. A new aristocracy was born before which the old aristocracy paled into insignificance.

Sheikh Mohammad Abdullah was again arrested on the night of April 29 under Security Act and removed to Kud Jail. During his previous detention for about 53 months his maintenence as a special class prisoner cost nearly Rs. 1,70,000/- since his release on January 8 last Sheikh Mohammad Abdullah was demanding plebiscite to which Security Council and the Republics of India and Pakistan were committed. No popular commotion followed his arrest as had taken place in 1953. It was not due to that he had lost hold on people. Financial Integration of the State with India formally took place on 1st May when Audit and Accounts were transferred to Auditor-General of India. Earlier a non-Kashmiri was appointed a High Court Judge by the President of India. As department after department dropped out and as Indians came in one by one to take over control the reaction among the people worsened. But the feeling did not express itself. While jeeps and cars moving freely were a reminder.

Jashne Kashmir started in 1956 was split up into two—Jashne Bahar and Jashne Khazan. Jashne Bahar started from 19th May and lasted till the first of the next month. High lights of this celebration were youth rally, illumination, gymkhana, matches, mushaira, baby and flower shows, drama, dance, Nadim Day at Bandipore, Shami Shalmar, Haba Khatun Day at Pampore, River pageant, torch light, tattoo and Abu-ul-Kalam Azad Seminar. Industrial and agricultural exhibition which is usually held in August/September was also opened the same day to cater to all types of tourists from all corners of India. Total inflow of visitors ending May 1958 was registered at about twenty thousands which showed substantial increase over previous figures. All available accommodation being over full tents were pitched in Polo Ground, Gandhi Park and Hazuri Bagh which posed the problem of housing expansion.

Complaint was filed in the court in May 2 against Mirza Afzal Beg and twenty others including four Pakistan Intelligence officers under Section 121A and 120A of Ranbir Penal Code read with Rule of 32 J.&K. Security Rules charging them with conspiracy to overthrow the State government and to facilitate wrongful annexation of Kashmir by Pakistan. Trial started in Kud (a hill station on Srinagar—Jammu road) from 11th June and was later shifted. President of India promulgated "Code of Criminal Procedure (Amendment) Ordinance 1958" inserting a subsection after Section 105 of the Code of Criminal Procedure of 1898 regarding execution of certain processes issued by courts in Jammu and Kashmir in the rest of India and vice versa.

Through the installed capacity of 6,000 k.w. from Sindh Valley Hydro Electric Project and bulk purchase of 3,000 k.w. from Joginder Nagar in Punjab, forty-three towns and villages in Jammu Province and eighteen towns and villages in Kashmir Valley were electrified under the development scheme.

The month of June was a month of great political excitement. Ch. Ghulam Abbas of "occupied Kashmir" had started Kashmir Liberation movement to cross cease fire line on 27th. But Pakistan did not approve of such a step. Forces on the Indian side of the cease fire were alert to meet any situation. When the zero hour approached bathces of volunteers on the other side of the cease fire were stopped by Pakistan forces. Even the "occupied Kashmir" Government was against such a move. But it appeared in inspired move to awaken conscience of the world and to draw the attention of the Security Council to Graham Report for an early consideration thereof. Sixteen persons from "occupied Kashmir" violated the cease fire line and crossed into Jammu near Janghar on July 3. These persons were arrested and detained by the civil authorities. The movement gained no ground. Thirty-one bomb explosions were reported in the State between January and June 1958. This was an indication of under current feeling. Total explosions during 1957-58 mounted to 91 and 53 in 1958-59.

The sum of Rs. 77,000/- was earmarked for grant of allowances to dependents of 140 martyrs who had lost lives in the cause of States' freedom. A big fire broke out on the night of 19th August in Fateh Kadal. It was traders' locality and the loss was about rupees one lakh, involving twelve houses, police station and a saw mill—

Food subsidy received from India during 1957-58 was distributed as under:—

5,88,354 mds.	wheat	Kashmir
1,85,645 "	maize	
38,950 "	flour	
42,017 "	rice	
3,32,472 "	wheat	Jummu
21,800 "	wheat seed	
20,575 "	maize	
5,000 "	bajra	Kishtwar
6,013 "	shali	Leh
1,361 "	rice	
1,565 "	bajra	
700 " grain		Kargil

As assessed in 1958 the food deficit of 3.6 million mds. a year was reduced by 8,00,000 mds. A rise of 11 per cent in the per capita income of the people, 25 per cent increase in literacy and growth in trade from 3.8 crores to 8.5 crores were noticed. Revenue which stood at Rs. 4.12 crores in 1950-51 went up to Rs. 11.54 crores in 1957-58. Before 1947 hardly 10 per cent girls were literate and in 1958 the percentage rose very high and they are taking part in every walk of life side by side with boys particularly in medicine, education etc. Development of cattle wealth and establishment of Goshalas were stressed at the first All-India Four-Day Gosamvardhan Seminar inaugurated by Sadar-i- Riyasat on 21th August. Acute shortage of cattle was not so much due to paucity of fodder as indiscriminate killing of cows and bulls in spite of prohibitory law on the Statute Book.

September-October is usually harvest time in Kashmir. The fact that Government fixed a target of 23 lakh maunds of grain [collection by voluntary effort at (a) Shali Rs. 16/-per khirwar and (b) Maize Rs. 14/- per khirwar at the village centre] makes it clear that the farmer also was going healthier along with others. He has not to face Mujwaza, begar or Wad system. When Mujwaza was introduced during World War I the price paid for was Rs. 4/- at the Ghat.

Dispensaries in the State rose to 235 in 1958 as against 85 in 1947.

Arts and Crafts centres were started at Anantnag, Shopian, Bandipore, Doda, Kathua, Poonch and Leh at an annual expenditure of Rs. 3,70,000/-. Expenditure on administration rose from Rs. 24,32,000/- in 1947 to Rs. 48,36,000/-in 1957 as per detail below:—

Gazetted Officers rose from 512 to 1,325. Non-Gazetted from 14,176 to 22,196 and Menials from 10,820 to 14,135 (in personnel). There are very few parallels in local annals of this year's land revenue remission to the tune of rupees one crore and manure remission amounting to Rs. 12,00,000/-. Besides food imports amounted to about Rs. 4 crores. National Extension service for 1958-59 received a grant of Rs. 12,57,000 as loan and Rs. 14,97,000 as aid from the Central Government.

Sheikh Mohammad Abdullah was also put on the list of accused in the Kashmir Conspiracy case on a supplementary complaint filed in the court of Special Magistrate trying the case under Section 121-A in which 24 persons already stand accused. Abdullah was produced before the court on 24th October at Jammu.

Sunwaar (low level ground) is a tract of land from Shalteng to Pattan and Sopore which in local annals is known as Kamraj (deficit area). This is being converted into Sonwaar (golden garden) for the first time in known history. The winter of 1958 saw mass concentration of energy employed in this conversion. This will go down as one of the main achievements of the present Government—canals, huts, schools, dispensaries, Panchayat Garhs and what no where before scarcity and grim poverty stared the eye. It is here that Bakhshi broke the record of Lalitaditya. Of all the development projects undertaken in the First and Second Five-Year Plans Sonwaar was a model project in which local population offered willing co-operation to authorities. Price paid for should be no consideration.

The western tube of Jawahar Tunnel was thrown open to Public traffic on 21th December. Heavy snow fall the same day frustrated for a while physical greetings from trucks and buses plying to and fro across the tunnel. This is yet another feat of people's will.

The year 1958 is coming to close and the Second Five-Year Plan is still on. A shop in Ward No. 1 which could be obtained at Rs. 200 a year before partition has been auctioned for Rs. 3,000 to Rs. 4,000. This is due to concentration of offices, business firms and settlement of non-Kashmiris in this area, not to mention visitors. Prices of land are on the increase and as one moves down the river prices also go down. The development of this ward received priority at the cost of other wards during Pathan, Sikh and Dogra rulers. The present government is adhering to the same policy with the result that the rest of the city continues to be neglected. Land prices in the city need be more or less uniform and this is possible when concentration is broken up and most of the offices as well as business firms diverted and evenly distributed. Inflation and growing population have failed to attract attention of the politician. Chatabal, Rainawari, area round Mal Khah, Idgah and Chandmari could as well cater to visitors. Why Sonwaar to Amirakadal only for all official as well as unofficial purposes. A person from Safa kadal going to Sopore comes to Amirakadal to catch his bus. The new year (1959) dawned with a fresh agrarian policy introducing joint co-operative farming in the State. January and February were one of the severest winters that history has known. In Northern areas there was a snow fall of about 9 feet. Food situation was worse in spite of bumper crop. Monthly ration not being adequate rice in the black market sold at about Rs. 5.00 per trak (5 seers 3 chataks). Entry of food grains into the city was already under ban. Even vegetables disappeared due to official intervention. During this season road and air traffic came to standstill too often because of heavy snow. In 1958 there was plenty amidst shortage, but this year it was shortage amidst plenty. Even the fixation of Rs. 16/ as purchasing price per khirwar of Shali could hardly bring to the Government about four lakhs (8,00,000 mds.) against the speculated target of twelve lakh khirwars (24,00,000 mds.). The soaring price and scarcity became unanswerable.

The revolt of Hamid Bakhshi (younger brother of Bakhshi Ghulam Mohammad—they are 6-1) from the National Conference and against his own brother provided fodder to all opposition camps. His criticism of the ruling class was the feeling of the public pulse—failure of food policy, Peace Brigade terror, corruption etc. Later he repudiated his stand.

A fresh census of Srinagar city was taken in February in response to a demand for revision of ration tickets which resulted in an increase of about 31,000 in city's population under rationing.

Rs. 2,67,000 were distributed as industrial loans and Rs. 3,96,000 paid to Town Area Committees as aid under Second Five- Year Plan Rs. 6,03,000 was given as aid and Rs. 3 crores as loan to refugees in the State, since 1947.

Financially 1959-60 was a bumper year. Revenue of the State rose to Rs., 11,77,39,000 which gave a saving of Rs. 3,61,16,000 after meeting with an expenditure of Rs. 8,62,30,000.

A.A. Andreyey, leader of Soviet Goodwill Delegation which visited Kashmir in the second week of March, reiterated that Kashmir was one of the States of the Republic of India and that the question of its future was an artificial creation. This was closely followed by yet another important event in the third week of March—visit of Hammarskjold, Secretary General of United Nations Organisation where the Kashmir dispute is still pending. He inspected the cease fire line on spot and contacted U.N. Observers. No Secretary General had come before.

Permit system which was introduced in 1947 controlling entry into and from the State against which Dr. S.P. Mukerjee had also raised his voice was abolished with effect from 1st April and was followed by expanding jurisdiction of Supreme Court and Election Commission through a vote of State Legislature. A mushroom political body called "United Democratic Front" came into being asking for special privileges of the State to continue but the move was against the current. All Archaeological Remains in the State were formally haned over to the Central Government.

Almost all detenues were released before the first week of May, prominent among whom were Kashyapa Bundhu, Ghulam Mohammad Shah and others.

For the first time the head of the State Sadar-i-Riyasat Karan Singh accompanied by his wife left for a three-week official tour of Soviet Russia on April 20 at the invitation of Russian Government. Another landmark which closely followed was the visit of Vinoba Bhave, Bhoodan leader, into the State. From May 22 onwards he made Padyatra (foot journey) from village to village and addressed huge gatherings asking for free gifts of land and money. His four months stay brought into his bowl, about 16,883 kanals of land.

By an Act of Parliament census operation due in 1961 were extended to the State of Jammu & Kashmir. No census was taken in 1951.

Formation of 1,000 Service Co-operatives was under contemplation towards the end of 1951 (Second Five-Year Plan) for promotion of agricultural production, each unit to consist of two to five villages with an approximate population of 1,000 people.

A survey was prompted by the growing tourist industry in the State showing 76 per cent Indians, 9 per cent Americans, 6 per cent Britons, 6 per cent Ceylonese and others, 3 per cent Business men. On an average a tourist spent about Rs. 275/- during his stay in the valley. Roughly speaking tourism brings about one and a half crore of rupees every year and the industry has rightly focussed attention in the public as well as private sections.

Disturbances in Tibet in March-April created some concern among 42,000 Buddhist followers of Dalai Lama in Ladakh particularly about the future of Mansar, an Indian enclave in Western Tibet which acknowledged sovereignty of Ladakh for the last 300 years or more. With the population of about 300 the enclave is situated 70 miles north of the nearest Indian border and 50 miles to the east of Gartok. The village paid land revenue to Ladakh when it was independent and to Kashmir Durbar since 1846. Purang, Rudok, Guge and Lowo were also parts of Ladakh State. The Lharai stream near the Pauggong lake was the boundary between Ladakh and Tibet. Chinese intrusion into this area should cause grave concern.

Before the formal introduction of Co-operative Farming or formation of Service Co-operatives about 8,000, acres of State land were distributed among landless cultivators—two acres of irrigated land or four acres of unirrigated land were allotted to a landless peasant. A dairy farm handling about 250 maunds of milk was set up at Chashmashahi (five miles from town) with four collective centres and thirty-five distribution centres. Subsidy of rupees 7 lakhs by the Central Government was available to make supply of fresh milk possible which had become a rare commodity. State contribution amounted to about Rs. 5 lakh. This milks colony was formally inaugurated on 30th November, 1959 by Bakhshi Ghulam Mohammad. An Industiral Finance Corporation was also set up with a resource of Rs. 10 lakhs to give further impetus to trade and industry.

Construction of roads included one to 8,000 ft. high beauty spot Gulmarg and second to Kishtwar, famous for saphire mines and rich forests. The latter in 40 miles long touching Doda which is already connected with Batote—Rs. 67 lakhs came the cost for this.

Katra town in Jummu is at the foot of Vaishnu Devi shrine. A yoga institute, the fist of its kind, is designed for this place at a cost of Rs. 10 lakhs. Two other projects—Engineering College and Cosmic Ray Laboratory are on anvil. The latter will be constructed at Khilanmarg (10,000 ft. high), 31 miles from Srinagar at a cost of Rs. 50,00,000 by the Atomic Energy Commission of India. A full-fledged Medical College has already come into operation. Economic position of the people could be read from the fact that over 250 pilgrims including some women left for Haj pilgrimage in May. This was the highest number so far recorded. During the last 64 years as many as 15 devastating floods were witnessed of which the flood of 1957 was worst on record. The capacity of the Jhelum is 36,000 to 50,000 cusecs but the flood was 90,000 cusecs. 10½ mile long Sindh Canal costing about Rs. 10,00,000 from Ganderbal to Harwan was completed. Besides irrigating land it will ensure 24-hour water supply to Srinagar with growing population and increasing water consumption.

Construction of Arts faculty of J. & K. University at the University campus near Naseem Bagh, seven miles from Srinagar, was taken up in hand. The University will be named after Maulana Abu-ul-Kalam Azad. Yuvraj Karan Singh donated land for the campus and the faculty is being built at a cost of Rs. 3.5 lakhs. The University may serve as beacon light for the whole of India as did once ancient University of Kashmir which produced historians, grammarians, surgeons, engineers, philosophers and what not.

But slums of Srinagar continue mostly as they did in feudal period in spite of I and II Five-Year Plans and tall talk by politicians. History does not take notice of parties, official or unofficial, that go round but progress that a country makes.

The month of July started with heavy rains which flooded the Jhelum and its tributaries submerging the valley in water. Level of Jhelum touched 30.25 ft. (six feet above the danger mark). Mohra Power House which had escaped the wrath of raiders in 1946 was hit hard. Ganderbal Power House collapsed. There was no light for about 10 days in the city. Water level in Wolur rose 2.4 feet above the 1957 record (highest was 5,185.8 feet above mean sea level against 5.183.4 feet in 1957). Ranbir Canal in Jammu also gave way. Death roll rose to 149 (127 civilian and 22 army) in the State—76 in Kashmir only (Anantnag 8, Baramulla 52, Srinagar 16). Jammu fared equally worse where the death figure rose to 86, 56 in Poonch alone. 300 miles of roadways and breaches including 18 bridges and culverts were affected. In Poonch 21 miles of roads and 7 bridges, in Jammu 100 miles of roads and in Leh one bridge and ten miles were affected. Loss was also heavy on account of timber that moved down to Pakistan. An estimate of loss was put as under—Rupees ten crores which affected about 4 lakhs of people and 1,000 villages. Sonawaar yielded no gold. Yields of I and II-year Plans were almost washed away. This flood was unprecedented as all tributaries in all directions rose simultaneously and yet the city was saved. In the thick of it the prices of shali and rice were abruptly raised from Rs.12/- to Rs. 16/-per Khirwar (shali) and four seers to three seers per rupee (rice). Political sagacity would defer this enhancement to a later date. Popular resentment expressed through mass procession and hartal was a natural corollary. And there were acts of incendiarism. Circuit House at Tosha Maidan and a bridge on Srinagar—Chrar Shariff road were burnt. An attempt was made to set Legislative Assembly Chamber on fire. And in spite of this all Vinoba Bhave climbed Pirpanchal and crossed into Gulmarg via Poonch on 15th July. Banihal Cart Road which had gone out of service from July 4 was available for traffic after eighteen days. Visitors who had come in large numbers were stranded at various spots. Many of them had reached the end of their resources and the hardships they faced were painful. The first convoy of 560 trucks and cars which carried about a thousand visitors was, inspite of free lift, a grim sight to look at the Tourist Reception Centre. While on its way a landslide caused many a death. Roughly estimated loss was put as under:—Live-stock 10,000; houses 14,000 plus 15,000 damaged; agricultural land 2,00,000 acres. Relief was given as under:—Rs. 500 to Rs. 1,000 per head in case of death, Rs. 30 lakhs taccavi loans, ordinance to prevent purchase, transfer, sale or lease of remission of land revenue. Since the construction of B.C. Road never had traffic come to standstill for a whole summer month. Nehru's flying visit on 27th July and Acharya Vinoba Bhave's entry in Srinagar on 2nd August via Gulmarg were a healing balm for a people facing a national calamity. Acharya Vinoba delivered about half a dozen surmons from New Kashmir Park. He is the third in line—Shankaracharya (Vedas), Shah Hamdan (Islam) and Vinoba (Bhudan) who enlightened Kashmir through the ages, the first two on spirituality and the third on economics. He went back via Banihal after a three week walking tour. India reacted to Kashmir's calamity with great generosity unparalleled in local annals. Donations and grants in cash and kind poured in abundantly.

A ropeway connecting Chinani in Jammu with Verinag in Kashmir is under survey. It will be the longest and highest (11,000 feet above sea level) ropeway. The first phase may cost about two lakhs of rupees.

Seventeenth of October became suddenly a jubilation day when restrictions on import of food grains into Srinagar were removed and city ration increased. The price of Shali was fixed at Rs. 16/- per khirwar and rice at Rs. 13.13 a maund in the open market as well. Food ration was increased from 12 seers to 15 seers per head per month from November i.e., 12 seers rice and 3 seers wheat four (the price of latter at 3 seers a rupee). The Government imported 3 million maunds of food-grains from India during the food-year 1959-60 to make up the loss caused by the floods. To supplement this Food-grain Regulation Order of 1958 and Guest Control Order continued to remain in force. Fixation of price was a thorn in the rose.

A big Indo-Chinese clash was reported from south Ladakh on October 21. Indian policemen were camping as part of their patrol duties at a place called Hot Springs in the Chang Chenmo Valley. This area is north of Spenggur, beyond the Khurnak Fort and some 100 miles from Leh. The party was attacked by the Chinese a a result of which nine men were killed, some injured and ten taken prisoner. The first Chinese attack had occurred on July 28 when six Indian policemen were taken into custody.

The first snowfall of the season came on 7th November, much earlier than usual and this also adversely affected harvesting of crops which was not completed.

Nehru will go down in the annals of Kashmir as a leader who fought against proverbial ignorance, poverty and starvation of the people during the last thirteen years which has hardly a parallel anywhere else.

A voluntary strain of about three quarters of a crore of rupees on the Exchequer was involved when third instalment of allowances for Government employees was announced by Bakhshi Ghulam Mohammad on December 7 payable from April last. The total burden was estimated to amount to Rs. 2 crores per year.

Since partition of India in 1947 the problem of refugees from areas now known as "occupied Kashmir" had, except periodic doles, remained practically unsolved. On January 7 the Government of India announced a grant of Rs. 15 crores. Every refugee settled on land was given Rs. 1,000 and every refugee not settled on land Rs. 3,500. The relief covered 35,000 refugee families. They were also assured that they would not be dislodged from lands or houses.

Except a small snowfall in the morning hours of 7th November which melted away before dawn, there was no snowfall of season, unusual again, up to 19th January, barring a nominal break on 14th—27th day of Chilakalan. Bright sunshine was considered a freak of nature.

A high-altitude cosmic research observatory at Gulmarg run by Aligarh and J. & K. Universities was transferred to the Department of Atomic Energy which is to build the laboratory at an altitude of 9,000 ft., costing Rs. 6,22,700/-.

The budget of the State rose to Rs. 1,569.93 lakhs (over 15 crores) for the year 1960-61. The Central assistance for the Plan during the year was estimated to be Rs. 706.74 lakhs.

Bakhshi Ghulam Mohammad stated in the Assembly that the State was getting Rs. 3 crore aid from the Centre while the Departments transferred like Customs, Income-tax, Telephone and Telegraph etc. would yield much higher income. Later he dissolved the Municipalities of Jammu and Srinagar.

The National Democratic Conference received a great set back when Ghulam Rasool Renzu, former Speaker of J. & K Assembly, resigned from it on the plea that communalism had entered into its ranks. It was Renzu episode which had given birth to the organisation.

Himachal slogan and Ladakh defence prompted Nehru's visit to the Valley on July 2. During his five day stay he made two trips to Ladakh.

King Mahendra of Nepal and his Queen arrived in Srinagar on 8th July. There were Gurkhas in the state army some of whom had acquired immoveable property but the visit of a King of Nepal (though private) was never heard before.

Eight bomb explosions in Lamandi at nightfall on 7th July were attributed to army agents which again shows that all is not well still.

The new Secretariat building at Shahid Gunj was taken up in August 1961 and completed in April 1963. About 400 labourers worked at it. The cost came to about Rs. 51 lakhs. The floor area is 140,000 sq. ft. 2500 tons of cement and 850 tons of iron were used in the Seven-storyed building—410 ft. x 53 ft. (12000 tons). Post office, Telephone Exchange and Cafetaria are attached to it.

The building was occupied on 6th May 1963 when offices moved from Jammu to Srinagar. The opening ceremony was performed on 3-5-63.

The decision of the Government to grant pensions to persons disabled or killed during the struggle movement since 1931 (belated though) from Rs. 40/- to Rs. 75/- per head per month was widely appreciated. Court-fine and punitive tax had already been remitted. But opportunists reaped better harvest than actual sufferers.

The first week of May was a time of great excitement at Delhi when America's Secretary of State, Britains Common-wealth Secretary, Foreign Secretary and Chief of Army Staff conferred with Indian leaders, Kashmir being the principal topic of discussion. But no honourable and equitable compromise between India and Pakistan was available.

The fifth round of ministerial talks on Kashmir which began at Karachi on 22nd April ended on 25th. Neither party won any Rubber.

The sixth round of talks started at Delhi on 15th May which ended dramatically on second day with no obvious gains or losses for either.

The sixteen year old Kashmir dispute will not be settled at the Conference table. Six rounds of ministerial talks have indicated this. Mediation, arbitration, partition or plebiscite are not acceptable. Two neighbours staring at each other with eagle looks while banking on a hostile population may one day flare up a situation that will be disastrous. Pakistan has already occupied over 28,000 sq. miles. Adjustment of Ceasefire Line would yield to her a little more but she insists on `pound of flesh'. India which claims legal sovereignty is not prepared to surrender more, come what may.

Kashmir presented Finance Minister of India 1.9 lakh grams of gold, 583,000 grams of silver, 168 sovereigns and a cheque for Rs. 30 lakhs on March 29 at a reception. Gold and silver was mostly taken from Toshkhana Department and passed on for Defence Fund. The amount in cash was the second instalment as collections had exceeded fifty lakhs by this time. Bakhshi Ghulam Mohammad presented a cheque for Rs. Ten lakhs to Jawahar Lal Nehru on his arrival here on 18th June as the state's further contribution towards National Defence Fund. The state has already contributed Rs. 30 lakhs plus $5\frac{1}{2}$ mds. gold and $15\frac{1}{2}$ mds. silver. Addressing workers Nehru stated that Pakistan had exploited Chinese aggression and black-mailed India at the most critical hour in her history. India still stood for honourable & equitable settlement but not for surrender.

